First and Second Kings

Westminster Bible Companion

Series Editors

Patrick D. Miller
David L. Bartlett

First and
Second Kings

TERENCE E. FRETHEIM

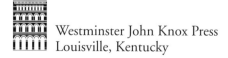

Westminster John Knox Press
Louisville, Kentucky

Book design by Publishers' WorkGroup
Cover design by Drew Stevens

First edition
Published by Westminster John Knox Press
Louisville, Kentucky

This book is printed on acid-free paper that meets the American National Standards Institute Z39.48 standard. ♾

PRINTED IN THE UNITED STATES OF AMERICA

99 00 01 02 03 04 05 06 07 08 — 10 9 8 7 6 5 4 3 2 1

Library of Congress Cataloging-in-Publication Data

Fretheim, Terence E.
　　First and Second Kings / Terence E. Fretheim. — 1st ed.
　　　　p.　　cm. — (Westminster Bible companion)
　　Includes bibliographical references.
　　ISBN 0-664-25565-5 (alk. paper)
　　1. Bible. O.T. Kings—Commentaries.　I. Title.　II. Series.
BS1335.3.F74 1999
222'.5077—dc21　　　　　　　　　　　　　　　　98-54747

Contents

SECOND KINGS

Series Foreword

This series of study guides to the Bible is offered to the church and more specifically to the laity. In daily devotions, in church school classes, and in listening to the preached word, individual Christians turn to the Bible for a sustaining word, a challenging word, and a sense of direction. The word that scripture brings may be highly personal as one deals with the demands and surprises, the joys and sorrows, of daily life. It also may have broader dimensions as people wrestle with moral and theological issues that involve us all. In every congregation and denomination, controversies arise that send ministry and laity alike back to the Word of God to find direction for dealing with difficult matters that confront us.

A significant number of lay women and men in the church also find themselves called to the service of teaching. Most of the time they will be teaching the Bible. In many churches, the primary sustained attention to the Bible and the discovery of its riches for our lives have come from the ongoing teaching of the Bible by persons who have not engaged in formal theological education. They have been willing, and often eager, to study the Bible in order to help others drink from its living water.

This volume is part of a series of books, the Westminster Bible Companion, intended to help the laity of the church read the Bible more clearly and intelligently. Whether such reading is for personal direction or for the teaching of others, the reader cannot avoid the difficulties of trying to understand these words from long ago. The scriptures are clear and clearly available to everyone as they call us to faith in the God who is revealed in Jesus Christ and as they offer to every human being the word of salvation. No companion volumes are necessary in order to hear such words truly. Yet every reader of scripture who pauses to ponder and think further about any text has questions that are not immediately answerable simply by reading the text of scripture. Such questions may be about historical and geographical details or about words that are obscure or so loaded with meaning that one cannot tell at a glance what is at stake. They may be about the fundamental meaning of a passage or about what connection a particular text might have to our contemporary world. Or a teacher preparing for a church school class may simply want to know: What should I say about this biblical passage when I have to teach it next Sunday? It is our hope that these volumes, written by teachers and pastors with long experience studying and teaching the Bible in the church, will help members of the church who want and need to study the Bible with their questions.

The New Revised Standard Version of the Bible is the basis for the interpretive comments that each author provides. The NRSV text is presented at the beginning of the discussion so that the reader may have at hand in a single volume both the scripture passage and the exposition of its meaning. In some instances, where inclusion of the entire passage is not necessary for understanding either the text or the interpreter's discussion, the presentation of the NSRV text may be abbreviated.

We hope this series will serve the community of faith, opening the Word of God to all the people, so that they may be sustained and guided by it.

Introduction

Kings and queens are far removed from the everyday life of most Americans. Though we may often be fascinated with the lives of royal figures (witness the British royal family), many would classify such an interest under the category of public relations or entertainment rather than religion or politics. Moreover, many of us are deeply suspicious of kings and associated royal trappings. Such mistrust is often grounded in issues of authority built up over generations of royal abuse. We live in a country established in order to get away from kings and their authoritative pronouncements. Our suspicions may also be related to issues of opulence and ostentation. The gold never seems to quit and the always evident wealth and rich living has certainly been gained at least in part on the backs of those who are less fortunate. Kings we don't need, thank you very much.

ISRAEL'S KINGS AND THE BOOK OF KINGS

It may come as something of a surprise to observe that Kings is comparably suspicious of kings. The book of Kings—it is actually one book divided into equal parts because of scroll length—begins and ends with a note of uncertainty about kings. David is "old and advanced in years" (1 Kings 1:1). Given this condition of the George Washington of Israel's history, political unrest reigns, with considerable intrigue out and about over who will succeed David. Kings ends on a comparable note. The sole survivor of David's house (Jehoiachin) is languishing in exile, and the reader is left in a vale of uncertainty regarding the future of the dynasty and the people (2 Kings 25:27–30).

In between these somewhat unstable and insubstantial bookends of Kings, the narrative takes its readers on a very bumpy ride. The book moves in and out of the lives of more royal figures than we care to remember (over

forty of them!), half of whose names we can't pronounce anyway; it's hard
to keep track even with a road map. Readers are treated to rhythms of good
and evil, reform and apostasy, peace and violence, and the regular drum-
beat of boring summaries of the lives of incompetent kings. Read 1 Kings
15–16 or 2 Kings 15 when you are having trouble getting to sleep! This is
the way it often is with kings, of course; yet, because kings are kings, such
a narrative journey usually means there will be trouble somewhere and people are going to suffer somehow. At the close of the day, the ups and downs
of Israel's history under its kings seem to have gone nowhere, except down
and out.

The title given this major block of the biblical story is, finally, somewhat misleading. "Kings" leads the reader to believe that royal figures will
be the major subject of concern. In some respects this is true, but, as we
shall see, their story is only part of the story of God's people. The reigns
of the various kings provide the overarching framework for the narrative
(though the chronology provided cannot always be sorted out). Their
reigns will be regularly (and often summarily) evaluated, but the narrator
will use criteria grounded in religious considerations rather than political.
Historians will often be frustrated by this ideological perspective (for an
assessment, see at 2 Kings 13–15). So much history is simply passed by in
the interest of tracking the relationship of these kings to their God. And
we as readers are asked to do the same.

The basic framework provided by the kings could be sketched as follows. The period covered extends nearly 400 years (from 960 to 586 B.C.).
The final stages of the Davidic era and the reign of Solomon anchor the
front end of the narrative and complete the story of the United Monarchy
(1 Kings 1–11). Upon the death of Solomon, and the division of the kingdom into two kingdoms during the reign of his son Rehoboam, the 200-
year history of the kingdom divided between North and South occupies
the broad middle of the book (1 Kings 12–22; 2 Kings 1–17). The ten
northern tribes had a total of nine dynasties (and nineteen kings) in its history. The southern tribes (Judah, with Benjamin) had only one dynasty
(and twelve kings) during this time, that of David; it was divinely chosen
and grounded in unconditional promises (2 Samuel 7). Yet significantly
more narrative space is given to the Northern Kingdom than to the Southern (approximately 80 percent to 20 percent). Among southern kings, only
the reign of Joash is given sustained attention in these chapters, probably
because the Davidic promise is endangered (2 Kings 11–12). This focus on
the North is surprising given the fact that the future of the people of God
will lie with the South rather than the North. We are asked to ponder why

this is so. After the Northern Kingdom falls to Assyria in 721 B.C. (2 Kings 17), the balance of Kings (2 Kings 18–25) is centered on the final years of the Southern Kingdom, which falls to the Babylonians in 586 B.C. The two best kings of Judah (Hezekiah and Josiah) undertake major reforms during this period, but their efforts are, finally, not able to stop the spiraling road to ruin. Over forty kings in all. Who they are and what they do have a cumulative effect and give decisive shape to the course of Israel's history, for good or (usually) for ill.

One may be given to wonder whether anything of genuine consequence has been accomplished by these kings along the way, and what all of this "history" has to do with the faith and life of the Christian in a postmodern world. Preliminarily, I suggest that this story of Israel's life mirrors the life of the people of God in our own time in more ways than might initially appear to be the case. People like ourselves have a way of thinking and acting like kings, not only because of our common humanity but also because most of us are in a position to affect the lives of others, for good or for ill. From another angle, we may well find ourselves caught up, willy-nilly, in the lives of "kings" around us and come under the spell of the influence they wield—one thinks of politics, sports, commerce, fashion, entertainment, or religion. Our lives get pushed and pulled around by "kings" more than we realize. Will we be as unflinching and relentless in our evaluation of them as Kings is? In view of such realities in our own lives, Kings may at times prove to be uncomfortable reading. Which is one good reason we should read it.

PROPHETS AND KINGS

For all the place given to royalty, Kings is concerned about much more than kings. Prophets will play an even more significant role in the book. The role of the prophets is crucial to Kings primarily because God raises them up to bring the word of God to bear on one crisis after another. The words they speak both interpret events from God's point of view and give shape to the development of Israel's history. The prominent place given to prophets and their message indicates that the word of God, both in grace and judgment, provides the sharpest perspective from which the history of Israel must finally be understood. The narrator often pauses to give special attention to their work.

A survey may help us see the dominant role of the prophets. The prophet Nathan is a key participant in the succession of Solomon (1 Kings

1–2), but the word of the prophet Ahijah will bring his reign to an igno-minious and divided end (1 Kings 11). Ahijah's word will in turn shape the beginning of the divided kingdoms, but he and two unnamed prophets will soon announce judgment upon the North (1 Kings 13–14). The prophet Elijah will come center stage in the Northern Kingdom in 1 Kings 17 and he and his successor Elisha will dominate the narrative through 2 Kings 9. Fully one-third of the book of Kings will be devoted to this period of Is-rael's history, covering just over fifty years out of four hundred (869–815 B.C.). The narrator obviously wants readers to pay special attention to this time. Micaiah and other prophets will also play a role during this time (1 Kings 20; 22). In the final section of Kings, the prophet Isaiah (2 Kings 19–20) and the prophetess Huldah (2 Kings 22) will speak for God re-garding both salvation and judgment. It should also be noted that two priests will surface in an important capacity at 2 Kings 11–12 (Jehoiada) and 2 Kings 22 (Hilkiah).

Unlike the role the prophets commonly have in the prophetic books as preachers to the people as a whole, in Kings the prophets relate primarily to royal figures. Used by God to serve as critics and counselors of kings, they are masters at discerning the word that needs to be spoken—affirm-ing or critical, uniting or dividing, saving or judging. Because the kings are increasingly reluctant to listen to prophetic counsel, the prophets' rela-tionship to the kings becomes more complex and tension-filled. Some prophets are unqualifiedly supportive of the king, while others are sharply critical; and prophets will not always agree (e.g., 1 Kings 22). An especially serious conflict between prophet and king (and prophet and prophet) emerges in the relationship between Elijah and Ahab and Jezebel. Their conflict over idolatry and syncretistic religious practice shows the extent to which Israel's faith was endangered.

For all their conflict, however, prophets and kings do come together at one key point. It is difficult to underestimate the power and symbolic value of the Davidic dynasty, even with all of its failures. One can observe to some extent how these images functioned for the Davidic monarchy in the so-called royal psalms, which were used in kingly rituals over the course of the Davidic monarchy. They include coronation hymns and liturgies (2; 72; 101; 110; 132), petitions and prayers of thanksgiving (18; 20–21; 89; 144), and a royal wedding song (45). Later messianic hopes would draw much of their imagery and energy from this royal tradition, especially the divine promises. The Davidic kings failed again and again, and their reigns betrayed the ideal of these psalms. But the prophets would pick up on these themes and project them into the future: Someday a king would arise who would truly mediate the rule of God (for example, Isaiah 7; 9; 11). The prophetic claim is that royal failure could not finally undo the promises of God. The Christian claim is that those promises are fully and finally realized in Jesus the Christ. But this fulfillment represents a shift in the divine strategy for the realization of the promises, for the crown Jesus would wear was made of thorns. The King of the Jews would reign from a tree.

Modern readers will not always welcome the words these prophets bring. We will cling to the promises, and at times we will appreciate the critical word they have to speak. At other times, however, their engagement with the political side of life and their uncompromising language or bizarre actions may make us feel ill at ease. Again, we must be careful not to dismiss the prophets simply because they may make us uncomfortable. Precisely at such disquieting and unsettling moments we may be called upon to listen very carefully. Perhaps it will be a word about our divided allegiance to God, our less than faithful worship, our lack of care for the needy neighbor, or our tendency to sever our religious life from the social, economic, and political realities with which we have to do.

PROPHETS, KINGS, AND GOD

Above all, the prophets (and a few kings) will bring God to the forefront of the narrative. In fact, God is the only character who moves across the pages of the book from beginning to end. Kings is not only about kings and prophets; it tells a story *of* God (and not just about God). God, too, takes a journey here that is of great consequence for Israel and for the divine purposes in the world. God is the subject of more verbs in these narratives than we may be used to; certainly no modern history is like this. At times we may be comforted by the God presented here. Divine promises and saving actions punctuate the narrative, though less frequently than we might like. Moreover, not unlike ourselves, God often gets tired and frustrated with kings. Most of what they do provokes God to anger again and again. That God, though often frustrated and disappointed, continues to hang in there with this recalcitrant people may also be reassuring.

At other times, however, talk of God's anger and judgment never seems to quit and that may get under your skin. This God seems so uncompromising in holding kings and people to fidelity within their relationship. Again and again, God brooks no rivals and holds people to high standards in daily life. And, in God's created order, what goes around usually comes around; and it may come around with a vengeance, because as kings go so

goes the nation. The result is that more than kings get hurt when all hell
breaks loose across the land. Moreover, many readers will not be altogether pleased with the ending of the book; it may leave you wondering
about this God and whether he has packed up and gone elsewhere. The
ending will send readers back into earlier chapters to see if there is not
some word of hope to which one might cling (see the discussion at 2 Kings
23–25). Finally, however, readers will need to go to other biblical texts for
a clearer word.

When you take the journey of reading Kings, one helpful way to read
would be to track this portrayal of God. Most of the brief essays interspersed throughout the commentary will address God-related issues. You
might ask what this long story must have been like for the one who created this world and redeemed this people and who remains involved with
them through thick and thin. And remember that in some basic respects
this is a journey not unlike the one that God takes with us.

With all of this attention given to kings, prophets, priests, and God, you
may wonder about the common people at times. They seem to be carried
along on the waves stirred up by the powers that be, rejoicing or suffering
in the wake of what they do and say. This is basically because Kings recognizes that what leaders do decisively shapes the life of the people (not
unlike today, as we have noted). All too often the sins of the kings become
the sins of the people and they suffer the adverse effects together (e.g.,
2 Kings 17:7–23). At the same time, the reader should be alert to the place
Kings gives to individuals who are not leaders, both men and women (e.g.,
2 Kings 4–8). They are given a more important role in this story than has
been commonly recognized, and you may find a home in their stories.

KINGS IN CONTEXT

The book of Kings is usually considered to be a "chapter" in a larger vol-
ume called the Deuteronomistic History, which includes Joshua, Judges,
Samuel, and Kings, with Deuteronomy as an introduction. The link of
Kings (and other Deuteronomistic History books) to the book of
Deuteronomy is seen especially because of the similar literary style and
theological interests (compare, e.g., the reform of Josiah in 2 Kings 23 and
Deuteronomy 12). We will look at some of these interests below (see
Fretheim, *Deuteronomic History*, 15–27, 44–48).

The person(s) responsible for the Deuteronomistic History were more
editors than authors. They wove together a variety of heterogeneous

sources and edited—selected, arranged, and interpreted—them in varying ways. Their point of view is more prominent in some sections of the work than at others. Sometimes they allow their sources to speak largely in their own voice (e.g., stories of Elijah and Elisha); at other times they place a distinctive interpretive stamp upon the material (e.g., 2 Kings 17:7–23). Within the text itself, Kings testifies to the use of several sources, no longer extant. For example, the Book of the Acts of Solomon (1 Kings 11:41) and, frequently, the Book of the Annals of the Kings of Judah (or Israel; 1 Kings 14:19, 29). First Kings 1–2 is often thought to be the conclusion of an originally independent Succession Narrative (including 2 Samuel 9–20). While scholars have sometimes argued that one or more of the putative Pentateuchal sources extended as far as Kings, this view has not commonly been followed.

The "Deuteronomic" perspective (that of the book of Deuteronomy) is particularly present in certain prayers and speeches spoken by leaders at key junctures in the story, as well as in some transitional pieces (especially those between the stories of the judges and the kings). These segments are often hortatory in character and tend to look both to the past and to the future. For example, the transition from the early monarchy under Saul to the era of the Davidic covenant is marked by the oracle of Nathan and a prayer by David in 2 Samuel 7. The promise to David provides the backdrop for many a story in Kings (e.g., 1 Kings 2:2–4; 9:1–9). In Kings itself, Solomon's prayer at the dedication of the temple (1 Kings 8) presents a key perspective for the larger narrative. The prophecy of Ahijah in 1 Kings 11:29–39 closes the United Monarchy and opens up the period of the divided kingdoms. The history of the Northern Kingdom is closed with the theological narrative of 2 Kings 17:7–23 and that of the Southern Kingdom with 2 Kings 21:7–15; 22:11–20; 23:26–27; and 24:2–4.

Most scholars understand that this editorial process took place in several stages, with the final form of the book completed sometime after 561 B.C. (the date for the events in 2 Kings 25:27–30). A common proposal speaks of two major editions of the Deuteronomistic History: (a) A thoroughgoing preexilic edition, dating from the time of Josiah. This edition promoted the reform of Josiah and urged repentance. This was supplemented by (b) a modest exilic redaction—the extent of which is much debated—in view of the fall of Jerusalem. It presented a more ambiguous view of Israel's situation in exile. It is usually thought that this context— Israel in exile—provides the setting for the final form of the book. Kings can be profitably read with this exilic audience in view.

Through the years there has been greater focus on the history of Israel that lies behind the present text, or the history of how the text has come to be the way it is, than in viewing the text as it presently stands. In the present time, there is greater interest in viewing the text in its present (final) form. This commentary will follow the latter approach.

Scholars have also shown how Kings is in dialogue with other biblical literature. This is most obvious at those points where verbal parallels are often identical, for example: 2 Kings 18:17–20:19 and Isaiah 36–39; 2 Kings 24:18–25:30 and Jeremiah 52. This supports the view that a prophetic perspective is at work in Kings. Other verbal parallels exist and invite correlation. For example, 1 Kings 22:28 parallels Micah 1:2; the description of Jeroboam's worship practices in 1 Kings 12 recalls the story of the golden calf in Exodus 32 (compare 1 Kings 12:28 with Exod. 32:4); the stories of Elijah often recall the traditions of Moses and Sinai. Generally, this means that Kings cannot be interpreted—theologically or otherwise—in isolation from other biblical traditions.

THE RHETORICAL STRATEGY OF KINGS

The Deuteronomistic History, and 1 and 2 Kings within it, was written to have an effect upon readers. The general objective was to bring about change in these readers, to create persons different from what they were before the reading took place. We as contemporary readers seek to identify and describe these (implied) readers, the kind of effect on them the text aims to have, and the rhetorical strategies used to accomplish it.

The identity of these readers is inferred from the data within the text itself. Several key texts, including the final datable events reported in 2 Kings (561 B.C.), imply that these readers can be identified with the exiles in Babylon (1 Kings 8:34, 46–53; 9:6–9; 2 Kings 21:8–15; cf. Deut. 4:25–31; 29:22–28; 30:1–10). These exiled readers had been involved in the apostasy of idolatry and had experienced the devastation of Jerusalem and the deportation to Babylon. They now had to struggle with the realities of captivity and dispersion, to reflect upon what had brought them to such a place, and to wonder about the continuing validity of the divine promises and the possibility of returning to the land. While different readers were no doubt in view in pre-Deuteronomistic forms of this material (e.g., the stories of Elijah and Elisha), they are largely hidden from view in the present form of the text.

Certain rhetorical strategies are employed to speak to these readers. The rhetorical strategy of the Deuteronomistic History is most clearly visible in the hortatory language of key texts (e.g., 2 Kings 17:7–23) and, especially, in the book of Deuteronomy, the introduction to that History. The beginning of any book is key to a proper discernment of its rhetorical strategy. The entire Deuteronomistic History, including Kings, is thus to be viewed through the lens provided by the book of Deuteronomy. Deuteronomy's prominent use of exhortation suggests an effort to move the readers, to speak to both mind and heart regarding matters of deep religious concern. This hortatory material presents to the reader sustained, intense, and urgent appeals for a faithful and obedient response to their God. The use of such language implies a claim that Israel has a future beyond disaster—because of the kind of God with whom the people have to do.

The Deuteronomistic material roots the entire range of the history of Israel from Joshua to Kings in the constitutive period of the exodus redemption and the giving of the law. Significant also is Deuteronomy's emphasis on the themes of judgment and promise, both of which will be woven in and out of the story that follows. It is noteworthy that, while not relaxing the import of the people's faithful response, the Deuteronomic law is enclosed by the promise (Deut. 4:31; 30:1–10) and the conviction that the exile is not God's final word to Israel. At the same time, the ending of Deuteronomy (and Kings) defers the fulfillment of the divine promises. The situation of the people of Israel under Moses, not yet in the land but on the eve of entry into it, is parallel to that of the exiles. The people are fearful and dispirited (Deut. 31:6), for that uncertain future is fraught with danger, and that danger comes not just from the difficulties of physically entering into the land, but also from the inner recesses of their own hearts (31:20–29). Deuteronomy makes clear that the promises do not set human responsibility aside; how people respond to their God *outside* the land is basic to the shape their future will take. The people of God are faced with clear choices, including blessing and curse, life and death (Deut. 30:15–20).

In pursuing its rhetorical strategy, the Deuteronomistic History uses the medium of telling a story about the past. Kings in particular is concerned to be specific about that past; it has an interest in matters of chronology and the cumulative effect over time of, say, royal policies. These texts may be considered history or history-like. This is not, however, to say that the interests are fundamentally historiographical—that is, writing a history of Israel for the purposes of reconstructing the history of the period involved.

The question of the historical value of the material in Kings has been raised afresh in light of newer literary perspectives. It is not uncommon, for example, to make a distinction between "biblical Israel" and "historical Israel," and to suggest that the former is presented with such a religious bias as to reveal little of the actual or historical Israel. This perspective certainly constitutes an overreaction to the religious nature of the text's interests, but it must be recognized that considerable imagination has been used to tell this story of the past (for criteria to be used in evaluating these texts for historiographical purposes, see Fretheim, *Deuteronomic History*, 27–35)).

Many scholars would claim that the narrator's strategy is didactic, to teach the basics of the faith to the exiles. Kings would thus be part of a larger religious education enterprise or reform program. Yet the strategy used does not seem to focus on instruction in liturgical or theological matters as such. The text is obviously interested in such realities, but they serve a more comprehensive strategy. The issue is not so much a matter of learning about the faith but the very existence of faith itself. To use the language of Deuteronomy 31:12–13: "Assemble the people—men, women, and children, as well as the aliens residing in your towns—so that they may hear and learn to fear the Lord your God and to observe diligently all the words of this law, and so that their children, who have not known it, may hear and learn to fear the Lord your God."

One might call this approach a prophetic strategy. Kings has long been considered a part of the "Former Prophets," the first section of the second division of the Hebrew canon ("The Prophets"). This language is supported by the extent to which words of the prophets and stories about them are incorporated into the book. To speak of a prophetic strategy would be to claim that these books constituted a word of God to the readers. In essence, Kings is proclamation.

THEMES IN SERVICE OF THIS STRATEGY

A commonly noted perspective of the Deuteronomistic History is that God's word spoken by prophets shapes Israel's history. In view of this, I highlight three major themes present in Kings and in prophetic literature more generally: indictment for apostasy, word of judgment, and word of promise.

1. *Apostasy* shapes Israel's history. The book of Kings is relentless in speaking sharply about the basic reason for Israel's tragic history. Israel's fundamental failure is not to be found in the political or military sphere, but in its relationship with God. In a word, apostasy. First Kings 9:8–9,

written in light of the destruction of Jerusalem, puts the issue this way: "Why has the LORD done such a thing to this land and to this house?" The reply gets to the point quickly: "Because they have forsaken the Lord their God . . . and embraced other gods, worshiping them and serving them."

Israel's apostasy is unfaithfulness to God, manifested fundamentally in the worship of other gods. The issue is the First Commandment (Deut. 5:7–10; 6:5). The problem at its heart is thus a matter of faith and unfaith, and not (dis)obedience of an external code. The failure to keep the commandments is understood to be symptomatic of a more pervasive problem, namely, Israel's disloyalty to God and its refusal to heed the prophetic call for repentance. Second Kings 17:7–18 is a key theological statement that explains the factors at work in Israel's fall to Assyria. All the specific sins cited have to do with the service of other gods (see also 1 Kings 11:4–11; 2 Kings 23:4–25). The First Commandment is the focus of what it means to "forsake" the covenant (Deut. 29:25–26; 1 Kings 11:9–11; 2 Kings 17:15, 35–38).

Idolatry is the force of the repeated evaluation of kings in the book of Kings regarding "the sin of Jeroboam." The idolatrous practices he introduced drew the people away from Yahweh (e.g., 1 Kings 15:30–34; 16:19–31; 2 Kings 17:21–22). But it was under Ahab and Jezebel that especially virulent forms of idolatry—particularly the worship of the Canaanite god Baal—were practiced and became entrenched in Israel's worship, both in the North and in the South. It assumed a syncretistic form, that is, a blending of Baal and Yahweh commitments. Such a syncretism deeply compromised Israel's commitment to Yahweh, the only God. Early prophets, especially Elijah, entered into this crisis for Israel's faith and life, rejected the syncretistic tendencies, and insisted that Israel is called to worship Yahweh alone. The prophet Elijah states the issue squarely: "How long will you go limping with two different opinions? If the LORD is God, then follow him; but if Baal, then follow him" (1 Kings 18:21).

2. God's word of *judgment* shapes Israel's history. Apostasy leads to judgment. The prophetic announcement of judgment is not an arbitrary divine move. Indeed, God introduces nothing new in judgment; that is why the language of punishment is not helpful in thinking through this issue. Rather, the people's apostasy carries within itself the very seeds of disaster. The people's evil (Hebrew: *ra͘*) issues in disaster (1 Kings 9:9; 2 Kings 22:16, 20; Hebrew: *ra͘*). This move from sin to consequence is a part of God's created moral order. God is not removed from this order however; God *mediates* the move from sin to disastrous effect.

Many texts can be cited wherein the word of judgment spoken is fulfilled later in the history (e.g., 1 Sam. 2:31 with 1 Kings 2:27). Such words of judgment are understood to have shaped the course of Israel's history, from the divided kingdoms (1 Kings 11) to the fall of the North (1 Kings 17) and South.

Yet to speak of fulfillment is not the only story to tell about prophetic words of judgment. Now and again, the judgment word of God spoken through the prophets is not (literally) fulfilled. Isaiah announces to Hezekiah (2 Kings 20:1–6) that he will die and not recover. Yet in response to Hezekiah's prayer the prophetic word is reversed through a direct word from God. Similarly, when Ahab repentantly responds to God's word through Elijah, God delays the fulfillment of the word (1 Kings 21:27–29; cf. 2 Chron. 12:1–12). Or, God's word to Elijah in 1 Kings 19:15–18 is only partially fulfilled in the ministry of Elijah; aspects of this word remain for others to accomplish (2 Kings 9–10). In addition, God's ongoing merciful interaction with the people affects the course of Israel's history, even in the face of contrary prophetic words (cf. 2 Kings 13:4–5, 23; 14:26–27).

The fact that *some* prophetic words are not (literally) fulfilled means that, in *every* such case, the future is understood to remain open until fulfillment actually occurs. Israel's future is not absolutely determined by the prophet's word. In other words, prophetic words of judgment do not function mechanistically, as if the word were some autonomous power beyond the reach of God's continuing attention. Even more, this "play" in the time between the word and its (potential) fulfillment gives room for the promise to be at work, even in the midst of judgment. Indeed, finally, God *uses* judgment, not as an end in itself, but as a refining fire for salvific purposes—in the service of the word of promise. Unlike love, wrath is not a divine attribute but a contingent response to Israel's sin (if there were no sin, there would be no wrath). God's wrath is always "provoked" (see the discussion at 1 Kings 14–16).

3. God's word of *promise* shapes Israel's history. The Deuteronomistic History specifies the word of promise as an unconditional word, either to David or to the people of Israel (Deut. 4:31; Judg. 2:1; 1 Sam. 12:22; 2 Sam. 7:16; 2 Kings 13:23). The ongoing fulfillment of that promise in Israel's history is noted (1 Kings 8:20, 56), and that word is fulfilled by God's own hand (1 Kings 8:15, 24; cf. 2 Sam. 7:25), not by some power that the word itself possesses. But even when fulfillment occurs, a literal interpretation may not be in view. For example, the strong words of Joshua 23:14 (cf. 11:23; 21:43–45; 1 Kings 8:56) that every word of God regarding the land has been fulfilled stands in tension with other notices that territory re-

mains to be taken (cf. Josh. 23:4–13; Judges 1). The word of promise did come to pass, but not with the literal precision one might expect from the word as originally spoken.

A comparable perspective on the fulfillment of words of divine promise is present in the Davidic texts. The unconditional promise of 2 Samuel 7:16 appears to be conditioned in the word to Solomon in 1 Kings 9:5–7 (see the discussion at 1 Kings 2). It becomes clear in the subsequent narrative, however, that this condition is limited in its scope. The fundamental Davidic promise is reiterated by the prophet Ahijah, albeit in more restrictive terms (1 Kings 11:11–13, 36–39). This promise continues to be articulated, in times of apostasy (1 Kings 15:4–6; 2 Kings 8:19) and faithfulness (2 Kings 18:3–7). This promise is endangered from time to time, particularly at the time of Joash (see at 2 Kings 11–12). That the promise is preserved at this point seems to be emblematic of a promise that will not fail more generally (see Provan, *1 and 2 Kings*, 92).

At the end of the Deuteronomistic History, however, the word of judgment on Judah seems to be expressed in unequivocal terms (2 Kings 23:26–27), and the fulfillment of the promise is stated in more ambiguous language in the reference to the release of the Davidic king Jehoiachin (2 Kings 25:27–30). Yet, even in the darkest of these passages, the Davidic promise articulated in earlier texts is not denied (see the discussion at 2 Kings 25:27–30). The ambiguity in the narrative portrayal corresponds to Israel's *experience*, wherein the promise is clouded by the disastrous events. But the promise remains for the believing to cling to, even through the most devastating fires of judgment, and divine forgiveness remains available to a repentant people (1 Kings 8:46–53), even the possibility of a return to the land of promise (1 Kings 8:34). This repentance is not finally a bootstrap operation on the part of the people, but a reality that God works within them (1 Kings 8:57–58).

This tension carries forward the ambiguities present at the end of Deuteronomy, wherein the promise is articulated clearly (30:1–10), but only within the context of certain apostasy and judgment (28:45–57; 31:16–29). Yet, even for Deuteronomy, the promise takes priority in its thinking about Israel's future (Deut. 30:4–5; cf. 4:31; Lev. 26:40–45). Indeed, God's promise includes a unilateral circumcising action on Israel's heart so that the people will unfailingly obey the First Commandment (30:6; note that the command to circumcise the heart in Deut. 10:16 here becomes promise). The priority of the promise is such that, in effect, God himself will see to the obedience of God's own law. These themes of judgment and promise are both poetically represented in Deuteronomy 32–33, but promise retains the climactic position with its strong concluding word in 33:26–29. Deuteronomy and the Deuteronomistic History seem finally to value Davidic promise over obedience to Sinaitic law. In the end, it is God who will see to both, but only on the far side of a devastating judgment.

Generally, it may be said that God's word of promise through the prophets will not fail; as far as God is concerned, the promise will never be made null and void. The promise is finally dependent only on the faithfulness of God. This promise can be relied on, though a rebellious generation may not live to see the fulfillment, and those who remain alive can claim the promises only through a refining fire. The prophetic word of disaster and death, however, does not become a word of eternal death or annihilation. No word of final rejection is pronounced or announced.

Israel's history is lived out within a tension of judgment and promise, but it is important to state clearly that no inherent theological contradiction exists between God's death-dealing judgment and the divine promise. God's move through death to life is a prominent biblical theme. The word of promise finally proves decisive for the continuing existence of Israel beyond the apostasy and consequent judgments.

The book of Lamentations, written in the wake of the fall of Jerusalem in 587 B.C., is not unlike the books of Kings in this regard. Trust in a God of love and faithfulness is sharply attested in the midst of an experience of uncompromising devastation (3:22–33). Trust in this kind of God resounds clearly even though it stands together with the ambiguity of the Kings-like ending of Lamentations 5:20–22. Because of the kind of God Israel's God is, there is hope for the future.

THE SCOPE OF THIS BOOK

This volume consists of two types of material, both of which approach the book of Kings as theological literature.

First, the commentary portion seeks to retain the narrative form of the book in its exposition rather than follow a verse-by-verse format. There are good reasons to do this. The narrative form may be able to reflect the meaning and import of the biblical narrative most accurately and effectively. Moreover, most people, both within and without the churches, have little knowledge of these stories. To move through the texts narratively in a more modern idiom may help to draw the reader into the stories and help recapture them for the Christian community. That the common lectionary moves through major portions of the Kings story may assist the church in this recovery.

Second, interspersed among the commentary sections throughout the volume are forty-three theological reflections. These brief essays pick up on key themes and concerns of the texts and reflect theologically upon their continuing significance for faith and life. These reflections have to do particularly with God, the chief subject of the book and the only character that remains engaged across the entirety of Kings. The God that emerges from this narrative is a very complex character. Readers will not be able to bring this character under control so as to make available a finished divine portrait. Readers will be able to observe a "core character" that the God of Kings has; but this God surprises the reader ever anew. In seeking to understand this God, it will be wise to recall that Kings is not an isolated volume. As we have noted, it is a part of the Deuteronomistic History and, beyond that, a part of the biblical canon. These additional texts should often be drawn upon to assist us in our search for understanding. Finally, though these essays fall under the rubric of "faith in search of understanding," the God whom Kings presents also seeks our trust and loyalty. Kings thereby encourages its readers to keep mind and heart together.

First Kings

1. The Reign of Solomon
1 Kings 1:1–11:43

The key issue that has been raised in the preceding scriptural books, especially from 2 Samuel 9 on, is this: Who shall succeed David on the throne of Israel and restore order to the kingdom? Various candidates have been eliminated over the course of the narrative, including David's sons Amnon and Absalom. The only sons of David remaining are Adonijah and Solomon; 1 Kings begins by resolving this issue in favor of Solomon. But this succession is accomplished only through shrewd and ruthless, even Machiavellian, political maneuverings; the narrative does not flinch in laying the story out in realistic, if at times apologetic, terms. It should be remembered that this is a dispute within the family—David's highly conflicted family; this in turn catches up an entire nation. It echoes another biblical story—that of Cain and Abel.

Chapters 3–11 detail the actual reign of Solomon, though it is important not to separate chapters 1 and 2 too sharply from what follows. Chapters 1 and 2 lay important groundwork, not least the links between David and Solomon, as Solomon resolves key issues remaining from David's reign (cf. 2:5–9 with 2:13–46), sits on David's throne (2:12), and assumes the Davidic promises, voiced by both David (1:30, 48; 2:4) and Solomon (2:24, 33, 45). In what follows, both God and Solomon present his rule as decisively continuous with that of David (3:3–14; 5:3–5; 6:12; 8:14–26; 9:4–5). The two kings are an ideal pair, bringing unprecedented splendor to Israel. But Solomon's rule stands in contrast to that of David (11:4–6), so that it is finally only David's rule that grounds any hope for the future (11:12–13, 32–39).

Readers may observe several different ways in which the story of Solomon's rule is laid out. One is chronological, from early years (3:1–9:9) to middle years (9:10–10:29) to "when Solomon was old" (11:4). Another way is in terms of his major functions. After a programmatic beginning (3:1–15), the narrative moves through wisely exercised, wide-ranging responsibilities that are basically judicial (3:16–28), administrative (4:1–28), instructional (4:29–34), building (5:1–7:51), priestly (8:1–66), and commercial (9:10–10:29). All of these dimensions of Solomon's wise rule are considered important and contribute to the Davidic ideal (see below). Interspersed are key summary and interpretive pieces (2:2–4; 3:1–15; 6:11–13; 9:1–9), often giving theological perspectives that mix divine promise and warning. A further way to view chapters 3–10 is in terms of internal activities (3:1–9:25) and external dealings (9:26–10:29).

The most obvious structure is to make a break between chapters 3–10 (or 2–10), which depict Solomon's rule in almost completely positive and idealistic terms, and chapter 11, which is sharply negative and portrays his downfall. This break is not as stark as at first appears; the narrator does prepare the reader in chapters 2–10 for the "fall" in chapter 11. Yet generally this division does present the reign of Solomon as both a positive and a negative example. On the one hand, the proper rule of a king of David ought to be like this. The king follows a divinely ordained pattern for kingship (3:1–15), the people of Israel eat and drink and are happy, live in safety, all of them under their vines and fig trees (4:20, 25), and they are joyful and in good spirits because of all the goodness that the Lord had shown to his servant David and to his people Israel (8:66). On the other hand (chap. 11), the rule of the king can become idolatrous and oppressive, following other gods, and not walking in God's ways and doing what is right (11:10, 33, 38), with disastrous effects on the unity and welfare of the community. There is ample warning in chapters 3–10 that this could happen (e.g., 9:6–9), and the repeated and strong understanding of sin and its effects in 8:31–50—for there is no one who does not sin (v. 46) and God knows the heart (v. 39)—make clear that, among others, Solomon is not exempt from sin and its disastrous effects, though forgiveness is available for those who turn to God.

SOLOMON SUCCEEDS DAVID
1 Kings 1:1–2:46

1 Kings 1–2 are "swing" chapters; they conclude the reign of David and begin that of Solomon (cf. 2 Samuel 1–2, the transition from Saul to David; 2 Kings 1–2, the transition from Elijah to Elisha). The repeated acclamation "Long live King Solomon" (1:34, 39) is the climactic point of the first chapter. David's confirming words are important to this end (1:30, 48), but finally Solomon stands alone as the royal figure, active for the first time

(1:51–53). In chapter 2, building on David's final instructions (2:1–12), Solomon consolidates his reign (vv. 13–46).

David's Succession Resolved
(1 Kings 1:1–53)

1:1 King David was old and advanced in years; and although they covered him with clothes, he could not get warm. ² So his servants said to him, "Let a young virgin be sought for my lord the king, and let her wait on the king, and be his attendant; let her lie in your bosom, so that my lord the king may be warm." ³ So they searched for a beautiful girl throughout all the territory of Israel, and found Abishag the Shunammite, and brought her to the king. ⁴ The girl was very beautiful. She became the king's attendant and served him, but the king did not know her sexually. ⁵ Now Adonijah son of Haggith exalted himself, saying, "I will be king"; he prepared for himself chariots and horsemen, and fifty men to run before him. ⁶ His father had never at any time displeased him by asking, "Why have you done thus and so?" He was also a very handsome man, and he was born next after Absalom. ⁷ He conferred with Joab son of Zeruiah and with the priest Abiathar, and they supported Adonijah. ⁸ But the priest Zadok, and Benaiah son of Jehoiada, and the prophet Nathan, and Shimei, and Rei, and David's own warriors did not side with Adonijah. ⁹ Adonijah sacrificed sheep, oxen, and fatted cattle by the stone Zoheleth, which is beside En-rogel, and he invited all his brothers, the king's sons, and all the royal officials of Judah, ¹⁰ but he did not invite the prophet Nathan or Benaiah or the warriors or his brother Solomon. ¹¹ Then Nathan said to Bathsheba, Solomon's mother, "Have you not heard that Adonijah son of Haggith has become king and our lord David does not know it? ¹² Now therefore come, let me give you advice, so that you may save your own life and the life of your son Solomon. ¹³ Go in at once to King David, and say to him, 'Did you not, my lord the king, swear to your servant, saying: Your son Solomon shall succeed me as king, and he shall sit on my throne? Why then is Adonijah king?' ¹⁴ Then while you are still there speaking with the king, I will come in after you and confirm your words." ¹⁵ So Bathsheba went to the king in his room. The king was very old; Abishag the Shunammite was attending the king. ¹⁶ Bathsheba bowed and did obeisance to the king, and the king said, "What do you wish?" ¹⁷ She said to him, "My lord, you swore to your servant by the LORD your God, saying: Your son Solomon shall succeed me as king, and he shall sit on my throne. ¹⁸ But now suddenly Adonijah has become king, though you, my lord the king, do not know it. ¹⁹ He has sacrificed oxen, fatted cattle, and sheep in abundance, and has invited all the children of the king, the priest Abiathar, and Joab the commander of the army; but your servant Solomon he has not invited. ²⁰ But you, my lord the king— the eyes of all Israel are on you to tell them who shall sit on the throne of my lord the king after him. [21] Otherwise it will come to pass, when my lord the king sleeps with his ancestors, that my son Solomon and I will be counted offenders." [22] While she was still speaking with the king, the prophet Nathan came in. [23] The king was told, "Here is the prophet Nathan." When he came in before the king, he did obeisance to the king, with his face to the ground. [24] Nathan said, "My lord the king, have you said, 'Adonijah shall succeed me as king, and he shall sit on my throne'? [25] For today he has gone down and has sacrificed oxen, fatted cattle, and sheep in abundance, and has invited all the king's children, Joab the commander of the army, and the priest Abiathar, who are now eating and drinking before him, and saying, 'Long live King Adonijah!' [26] But he did not invite me, your servant, and the priest Zadok, and Benaiah son of Jehoiada, and your servant Solomon. [27] Has this thing been brought about by my lord the king and you have not let your servants know who should sit on the throne of my lord the king after him?" [28] King David answered, "Summon Bathsheba to me." So she came into the king's presence, and stood before the king. [29] The king swore, saying, "As the LORD lives, who has saved my life from every adversity, [30] as I swore to you by the LORD, the God of Israel, 'Your son Solomon shall succeed me as king, and he shall sit on my throne in my place,' so will I do this day." [31] Then Bathsheba bowed with her face to the ground, and did obeisance to the king, and said, "May my lord King David live forever!" [32] King David said, "Summon to me the priest Zadok, the prophet Nathan, and Benaiah son of Jehoiada." When they came before the king, [33] the king said to them, "Take with you the servants of your lord, and have my son Solomon ride on my own mule, and bring him down to Gihon. [34] There let the priest Zadok and the prophet Nathan anoint him king over Israel; then blow the trumpet, and say, 'Long live King Solomon!' [35] You shall go up following him. Let him enter and sit on my throne; he shall be king in my place; for I have appointed him to be ruler over Israel and over Judah." [36] Benaiah son of Jehoiada answered the king, "Amen! May the LORD, the God of my lord the king, so ordain. [37] As the LORD has been with my lord the king, so may he be with Solomon, and make his throne greater than the throne of my lord King David." [38] So the priest Zadok, the prophet Nathan, and Benaiah son of Jehoiada, and the Cherethites and the Pelethites, went down and had Solomon ride on King David's mule, and led him to Gihon. [39] There the priest Zadok took the horn of oil from the tent and anointed Solomon. Then they blew the trumpet, and all the people said, "Long live King Solomon!" [40] And all the people went up following him, playing on pipes and rejoicing with great joy, so that the earth quaked at their noise. [41] Adonijah and all the guests who were with him heard it as they finished feasting. When Joab heard the sound of the trumpet, he said, "Why is the city in an uproar?" [42] While he was still speaking, Jonathan son of the priest Abiathar arrived. Adonijah said, "Come in, for you are a worthy man and surely you bring good news." [43] Jonathan answered Adonijah, "No, for our lord King David has made Solomon king; ⁴⁴ the king has sent with him the priest Zadok, the prophet Nathan, and Benaiah son of Jehoiada, and the Cherethites and the Pelethites; and they had him ride on the king's mule; ⁴⁵ the priest Zadok and the prophet Nathan have anointed him king at Gihon; and they have gone up from there rejoicing, so that the city is in an uproar. This is the noise that you heard. ⁴⁶ Solomon now sits on the royal throne. ⁴⁷ Moreover the king's servants came to congratulate our lord King David, saying, 'May God make the name of Solomon more famous than yours, and make his throne greater than your throne.' The king bowed in worship on the bed ⁴⁸ and went on to pray thus, 'Blessed be the LORD, the God of Israel, who today has granted one of my offspring to sit on my throne and permitted me to witness it.'" ⁴⁹ Then all the guests of Adonijah got up trembling and went their own ways. ⁵⁰ Adonijah, fearing Solomon, got up and went to grasp the horns of the altar. ⁵¹ Solomon was informed, "Adonijah is afraid of King Solomon; see, he has laid hold of the horns of the altar, saying, 'Let King Solomon swear to me first that he will not kill his servant with the sword.'" ⁵² So Solomon responded, "If he proves to be a worthy man, not one of his hairs shall fall to the ground; but if wickedness is found in him, he shall die." ⁵³ Then King Solomon sent to have him brought down from the altar. He came to do obeisance to King Solomon; and Solomon said to him, "Go home."

The transition from David to Solomon is not accomplished without intrigue, no doubt complicated by David's failing health, the theme with which Kings begins. What a contrast from the David of 1 and 2 Samuel! His servants procure a beautiful virgin named Abishag, probably hoping thereby to test his potency more than simply to make him comfortable. The knowledge gained intensifies the intrigue between rival factions, right under David's nose within the palace precincts.

The supporters of David's only two living sons, Adonijah (the oldest and hence the logical choice) and Solomon, seek to take advantage of the power vacuum. Matching his sexual incapacity, David is blissfully unaware of these developments (contrast the claims regarding his wisdom in 2 Sam. 14:20). Both political and religious leaders, the most powerful figures of the time, are engaged in this intrigue. Priestly and military leaders are divided (Abiathar and Joab for Adonijah; Zadok and Benaiah for Solomon). The only prophet mentioned is not. Nathan's effort on behalf of Solomon is especially notable. His strategy is clever and manipulative; he enlists Bathsheba, carefully orchestrates Soloman's entrance, and uses exaggerated rhetoric (e.g., in stating that Adonijah actually had become king, vv. 13, 25). Solomon's mother, Bathsheba, plays a key role with Nathan in bringing the matter before David. Given the powerful role of the queen mother, she would have had more than a personal interest in Solomon becoming king. She enhances Nathan's rhetoric in her own direct and clever way, introducing God language (v. 17), playing on David's reputation before "all Israel" (v. 20), and suggesting that her life and Solomon's are in jeopardy (v. 21; see v. 31). In tandem Nathan and Bathsheba deferentially stress their own loyalty to David while implicating others. In a key move they remind him of his previous oath about Solomon (vv. 13, 17; cunningly put in the form of a question in v. 24); though this oath has not been previously mentioned in the narrative, David confirms it, whether it happened or not (v. 30; cf. v. 48). These key verses recall Nathan's original oracle of promise to David regarding an eternal dynasty (see 2 Samuel 7), and link Solomon to its fulfillment. Solomon is *God's* choice.

A key difference between the candidates to succeed David is made very clear. Adonijah (in the manner of treasonous Absalom, cf. 2 Sam. 14:25–26; 15:1) takes the initiative, is actively and conspiratorially engaged in his own promotion, and confidently acts to ensure his enthronement apart from any word from David. He is ironically portrayed (cf. all his feasting) as thinking everything has been resolved in his favor. In contrast, Solomon is represented as neither speaking nor acting on his own behalf. Solomon's wisdom is indirectly manifested thereby; he lets others do the dirty work.

The strategies of Nathan and Bathsheba, however questionable, are successful in moving David to act. Notably, David reports his decision to Bathsheba, not Nathan (v. 28). Although David is near death and has to be prompted by Solomon's supporters, he retains enough authority to name Solomon as his successor. David's word is effective in starting the process that brings Solomon to the throne (as co-regent until David's death). David confirms the oath to Nathan (v. 30) and even specifies the nature of the enthronement rite (vv. 33–35). The military leader Benaiah replies with a blessing (vv. 36–37), and the rite is carried out with full priestly, prophetic, and military participation (vv. 38–40; the mule carried royal symbolism). Though David does not participate, we hear indirectly that he responds to the news in language that again echoes the fulfillment of Nathan's oracle (v. 48; 2 Sam. 7:12). "All the people" participate in the occasion with much rejoicing, and even the earth resounds (v. 40).

But "all the people" does not include Adonijah and "all the guests" who were feasting with him (1:41). When these events are reported in no uncertain terms to Adonijah (vv. 43–48), "all" his guests disappear and, in a remarkable reversal from his earlier situation, he is left alone and fearful. He seeks asylum at the altar and pleads for clemency from Solomon. The new king, in his first act, links Abiathar's continuing life to the worthiness of his future behavior and sends him home. Chapter 2 will reveal that Adonijah does not "prove to be a worthy man."

Solomon Consolidates His Reign
(1 Kings 2:1–46)

The narrative in chapter 2 brings the reign of David to an end (vv. 1–12) and reports the first public actions of Solomon, which consolidate his power (vv. 13–46). In David's farewell speech (2:1–9; cf. Josh. 23:1–2) the dying king charges Solomon with keeping "the law of Moses" (2:3; the first use of this phrase), reiterates the promise given to David (in a qualified form), and reviews relationships with key individuals, stressing the wisdom of Solomon (vv. 6, 9). These themes set the agenda for the narratives that follow: law, promise, and wisdom. Solomon turns out to have a somewhat ambiguous relationship to these Davidic charges, and his wisdom will finally prove to be insufficient for the task.

After the initial reference to law and promise (2:2–4; see below), David's charge (2:5–9) turns to very particular political issues to be addressed by the new king. The immediate juxtaposition of personal faithfulness and public actions, both merciful and merciless, is striking; it suggests that public acts, as messy as they might be, must be informed by personal integrity and a right relationship with God. Yet the reader cannot but wonder if David hasn't slipped on this one. For David, this means that Solomon, in consolidating his reign, is to use wisdom (vv. 6, 9) in rewarding some friends and settling some scores. The friends David wants remembered are the sons of Barzillai, who provided support for him at a crucial time (see 2 Sam. 17:27–29; 19:31–40); the narrative does not report Solomon's response to this request.

Regarding the scores to be settled, David wants action taken against Joab, who had served him faithfully, for some old killings (see 2 Sam. 3:6–39; 7:12–16; 17:25; 19:11–15; 20:4–10) and against Shimei for an old curse (see 2 Sam. 16:5–13). In each case, David speaks of Solomon using his wisdom (vv. 6, 9), but it is clear what David wants; wisdom has the meaning here of shrewdness, and it may be used ironically. In Joab's case, the issue is stated in terms of an objective guilt for wrongful killings that remained to be dealt with; the guilt should be borne by Joab, not the Davidic house (2:5, 31–33). At the same time, Joab's support of Adonijah (1:7, 25; 2:28) is certainly in mind. David in effect gives Solomon another reason to eliminate Joab in order to consolidate his power and to install his own supporter (Benaiah, 1:8) as commander of the army (2:35). In Shimei's case, even though David had pardoned him (2 Sam. 19:16–23), he makes it clear that Solomon would not be bound by that oath.

Upon David's death after a forty-year reign, Solomon moves on four fronts to consolidate his position. Solomon follows through on David's charge with respect to Joab (2:28–35)—though Benaiah has reservations (2:28–30)—and Shimei (2:36–46); though the latter had been his supporter (1:8), he is executed after violating an agreement with Solomon to stay in Jerusalem. The new king also moves against another Adonijah supporter, the priest Abiathar (2:26–27), no doubt for backing the wrong horse. He is banished and replaced by his supporter, Zadok (1:8; 2:35), thus fulfilling the word of judgment announced to the corrupt house of Eli (of which Abiathar was a member) in 1 Samuel 2:27–36. With respect to Adonijah himself, the situation is more complex (2:13–25). Adonijah's attempt to procure Abishag as his wife may have been considered an effort to establish himself in a key position by marrying a woman closely associated with David (see 1:1–4; cf. 2 Sam. 16:21–22). Though Bathsheba agrees to intercede on his behalf, her commitment to Solomon raises the issue of her motives for doing so. Solomon interprets Adonijah's move as a threat to his throne (2:22–24) and reneges on his promise to her (2:20), a move probably welcomed by Bathsheba.

Politics as Usual and Narrative Justification

The initial impression that many modern readers will take away from this account is that Solomon has an "enemies list" and methodically moves to eliminate them, each in turn. This seems to be politics as usual, but with more than the usual complement of ruthlessness. Yet for all of the reader's legitimate suspicions about political chicanery, the narrator goes to great lengths to protect Solomon's motives. With regard to Joab and Shimei, he simply follows David's charge. Also, all but Abiathar act in ill-advised ways that give Solomon additional reasons to move against them. Even more, Solomon is given justifying speeches that link his actions to the good of the community and the Davidic dynasty (2:22–24, 31–33, 42–45). Moreover, in each case, God's own work is tied to his deeds (2:23–24, 27, 32, 44). Even Adonijah is said to confess that Solomon's reign is "from the Lord" (2:15); the point is made publicly, even if not sincerely.

Even so, the reader does need to raise queries regarding the perspective of the narrator (see also at 9:15–10:29). Has the narrator softened or justified actions that should be condemned, or at least sharply questioned? Perhaps so. The narrator's perspective must be considered in assessing Solomon's actions. At the same time, the bias evident in this account does not prevent the narrator from later being highly critical of Solomon's reign (chap. 11). Moreover, the considerable effort made to defend Solomon's motives suggests that the narrator would not approve such political activity as a matter of course. It may even be that the narrator has introduced subtle reservations into the account, for example, Benaiah's misgivings regarding the violation of sanctuary for Joab (2:28–30), Bathsheba's support of Adonijah's request and Solomon's angry and peremptory reneging on his promise to her (2:19–24), and Shimei's seemingly innocent violation of the agreement with Solomon (2:39–43). The narrator seems to have introduced enough ambiguity into the account of Solomon's actions to stop the reader from simply adopting an unquestioning stance toward what he has done. Such narrative ambiguities are also present in the narratives that follow (e.g., 3:1–3; 4:6; 5:13–14 on forced labor). One wonders why the narrator found it necessary to be critical in relatively subtle ways (some scholarly claims to find much negative comment about Solomon tend to forget this point). At the least, this narrator is more realistic than 1 Chronicles 28–29, which tells the story of the transition only from a positive perspective.

Divine Purpose and Human Intrigue

How the divine purpose is to be related to this human intrigue is an important issue to be addressed. Initially, David, though in failing health, sees through all the maneuvers and manipulations and recognizes that God's will has been done here. God has worked in, with, and under human intrigue to accomplish the divine purposes. God's action has been key to Solomon's becoming king.

It would not be true, however, to say that *only* God has brought this event about, as if the human actions involved were finally of no account. What the supporters of Solomon did, not least the cleverness and heightened rhetoric of Nathan and Bathsheba, truly counts for something in bringing about the desired result. Moreover, the wisdom of Solomon is specifically associated (by David, 1:6, 9) with his elimination of threats to his power. In pursuing the divine purposes, God does not act alone, but works with what is available, with human beings as they are, with all their foibles and flaws as well as their wisdom. God does not perfect people before working in and through them; God can work even through evil toward the divine purposes (see Gen. 50:20). These chapters are "a summons to the man or woman of God to be in the midst of the rowdy, untidy push and shove of human striving where God's purposes are at stake and to act with the boldness and astuteness of a Nathan. Bad leadership and evil can succeed only with the consent of the righteous. 'I told you so' is no substitute for responsible action" (Rice, *Nations under God*, 17).

It is important to say, however, that this divine action does not necessarily confer a positive value on the specific human means through which God chooses to work. The human means and methods that God uses here (and elsewhere) are not held up as exemplary behaviors, applicable to any situation. Richard Nelson's claim that "Yahweh's plan and will must be effected, and for God, at least, the ends justify the means" (*First and Second Kings*, 22) needs several qualifications. God's "plan" must not be reduced to specific details, God's will must not be considered irresistible in every respect, and the ends do not "justify" the means. Nelson's sentence is apt, "Yahweh is an unindicted co-conspirator in this palace intrigue." At the same time, it is not helpful to understand this claim in such a way that God's actions in the event are reduced to these human proportions. To speak unqualifiedly of God being "in charge" or "in complete control of events," as if everything that happens conforms to God's will, is to engage in such a reduction. The God of Kings (and the Bible!) is neither limited to human means (as if "God has no hands but our hands") nor all-determining of human action (as if God micromanages the life of the world). At the same time, between those two ditches, it is not possible to define precisely just how God has been at work in these events.

Davidic Covenant:
Conditional or Unconditional?

David's charge to Solomon in 2:2–4, filled with language from Deuteronomy, includes a reiteration of the promise made to David in 2 Samuel 7:12–16, but David conditions the promise, making it dependent upon the royal figure's remaining faithful (see Ps. 132:12). What are we to make of this condition in view of the unconditional character of the original promise? For one thing, the speaker of this text is not God. This is David's point of view (which Solomon reiterates in 8:25; cf. 3:6). Though God is quoted in verse 4, the prior narrative gives no indication that God has adjusted the original unconditional promise in this way. This text might reflect David's actual understanding of the promise, or it might be the way in which David chooses to put the matter to Solomon at this juncture in his life. The text does not make this clear, though from David's own life we know that faithfulness does not mean sinlessness or unbroken obedience (this is recognized in 1 Kings 15:5; cf. 8:46). At the same time, God does restate the promise in these conditional terms in 9:4–5, though this is not a conditioning of the *dynasty* of David, but Solomon's occupancy of the throne. In 11:11, Solomon's removal is what occurs, and the dynasty remains intact. At the least, this element recognizes that royal leadership will conform to God's will for Israel and be truly effective in bringing life and well-being only if kings walk before God "in faithfulness with all their heart and with all their soul" (2:4).

This conditional language must be set alongside continuing unconditional understandings, by Solomon himself (in 2:33, 45) and in the subsequent narrative (11:36–39; 15:4; 2 Kings 8:19). The conditional statements of the promise regarding "the throne of Israel" (2:4; 8:25; 9:4–6) refer not only to the Northern Kingdom (though Israel and Judah are recognized entities *within* the United Monarchy [2 Sam. 12:8; 1 Kings 1:35], "Israel" may also refer to all Israel, 1:34). "Israel" need only refer to *all* Israel to make the same point. These texts thus anticipate chapter 11, when the Northern Kingdom was in fact taken away from the Davidic dynasty and given to Jeroboam (11:38) in view of Solomon's unfaithfulness. But the Davidic dynasty, and God's promise relating thereto, remains in place (11:36–39), even if somewhat tenuously at the end of Kings (see at 25:27–30); at no point in these last chapters is the Davidic promise set aside.

The conditional and the unconditional thus stand in no little tension in Kings. This dissonance is at least in part due to multiple voices in the text (God, David, Solomon, and the various prophets) and to difficulty in assessing their place in the overall work. It may also be due to multiple editors. But the canonical form of the text invites the reader to retain the tension provided by the voices. In any case, it remains clear throughout that the problem is not with God. God will remain true to the divine promises; they will never be made null and void as far as God is concerned. The promise is an everlasting one, but people can, by their unfaithfulness, remove themselves from the sphere of the promise and suffer the consequences, a move that God will honor. And one way of being unfaithful would be to justify every personal agenda by an appeal to theological claims regarding divine commitment. But God's promise is always there for the believing to cling to, or the repentant to return to (see 8:1–66). They can be assured that God's work in the world, even in the midst of judgment and seeming "breaks" when the promise is not externally visible or embodied, will always be shaped by a drive to include all within the sphere of the fulfillment of that promise (for issues of God and the future, see the discussion at 9:1–9; 11:26–43).

A ROYAL PARADIGM
1 Kings 3:1–15

> 3:1 Solomon made a marriage alliance with Pharaoh king of Egypt; he took Pharaoh's daughter and brought her into the city of David, until he had finished building his own house and the house of the LORD and the wall around Jerusalem. [2] The people were sacrificing at the high places, however, because no house had yet been built for the name of the LORD. [3] Solomon loved the LORD, walking in the statutes of his father David; only, he sacrificed and offered incense at the high places. [4] The king went to Gibeon to sacrifice there, for that was the principal high place; Solomon used to offer a thousand burnt offerings on that altar. [5] At Gibeon the LORD appeared to Solomon in a dream by night; and God said, "Ask what I should give you." [6] And Solomon said, "You have shown great and steadfast love to your servant my father David, because he walked before you in faithfulness, in righteousness, and in uprightness of heart toward you; and you have kept for him this great and steadfast love, and have given him a son to sit on his throne today. [7] And now, O LORD my God, you have made your servant king in place of my father David, although I am only a little child; I do not know how to go out or come in. [8] And your servant is in the midst of the people whom you have chosen, a great people, so numerous they cannot be numbered or counted. [9] Give your servant therefore an understanding mind to govern your people, able to discern between good and evil; for who can govern this your great people?" [10] It pleased the LORD that Solomon had asked this. [11] God said to him, "Because you have asked this, and have not asked for yourself long life or riches, or for the life of your enemies, but have asked for yourself understanding to discern what is right, [12] I now do according to your word. Indeed I give you a wise and discerning mind; no one like you has been before you and no one like you shall arise after you. [13] I give you also what you have not asked, both riches and honor all your life; no other king shall compare with you. [14] If you will walk in my ways, keeping my statutes and my commandments, as your father David walked, then I will lengthen your life." [15] Then Solomon awoke; it had been a dream. He came to Jerusalem where he stood before the ark of the covenant of the LORD. He offered up burnt offerings and offerings of well-being, and provided a feast for all his servants.

This section presents the religious grounding for Solomon's reign; it parallels the more "earthly" perspective provided in chapters 1–2. God legitimates Solomon's kingship and extends to him the gifts that make it possible. A succession of chapters follows (3–10), chapters that are mostly positive in their assessment of Solomon. In chapter 11 a negative portrait comes to the fore and some contrary voices are heard, albeit softly, along the way (including this text).

The notice regarding the consolidation of Solomon's reign (2:46b) is immediately followed with some remarkably ambiguous comments. While Solomon's growing power is implied and his major building programs are anticipated, his later troubles are also signaled. Solomon's alliance with Egypt is sealed with his marriage to the Pharaoh's daughter; it is Solomon's tolerance of the worship practices of his foreign wives and his "love" for them that will eventually lead to his downfall (see 9:24; 11:1–8). The latter may also be embedded in the repeated reference to worship at the high places (vv. 2–3). These were legitimate shrines for the worship of God before the temple was built. The narrator's evaluation that Solomon loved the Lord (see God's love for him, 2 Sam. 12:24) and was faithful in worship at such a shrine in Gibeon (vv. 3–4) makes this clear. Yet the high places soon emerge in the narrative as a troubling issue associated with apostasy (11:7; 14:23; 15:14).

During Solomon's visit to Gibeon, apparently a typical royal move to seek direction for one's reign, God appears to him in a dream. Dreams are a legitimate means for divine revelation in the Old Testament (though some may falsely claim to have so received a revelation, Jer. 23:23–32). They are understood to be generated by external realities rather than internal psychological processes, in this case a divine appearance or theophany. The realism associated with this appearance is intensified by the conversation within the dream between God and Solomon that ensues (cf. Gen. 20:3–7; 28:12–16). God will appear to him a second time in 9:1–9 (Solomon is the last king to whom God will appear or speak directly).

In a remarkably open divine move, God invites Solomon to request what he will (v. 5). Solomon's response (vv. 6–9) witnesses to his wisdom in several respects and reveals a pattern for kingship that is in tune with the ideal of Deuteronomy 17:16–17, the warnings of Samuel in 1 Samuel 8:11–18, the royal psalms (see Psalm 72), and the prophetic vision in Isaiah 11:2–5 (and see Jesus' own standards for his disciples in Mark 10:41–45). Especially notable are these factors: Solomon's repeated self-reference as "your servant" (vv. 7–9; which he shares with David, v. 6), his humility (a "little child" who has much to learn), his openness to and expressed need for divine instruction for the task of governing, and his repeated focus on the welfare of the community as God's chosen rather than his own glory or personal gain. In effect, Solomon himself sets the standards by which his own rule will be judged, finally, in negative terms. His rule is a good illustration of the disjunction between intention and action (see Rom. 7:15–23).

Before speaking his petitions, Solomon bears witness to God's history of steadfast love to David, that is, God's faithfulness to the covenant with David (2 Samuel 7). This covenant was established with a faithful David in the first place, was continued throughout his life, and included the gift of "a son" for the throne. (Solomon does not personalize the promise.) Solomon's repeated witness to God's uncompromising faithfulness implies a desire for that to be continued to him (his comparable prayer in 8:23–26 brings that testimony up to date). His most basic prayer is a request for an understanding mind (literally, "a listening heart") in order to govern the people well, especially an ability to discern between good and evil, that is, to rule with justice and righteousness (see 10:9). This includes a listening to both God and people. God reiterates these themes in his response (vv. 11–12).

God is delighted with Solomon's response (note the divine emotion expressed in 10:9) and commends him for his understanding of kingship, evident especially in his asking for wisdom rather than long life, riches, and the death of his enemies. In view of this request, God not only grants him unparalleled wisdom (illustrated immediately in vv. 16–28) but goes beyond the asking in extending riches and honor as well. In addition, and conditional upon his being faithful as David was (David is the model for kingship throughout Kings, 9:4; 11:4–6), God will grant him long life. This condition is a simple recognition of the way in which the moral order works, not a precise or mechanistic divine calculation, and, interestingly (see the discussion at 1:1–2:46), does not suggest that the basic covenant is conditioned. Upon waking from his dream, Solomon responds in turn by returning to Jerusalem and, before the ark of the covenant (anticipating the appropriate place for worship in the soon-to-be-built temple), expresses his thanksgiving through sacrifices and feasting.

Praying for Wisdom

Solomon's prayer for wisdom is efficacious; his prayer makes a difference with respect to the shape of his future (on prayer, see discussions at 8:1–66; 2 Kings 18:1–20:21). This efficacy is evident not only in God's response to the request but in Solomon's actual exercise of wisdom in what follows. The text also claims that the character of the prayer makes a difference; the way in which Solomon sorts out priorities in his petitioning counts with God. God is pleased that Solomon has not engaged in self-promotion and has placed the welfare of the community in the forefront of his request. In fact, when those priorities are in order, benefits beyond the asking will follow (see also the confidence of Paul in Eph. 3:20). At the same time,

God's gift of wisdom does not function in independence from Solomon's own use, misuse, or non-use of that gift. The story of Solomon, finally, testifies to his failure to use well the wisdom God has made available to him.

The wisdom that God grants Solomon is not a supernatural implantation of a body of knowledge or a miraculous reconfiguration of Solomon's brain cells. Rather, it is an ongoing effective divine presence that includes instruction (see 8:36; Deut. 1:17; Ps. 25:4–5, 8–10; 143:10). As 3:28 puts it, "the wisdom of God [!] was in him"; 4:29 and 5:12 speak of an ongoing divine granting of wisdom. In view of the references to the king's reading the book of the law in Deuteronomy 17:19 and 1 Kings 2:3, one might even think of a kind of "scriptural" guidance (see 2 Kings 23:3, 24). Christians could speak of the internal testimony of the Holy Spirit (see John 16:7–15).

SOLOMON'S WISDOM DEMONSTRATED
1 Kings 3:16–5:18

This section illustrates Solomon's wisdom is several ways: discernment in judicial matters (3:16–28); administrative appointments and decisions (4:1–28); breadth of knowledge and sharing of that wisdom (4:29–34); and preparations for the building of the temple, including relationships with foreigners (5:1–18). The narrative is punctuated throughout with Solomon's growing reputation, both within Israel and in the international community. Solomon embodies wisdom's claim: "By me kings reign, and rulers decree what is just" (Prov. 8:15).

Wisdom in Judgment
(1 Kings 3:16–28)

3:16 Later, two women who were prostitutes came to the king and stood before him. 17 The one woman said, "Please, my lord, this woman and I live in the same house; and I gave birth while she was in the house. 18 Then on the third day after I gave birth, this woman also gave birth. We were together; there was no one else with us in the house, only the two of us were in the house. 19 Then this woman's son died in the night, because she lay on him. 20 She got up in the middle of the night and took my son from beside me while your servant slept. She laid him at her breast, and laid her dead son at my breast. 21 When I rose in the morning to nurse my son, I saw that he was dead; but when I looked at him closely in the morning, clearly it was not the son I had borne." 22 But the other woman said, "No, the living son is mine, and the dead son is yours." The first said, "No, the dead son is yours, and the living son is mine." So they argued before the king. [23] Then the king said, "The one says, 'This is my son that is alive, and your son is dead'; while the other says, 'Not so! Your son is dead, and my son is the living one.'" [24] So the king said, "Bring me a sword," and they brought a sword before the king. [25] The king said, "Divide the living boy in two; then give half to the one, and half to the other." [26] But the woman whose son was alive said to the king— because compassion for her son burned within her—"Please, my lord, give her the living boy; certainly do not kill him!" The other said, "It shall be neither mine nor yours; divide it." [27] Then the king responded: "Give the first woman the living boy; do not kill him. She is his mother." [28] All Israel heard of the judgment that the king had rendered; and they stood in awe of the king, because they perceived that the wisdom of God was in him, to execute justice.

This familiar story was probably one of many that circulated about Solomon (see v. 28). The absence of names and places in the story suggests that the interest is its typicality, not particular individuals. The story served to illustrate Solomon's powers of discernment in judicial matters. Solomon's wisdom is demonstrated both in the procedure set up for deciding the issue as well as in the determination of which woman is the mother.

The identity of the speeches of the two mothers has provoked some debate. The narrator informs the reader in verse 26a that the speaker is the mother of the living son. The other mother's heartless response (v. 26b) seems to make Solomon's decision obvious, though not finally foolproof. Though verse 27 literally reads, "Give *to her* the living boy," the NRSV clarification that "the first woman" (that is, the speaker of v. 26a) is "his mother" is probably correct. The identity of the speakers in vv. 17–22 is less certain. Though most scholars consider verses 17–21 and 22b to be the speech of the mother of the living son, the ambiguity of the text invites the reader to read the verses from both perspectives.

Though the focus of the narrative is on Solomon's more general ability "to execute justice" (v. 28), this story also demonstrates Solomon's concern for matters that are personal and local. Solomon cares about and helps to sort out a family issue—matters having to do with mothers and children in everyday life. He is not just a government bureaucrat and international entrepreneur, focused on the nation's political and commercial interests. Even more, the two women are prostitutes (v. 1), individuals from the underside of Israel's society whose rights would be honored by few. While the hearing is carried out at a rather formal and objective level, as such proceedings should be, more personal and caring tones are evident in that Solomon (the king!) receives them into his presence, personally listens to their stories, and honors their participation in the decision-making process (the absence of witnesses is stressed, v. 18). The predominance of dialogue in this story is noteworthy and gives evidence that Solomon indeed has "a listening heart" (3:9). Also notable is that the mother who lied is not punished (because her identity is not absolutely certain?). Solomon here exemplifies the ideal royal paradigm that speaks clearly of the king as one who "defends the cause of the poor of the people" and "has pity on the weak and the needy," and adds that their life is "precious . . . in his sight" (Ps. 72:4, 12, 14).

God and Political Structures

While this story does focus on the wisdom of Solomon, the reference to "the wisdom of God" in the climactic position (v. 28) finally places the emphasis on God's gift, not Solomon's prowess (see also 4:29; 5:12). This reference makes sure that readers do not lose sight of the link between the public world with its various political and judicial structures and the work of God. God is concerned about all aspects of the life of the people of God, not just the spiritual and religious dimensions. And God will be at work in and through those "secular" structures and their related personnel on behalf of the life of the creation (not just Israel). The reader is asked to recall the lively concern for justice and its administration in the law given by God, especially Deuteronomy (e.g., Deut. 16:18–20). Concern for the disadvantaged is often a central concern in such laws (e.g., Exod. 23:6–9). God provides for these and other societal structures "so that you may live, and that it may go well with you, and that you may live long in the land that you are to possess" (Deut. 5:33).

The sharp separation between church and state in American society has often obscured God's connection with the "state side" of our life together. Texts like these should remind us that God has a lively concern that justice be done and that the rights of "the least of these" be protected. To that end, God has provided for judicial and other structures to order our life together. Even more, God does not just provide for the structures and then let them be. God continues to be at work in and through (and beyond!) persons charged with their administration, not least with the gift of wisdom. But how such individuals draw on and use that wisdom will make a difference in how and whether life and well-being are promoted and advanced. The Solomon of this text illustrates how such wisdom ought to be used.

Wisdom in Administration
(1 Kings 4:1–28)

The first part of this chapter consists of two registers of administrative officers for "all Israel" appointed by Solomon (vv. 1–6, 7–19). Various notices about the officers and more general statements about the splendor of the Solomonic reign and the breadth and depth of his wisdom have been appended to these lists (vv. 20–34). Though archival in character, the registers function as another example of Solomon's wise leadership. The references to peace and prosperity that are woven here and there into the administrative notices imply that wise leadership is integral to peace in the land. Wisely devised and administered political structures serve Israel's life and well-being (see preceding section). The reader might wonder about the wisdom of a growing and entrenched bureaucracy, especially in view of Samuel's warning in 1 Samuel 8:11–18, but there seems to be no doubt in the narrator's mind (though the reference to "forced labor" in 4:6 anticipates later troubles). Links with Egyptian court practice are evident, but this is not necessarily negative. Israel has no monopoly on good order in God's creation (see Exod. 18:13–27).

The list of "high officials" in Jerusalem (vv. 1–6) includes some holdovers from David's administration (Adoniram, Benaiah, Jehoshaphat, and Zadok; the presence of Abiathar may mean that this list predates his banishment, [2:26–27] or that he has been reinstated). That sons of both Nathan and Zadok are included suggests an interest in establishing a hereditary bureaucracy that mirrors the Davidic dynasty. The territories of the twelve district "officials" (vv. 5, 7–19, 27) are not altogether clear, but seem not to reflect the usual tribal divisions. This ordering may reflect a new way of organizing the entire country ("all Israel" in v. 7 is "Judah and Israel" of v. 20). These individuals, which include Solomon's sons-in-law (vv. 11, 15), were responsible for forwarding support to the regime (a form of taxation), one district for each month of the year (vv. 7, 27–28). The daily provisions needed by the court are specified in vv. 22–23, and no perishable food is listed! This extensive inventory of provisions, which includes the needs of a sizable army (vv. 26, 28; the many horses could be a negative comment in view of Deut. 17:16), shows the extent of the growth of the Solomonic court, which has become responsible for an empire that extends from the Euphrates River in the northeast (Tiphsah) to the border of Egypt in the southwest (vv. 21, 24).

These and other highly positive notices (vv. 20–21, 24–25) in effect announce the fulfillment of ancestral promises, including the extent of land (see Gen. 15:18–19; Deut. 1:7), the size of the community—as the sand of the sea (see Gen. 22:17), security from all their enemies (Gen. 22:17–18;

Deut. 12:10), and peace (see Lev. 26:3–13; Micah 4:3–4). They "ate and drank and were happy . . . all of them under their vines and fig trees" (vv. 20, 25). It sounds like paradise. One wonders how anything could go wrong. Though things do go dreadfully wrong, the narrator sees much that is good in these Solomonic accomplishments, and it is important not to skip past these emphases too quickly or simply dismiss them as a facade.

Wisdom as Breadth of Knowledge (1 Kings 4:29–34)

4:29 **God gave Solomon very great wisdom, discernment, and breadth of understanding as vast as the sand on the seashore,** 30 **so that Solomon's wisdom surpassed the wisdom of all the people of the east, and all the wisdom of Egypt.** 31 **He was wiser than anyone else, wiser than Ethan the Ezrahite, and Heman, Calcol, and Darda, children of Mahol; his fame spread throughout all the surrounding nations.** 32 **He composed three thousand proverbs, and his songs numbered a thousand and five.** 33 **He would speak of trees, from the cedar that is in the Lebanon to the hyssop that grows in the wall; he would speak of animals, and birds, and reptiles, and fish.** 34 **People came from all the nations to hear the wisdom of Solomon; they came from all the kings of the earth who had heard of his wisdom.**

The chapter concludes (vv. 29–34) with a reference to the extent of Solomon's wisdom and the worldwide reputation for it that he achieved. The claims made are extraordinary; his wisdom exceeds not only that of other known wise individuals but that of entire peoples and cultures! This wisdom has to do with both depth and range, including such matters as insight, intellectual acumen, wide-ranging knowledge, skills of various sorts, and good judgment. Solomon is named as the author of numerous songs and proverbs, which leads in time to his being credited or associated with much of the extant wisdom literature (see Prov. 1:1; 25:1; Eccl. 1:1; Song of Sol. 1:1; Wisdom of Solomon; *Psalms of Solomon*). His knowledge, including "scientific" knowledge, is so extensive that people travel to Israel to hear him speak. These international dimensions of Solomon's wisdom continue in chapter 10.

Wisdom in Temple Building (1 Kings 5:1–18)

The testimony to Solomon's wisdom moves to another front in this section (vv. 7, 12); the dealings with King Hiram of Tyre follow naturally from the reference to Solomon's international reputation in 4:29–34. The issue Solomon faces is the building of the temple and how best to proceed with preparations for that task (on the temple, see at 6:1–8:66). Solomon's wisdom is demonstrated by the way in which he works with a foreign king to achieve that purpose.

An interesting aspect of this text is the portrayal of King Hiram of Tyre. He, too, comes off as a wise individual. Tyre, the chief city of Lebanon (Phoenicia), was situated on the Mediterranean coast about fifty miles south of Beirut. It had control of the "cedars of Lebanon," famed for providing the wood for important buildings in that world (see 4:33; cedar is often mentioned in chaps. 5–7). Hiram had already had dealings with David and been involved in building a house for him (2 Sam. 5:11). So he was a natural candidate to help with Solomon's building of the temple. In fact, Hiram initiates contact with the new king (v. 1), no doubt anticipating such building projects. Hiram eagerly receives Solomon's word about the temple and even voices praise to Yahweh (!) for Solomon's wise leadership of a "great people" (v. 7). The reader has some room to be cynical about such praise in view of the obvious commercial benefits! Yet such a doxology on the lips of a foreigner ought not simply be dismissed as opportunistic (see the discussion at 8:1–66; 2 Kings 5:1–27), and Hiram is responding to a message that is filled with theological claims. Solomon states that his servants would join Hiram's (v. 6); Hiram's counteroffer—to involve only his own servants in the logging while Solomon provides food (v. 9)—is not accepted by Solomon, who sends his own servants after all (v. 14). The cost is high (compare 5:11 with 4:22). A treaty is signed and verse 18 witnesses to the high level of cooperation between them. Solomon's wisdom is demonstrated at least in part by the way he integrates Hiram's wisdom with his own (yet finally dominates their relationship; cf. 9:10–14).

Solomon grounds his temple building project in a word from God to David (v. 5) in language reflective of 2 Samuel 7:13–14. He also gives a reason (unlike 2 Samuel 7) why David was not able to build the temple—his kingdom had not been completely secured from enemy attack (v. 3), which is contrary to the claim of 2 Samuel 7:1. Perhaps Solomon is overly apologetic about his father, given the audience, or exaggerates his own accomplishments. His reference to the absence of adversaries and misfortune is optimistic in view of 11:14, 23; and the reader cannot but recall Solomon's methods in eliminating his adversaries (2:13–46). Yet Kings speaks of no wars in which Solomon was involved.

In order to complete the work, Solomon conscripts 30,000 men, sending them to the Lebanon in shifts. Allowing them two months at home for every month at work was probably viewed as generous, and was certainly viewed as being in the service of a worthy cause and less than enslaving (stressed in 9:22, in contrast to the enslavement of the Canaanites). Yet in view of later developments (12:4), such references to forced labor anticipate trouble—not least by the way in which help for a specific project, which could be justified as a religious and civic duty, will become an institution. In addition, Solomon puts 150,000 men to work quarrying, dressing, and transporting the huge stones needed for the foundation of the temple. The potential for injustice is great, and later worker rebellions indicate that Solomon did not always deal with these laborers wisely.

On the Use and Abuse of Wisdom

In 4:29 and 5:12 (cf. 3:28) the narrator again makes clear that these accomplishments of Solomon have been possible because God has been at work in his life. Political structures (see above at 3:16–28) are gifts of the Creator God and integral to the well-being of society, as recognized in Deuteronomy 16:18–17:20. But, as the reader will shortly learn, to be gifted with wisdom is one thing; to use it well is another. Good starts—and that is the basic, if not entirely unambiguous assessment of Solomon—may not be sustained. God gives, but God does not finally control, the way in which those gifts are put to use over time. Gifts can be misused and abused so that their effects cease to be blessings. Obedience does not necessarily follow from being wise, and only wisdom and faithfulness working together ("The fear of the Lord is the beginning of wisdom," Prov. 1:1) can assure a future of life and well-being, as will shortly become evident. Those who live in Solomon-like societies today (whose empires are more commercial than political), where peace and prosperity are often the order of the day, may properly think of these "blessings" as the effects of a God-given wisdom. But they also need to remember what happened to Solomon and to Israel when those marvelous gifts were used in unfaithful ways, and when "blessings" could finally only be named as ill-gotten gains. They also need to be alert to the possibility that God himself will raise up prophets and adversaries (11:14, 23) and be prepared to listen and to evaluate themselves in self-critical terms.

SOLOMON AND THE TEMPLE
1 Kings 6:1–8:66

This text is the centerpiece of the reign of Solomon. It describes the building and decorating of the temple and the cherubim (6:1–38)—the exterior

(vv. 2–14), then the interior (vv. 15–36)—and various temple furnishings (7:13–51). These passages bracket verses that speak of another Solomonic building project—the palace (7:1–12). This placement in effect makes it secondary to the temple, but the order is probably due to building first and then furnishing. The purpose for this report was certainly not to describe the temple and its construction fully; too many details are missing or obscure. Yet, enough detail is present regarding size, quality of materials, and skill of design and workmanship to generate a sense of wonder. But this is more than a simple building report. At one level, this is wonder at Solomon's achievement (with much help from others, 7:14), which continues the emphasis on his wisdom in the prior narratives. At another level, this was "the house of (for) Yahweh" (twenty-two references in chaps. 6–10), God's dwelling place; only the best would do. The character of the dwelling place would reflect upon the character of Israel's God. The temple is to show forth the glory of the God who dwells therein.

The concern for detail, identity of the furnishings, interest in measurements and materials, skill of the designer (7:14), and language of divine dwelling (6:13; 8:12–13) remind the reader of the tabernacle (Exodus 25–31; 35–40), early forms of which influenced the temple architecture. The specific references to the exodus and Moses (6:1; 8:9, 16, 21, 51, 53, 56; 9:9) affirm continuities with that formative period; at the same time, the temple is something genuinely new. Compare the temple account in 2 Chronicles 2:1–5:1, which has been edited to make the temple conform even more closely than Kings to the tabernacle in Exodus 25–40. The visionary temple in Ezekiel 40–46 is of uncertain relationship to Solomon's temple. While archival texts may have informed the Kings account, idealized memories may have outdistanced reality.

Solomon Builds the Temple
(1 Kings 6:1–38)

Solomon began to build the temple in April-May (Ziv) of the fourth year of his reign (c. 956 B.C.) and completed it seven years later (6:38). The claim that this took place 480 years after the exodus (6:1) marks the building of the temple as a comparably key event in Israel's history, though it raises chronological issues—most scholars consider the exodus to have occurred somewhat later (1300–1250 B.C.). The site north of the city had been acquired by David (2 Sam. 24:18–25).

No traces of this temple have been found, but the remains of other Syrian and Palestinian temples have helped us understand temples in that world. By calling on key help from non-Israelites for planning and construction, Solomon links this temple to a widespread architectural tradition. Efforts have been made to discern the function and symbolic value of various temple features in view of such parallels. The absence of such an interest in the text itself has made suggestions problematic. Yet the interest in cosmic symbolism seems apparent (e.g., the pillars of stability [the basic sense of the names Jachin and Boaz]; the "molten sea" which "contains" the chaos; the wisdom and skill of the craftsmanship that mirrors God's creative work; the intricately designed, functionally ordered, precisely built product; and the materials and designs from God's good creation, including precious metals and flowery ornamentation). In some basic sense the temple is viewed as a world in microcosm, well-ordered and secure, in which the God who dwells in the cosmos becomes intensely present for Israel. In the temple and its worship, a world is re-created in the midst of the chaos of Israel's larger experience. Such borrowings from the larger environment as there may be should not necessarily be considered a negative reality. In time, they may have opened Israel up to distorted understandings, but that is potentially true of any tradition (cf. Nehushtan, 2 Kings 18:4). It is also likely that Israelite tent traditions and related values (the tent of meeting, Shiloh, and David's tent for the ark) had some influence on the temple's construction.

The temple was smaller than readers familiar with modern cathedrals might imagine, though larger than other temples archaeologists have unearthed in that region. It did not function as a place of public worship for the general populace, who were never admitted to the interior of the temple. Indeed, even clergy had limited access; only the high priest could enter the Holy of Holies, and then only on the Day of Atonement. At the same time, the temple as an institution was important for the people, not only because of its religious associations (e.g., sacrificial acts) but also because of its links to political and economic life (as elsewhere in the ancient Near East). That God had chosen this temple for a dwelling place gave public legitimation to the rule of the Davidic monarchy that had built it, in the eyes of both Israelites and the international community.

Little information is given about the temple's external appearance; it was a rectangular hewn-stone structure and had latticed windows. The starkness of the exterior contrasted with the highly ornamental interior. Its interior length was about 90 feet, of which the nave was 60 feet; the Holy of Holies was a 30-foot cube. Its interior width was 30 feet, and its height 45 feet. Basically, the building was made of stone, with internal cedar beams and walls, cypress floors, and olivewood and cypress doors.

Palm trees, pomegranates, and open flowers—perhaps symbols of fertil-ity—as well as cherubim were carved into the wood, and everything was overlaid with gold. The temple was fronted by an unroofed entryway 15 feet long and 30 feet wide. Placed on the two longer sides of the building itself was a three-story structure to provide wall support and numerous rooms for storage (see 7:51).

Interestingly, the construction of the cherubim for the Holy of Holies (6:23–28) is separated out from that of other furnishings (7:13–51); they were understood to be integral to the temple building itself. The cheru-bim, which most readers would never have seen, were human-animal hy-brid figures shaped in such a way as to provide a protected throne for the invisible God; the ark of the covenant (6:19; see 8:1–12) constituted the footstool part of a throne complex. These elements, especially, designate the whole as a divine dwelling place.

The Temple and Faithfulness

Right in the middle of the description of the temple is a word from God to Solomon, interruptive both literarily and theologically (6:11–13). This placement suggests that, for all the splendor of the temple being described, the temple itself is not to be the focus of attention nor is it to be conceived in such a way as to "contain" God, or as a vehicle by which God can be controlled. The key concern for Solomon and Israel is faithfulness to God. This commitment must be basic to any talk about the temple as the divine dwelling place. Everything else is of secondary import.

To what does the "promise" refer (v. 12)? It probably refers to God's dwelling among the people of Israel (v. 13), rather than to the basic Da-vidic covenant (see 2 Kings 23:27, which puts these themes together). For the exilic audience of Kings the temple had been destroyed and its vessels broken up and confiscated (2 Kings 24:13; 25:9, 13–17). All of this Solomonic splendor had gone down the tubes. The conditionality of God's dwelling in the temple among the people of Israel (6:11–13; 9:6–9; see 2 Kings 23:27) had become all too apparent. As it turned out, Solomon's disobedience (11:9–10) in itself did not seal the fate of the tem-ple (because of divine patience?). Its fate would finally be sealed by a buildup of the effects of disobedience, especially evident in the apostate practices of king after king (e.g., 2 Kings 16:10–18; 21:4–7). The reforms of a few kings (e.g., 2 Kings 12:4–16; 22:3–7; 23:4–12) would not finally be sufficient to turn this downward spiral around. In view of this history, it is possible that the present account was intended to function as a model for future temple building and use. For even 2 Kings 23:27 does not suggest that the divine decision to reject the dwelling place is permanent (for issues of God and the future, see discussions at 9:1–9; 11:25–43).

Other Solomonic Projects
(1 Kings 7:1–12)

This textually unclear segment is an account of Solomon's other major building project (v. 1 refers to the entire project of vv. 2–12). Almost twice as much time is taken to build it as the temple, though that is probably not a negative judgment, given the buildings necessary for the state to function. The lack of clear detail may indicate a lack of interest (and/or knowledge) apart from highlighting Solomon as a wise builder. This complex, completed in thirteen years after the temple (9:10), consisted of five integrated buildings (south of the temple), including his own palace and one for his Egyptian queen (v. 8). The other three (named) buildings have public functions, though their relationship to one another is not clear; the third (v. 7) appears to function as a courthouse.

Temple Furnishings
(1 Kings 7:13–51)

7:13 **Now King Solomon invited and received Hiram from Tyre.** [14] **He was the son of a widow of the tribe of Naphtali, whose father, a man of Tyre, had been an artisan in bronze; he was full of skill, intelligence, and knowledge in working bronze. He came to King Solomon, and did all his work.**
7:51 **Thus all the work that King Solomon did on the house of the LORD was finished. Solomon brought in the things that his father David had dedicated, the silver, the gold, and the vessels, and stored them in the treasuries of the house of the LORD.**

This segment is a detailed account of the furnishings for the temple (on symbolism, see above), including two pillars of bronze with decorated capitals (vv. 15–22), a "molten sea" supported by a pedestal of twelve oxen (vv. 23–26), ten stands to support basins (vv. 27–39), various pots and shovels used in sacrificial rituals (vv. 40a, 45–47), and various gold vessels (vv. 48–50). Key to the quality and completion of this work was one Hiram of Tyre (7:13–14; not the king), a person with an Israelite mother and great skill in working bronze; his wisdom is emphasized, which in turn enhances the splendor of the temple and the results of his work (and of those whom he supervised). His work is summarized in verses 40b–45.

Solomon becomes the subject of the making verbs in verses 46–51, stressing his role in the entire project, especially regarding the gold items (again, cf. the tabernacle furnishings in Exod. 25:23–40; 30:1–10). The repeated emphasis upon gold in verses 48–50 is intended to stress the value and splendor of these vessels. Verse 51 summarizes the work, with the note that to these were added various precious items that David had dedicated to the Lord (see 2 Sam. 8:9–12; 1 Chron. 22:2–5).

The Temple and the Importance of Place

In choosing a place to dwell among the people, God enters into the life of those for whom place is important. If places are important for people, they are important for God. What I have elsewhere said about the tabernacle is also true of the temple: "To speak of divine presence at a place helps preserve the personal character of that presence, for persons are always associated with places. Because the human is so shaped by place as well as time, worship for Israel could never be careless of times and places. Because the human is not simply a spiritual creature but physical through and through, there had to be a tangible place, as well as sights and sounds, touch and movement, in Israel's worship" (Fretheim, *Exodus*, 273–74).

It becomes clear over the course of Kings that worship at the high places or under any green tree will not do. Worship is associated with a divinely chosen place because it brings order, stability, and discipline; it provides a tangible aspect that relates the divine presence to physical as well as spiritual life; and it gives a concrete shape to the divine promise to be present within the community. Moreover, this is a place where *God* has specifically chosen to dwell among the people (see the language of "desire" in Ps. 132:13–14). This place is important *for God* as well as for people because it enhances the relationship between them.

At the same time, it was important to guard against a "house of God" understanding, as if God's presence could thereby be localized and fixed. The presence of the ark and the cherubim (mobile creatures) in the temple may have represented, at least in part, a certain concern for mobility and portability. Moreover, the continuing role given to the carrying poles in 8:7–8 (as in Exod. 25:15) and other linkages with the sanctuary of the wilderness wanderings helped avoid notions of a static and domesticated God. The usage of tabernacle language for the temple in the Psalms also bears testimony to such a concern (see Ps. 15:1; 26:8; 43:3; 46:4; 74:7; 84:1). The God who dwells among the people is also a God who is on the move with the people (or, in judgment, a God who can move away from them!—see Ezek. 8:6; 2 Kings 23:37). For people in exile, this becomes an important witness to the presence of God in their midst (see the discussion at 8:1–66).

Dedication of the Temple
(1 Kings 8:1–66)

8:1 **Then Solomon assembled the elders of Israel and all the heads of the tribes, the leaders of the ancestral houses of the Israelites, before King Solomon in Jerusalem, to bring up the ark of the covenant of the LORD out of the city of David, which is Zion.** [2] **All the people of Israel assembled to King Solomon at the festival in the month Ethanim, which is the seventh month.** [3] **And all the elders of Israel came, and the priests carried the ark.** [4] **So they brought up the ark of the LORD, the tent of meeting, and all the holy vessels that were in the tent; the priests and the Levites brought them up.** [5] **King Solomon and all the congregation of Israel, who had assembled before him, were with him before the ark, sacrificing so many sheep and oxen that they could not be counted or numbered.** [6] **Then the priests brought the ark of the covenant of the LORD to its place, in the inner sanctuary of the house, in the most holy place, underneath the wings of the cherubim.** [7] **For the cherubim spread out their wings over the place of the ark, so that the cherubim made a covering above the ark and its poles.** [8] **The poles were so long that the ends of the poles were seen from the holy place in front of the inner sanctuary; but they could not be seen from outside; they are there to this day.** [9] **There was nothing in the ark except the two tablets of stone that Moses had placed there at Horeb, where the LORD made a covenant with the Israelites, when they came out of the land of Egypt.** [10] **And when the priests came out of the holy place, a cloud filled the house of the LORD,** [11] **so that the priests could not stand to minister because of the cloud; for the glory of the LORD filled the house of the LORD.** [12] **Then Solomon said,**

> **"The LORD has said that he would dwell in thick darkness.**

[13]   **I have built you an exalted house,
> a place for you to dwell in forever."**

[14] **Then the king turned around and blessed all the assembly of Israel, while all the assembly of Israel stood.** [15] **He said, "Blessed be the LORD, the God of Israel, who with his hand has fulfilled what he promised with his mouth to my father David, saying,** [16] **'Since the day that I brought my people Israel out of Egypt, I have not chosen a city from any of the tribes of Israel in which to build a house, that my name might be there; but I chose David to be over my people Israel.'** [17] **My father David had it in mind to build a house for the name of the LORD, the God of Israel.** [18] **But the LORD said to my father David, 'You did well to consider building a house for my name;** [19] **nevertheless you shall**

not build the house, but your son who shall be born to you shall build the house for my name.' ²⁰ Now the LORD has upheld the promise that he made; for I have risen in the place of my father David; I sit on the throne of Israel, as the LORD promised, and have built the house for the name of the LORD, the God of Israel. ²¹ There I have provided a place for the ark, in which is the covenant of the LORD that he made with our ancestors when he brought them out of the land of Egypt." ²² Then Solomon stood before the altar of the LORD in the presence of all the assembly of Israel, and spread out his hands to heaven. ²³ He said, "O LORD, God of Israel, there is no God like you in heaven above or on earth beneath, keeping covenant and steadfast love for your servants who walk before you with all their heart, ²⁴ the covenant that you kept for your servant my father David as you declared to him; you promised with your mouth and have this day fulfilled with your hand. ²⁵ Therefore, O LORD, God of Israel, keep for your servant my father David that which you promised him, saying, 'There shall never fail you a successor before me to sit on the throne of Israel, if only your children look to their way, to walk before me as you have walked before me.' ²⁶ Therefore, O God of Israel, let your word be confirmed, which you promised to your servant my father David. ²⁷ "But will God indeed dwell on the earth? Even heaven and the highest heaven cannot contain you, much less this house that I have built! ²⁸ Regard your servant's prayer and his plea, O LORD my God, heeding the cry and the prayer that your servant prays to you today; ²⁹ that your eyes may be open night and day toward this house, the place of which you said, 'My name shall be there,' that you may heed the prayer that your servant prays toward this place. ³⁰ Hear the plea of your servant and of your people Israel when they pray toward this place; O hear in heaven your dwelling place; heed and forgive. ³¹ "If someone sins against a neighbor and is given an oath to swear, and comes and swears before your altar in this house, ³² then hear in heaven, and act, and judge your servants, condemning the guilty by bringing their conduct on their own head, and vindicating the righteous by rewarding them according to their righteousness. ³³ "When your people Israel, having sinned against you, are defeated before an enemy but turn again to you, confess your name, pray and plead with you in this house, ³⁴ then hear in heaven, forgive the sin of your people Israel, and bring them again to the land that you gave to their ancestors. ³⁵ "When heaven is shut up and there is no rain because they have sinned against you, and then they pray toward this place, confess your name, and turn from their sin, because you punish them, ³⁶ then hear in heaven, and forgive the sin of your servants, your people Israel, when you teach them the good way in which they should walk; and grant rain on your land, which you have given to your people as an inheritance. ³⁷ "If there is famine in the land, if there is plague, blight, mildew, locust, or caterpillar; if their enemy besieges them in any of their cities; whatever plague, whatever sickness there is; ³⁸ whatever prayer, whatever plea there is from any individual or from all your people Israel, all knowing the afflictions of their own hearts so that they stretch out their hands toward this house; [39] then hear in heaven your dwelling place, forgive, act, and render to all whose hearts you know—according to all their ways, for only you know what is in every human heart— [40] so that they may fear you all the days that they live in the land that you gave to our ancestors. [41] "Likewise when a foreigner, who is not of your people Israel, comes from a distant land because of your name [42] —for they shall hear of your great name, your mighty hand, and your outstretched arm—when a foreigner comes and prays toward this house, [43] then hear in heaven your dwelling place, and do according to all that the foreigner calls to you, so that all the peoples of the earth may know your name and fear you, as do your people Israel, and so that they may know that your name has been invoked on this house that I have built. [44] "If your people go out to battle against their enemy, by whatever way you shall send them, and they pray to the LORD toward the city that you have chosen and the house that I have built for your name, [45] then hear in heaven their prayer and their plea, and maintain their cause. [46] "If they sin against you—for there is no one who does not sin—and you are angry with them and give them to an enemy, so that they are carried away captive to the land of the enemy, far off or near; [47] yet if they come to their senses in the land to which they have been taken captive, and repent, and plead with you in the land of their captors, saying, 'We have sinned, and have done wrong; we have acted wickedly'; [48] if they repent with all their heart and soul in the land of their enemies, who took them captive, and pray to you toward their land, which you gave to their ancestors, the city that you have chosen, and the house that I have built for your name; [49] then hear in heaven your dwelling place their prayer and their plea, maintain their cause [50] and forgive your people who have sinned against you, and all their transgressions that they have committed against you; and grant them compassion in the sight of their captors, so that they may have compassion on them [51] (for they are your people and heritage, which you brought out of Egypt, from the midst of the iron-smelter). [52] Let your eyes be open to the plea of your servant, and to the plea of your people Israel, listening to them whenever they call to you. [53] For you have separated them from among all the peoples of the earth, to be your heritage, just as you promised through Moses, your servant, when you brought our ancestors out of Egypt, O Lord GOD." [54] Now when Solomon finished offering all this prayer and this plea to the LORD, he arose from facing the altar of the Lord, where he had knelt with hands outstretched toward heaven; [55] he stood and blessed all the assembly of Israel with a loud voice: [56] "Blessed be the LORD, who has given rest to his people Israel according to all that he promised; not one word has failed of all his good promise, which he spoke through his servant Moses. [57] The LORD our God be with us, as he was with our ancestors; may he not leave us or abandon us, [58] but incline our hearts to him, to walk in all his ways, and to keep his commandments, his statutes, and his ordinances, which he commanded our ancestors. [59] Let these words of mine, with which I pleaded before the LORD, be near to the LORD our God day and night, and may he maintain the cause of his servant and the cause of his people Israel, as each day requires; [60] so that all the peoples of the earth may know that the LORD is God; there is no other. [61] Therefore devote yourselves completely to the LORD our God, walking in his statutes and keeping his commandments, as at this day." [62] Then the king, and all Israel with him, offered sacrifice before the LORD. [63] Solomon offered as sacrifices of well-being to the LORD twenty-two thousand oxen and one hundred twenty thousand sheep. So the king and all the people of Israel dedicated the house of the LORD. [64] The same day the king consecrated the middle of the court that was in front of the house of the LORD; for there he offered the burnt offerings and the grain offerings and the fat pieces of the sacrifices of well-being, because the bronze altar that was before the LORD was too small to receive the burnt offerings and the grain offerings and the fat pieces of the sacrifices of well-being. [65] So Solomon held the festival at that time, and all Israel with him—a great assembly, people from Lebo-hamath to the Wadi of Egypt—before the LORD our God, seven days. [66] On the eighth day he sent the people away; and they blessed the king, and went to their tents, joyful and in good spirits because of all the goodness that the LORD had shown to his servant David and to his people Israel.

The major portion of this text is a lengthy prayer of seven petitions by Solomon (vv. 22–53) on the occasion of the dedication of the temple in Jerusalem. The prayer is enclosed by Solomon's blessing of the assembly (vv. 14–21; 54–61), in which the fulfillment of God's promises to David and Moses is highlighted, concluding with a call to obedience on the part of the entire populace (v. 61). The chapter as a whole is enclosed by liturgical actions, the gathering of the people and the dedication itself (vv. 1–13), and concluding acts of worship and dismissal (vv. 62–66). The Deuteronomic editing is evident throughout in its vocabulary and themes; this chapter and the temple of which it speaks are central to the theology of Kings.

The dedication of the temple was a week long ceremony, with an impressive guest list (8:1, 65) and much feasting, celebration, and a multitude of sacrifices. Solomon himself carries out certain priestly responsibilities (vv. 14, 55, 62–64), as David had before him (2 Sam. 6:17–19). The dedication was delayed for almost a year after the completion of the temple (compare 8:2 with 6:38), perhaps to coincide with the harvest festival of Booths (see v. 65; Deut. 16:13–16). According to the Deuteronomistic tradition, the law was read at this festival in the hearing of all the people (Deut. 31:9–13), though the narrative does not report that a reading occurred on this occasion (see v. 9). The joyfulness of this occasion for the people is particularly evident in verse 66, and it is grounded in God's "goodness" toward them (not Solomon's).

The prayer itself (vv. 22–53) is carefully structured and formulated in such a way as to address God and the assembly and their future life situations (though second-person address occurs only in v. 61). The prayer's introduction (vv. 22–26) picks up on themes in Solomon's previous speech (vv. 14–21); it centers on God's incomparability and God's having acted to keep the Davidic covenant (see 2 Sam. 7:1–17 and the discussion at 2:4) both up to this point and into the future, a future that reaches into the time of the Babylonian exile (vv. 46–51). The conclusion of the prayer (v. 53) also focuses on divine promises, but they are the ones given to Moses (cf. v. 56).

Thus, a two-pronged appeal to divine faithfulness with respect to covenants at two major junctures in Israel's life opens and closes the prayer. In view of such a structure, God's action and God's faithfulness surrounds and grounds the prayer petitions. Solomon (and God's people, vv. 30, 52) can presume to pray in confidence because God is a promise-keeper. Because of the kind of God Israel's God is, the people can pray knowing that their prayers will be heard and graciously acknowledged, though return from exile seems but a faint hope in the seventh petition—grounded in God's exodus deliverance (vv. 51–53). At the same time, Israel's repentance and faithfulness to God remains integral to the relationship (vv. 23–25, 61), though it is recognized that such faithfulness is not possible without the Lord's action to "incline our hearts to him" (v. 58).

The second segment of the prayer (vv. 27–30) constitutes a request that God hear the prayer and (except for petitions five and six) forgive. This segment of the prayer finds its parallel in verse 52, which adds God's eyes to the ears of God in verse 30. In both segments God is understood to be present and within "praying distance." The opening question in verse 27 regarding the divine dwelling does not contradict verse 13; the point is that, in the strictest terms, no place (even heaven) can be considered *the place* where God dwells. God dwells *both* in heaven and in the temple (see Ps. 11:4; see below on differences in understanding divine presence in this text). While God's people can lay claim to the promises that God will hear, God's specific responses are not under the control of those who pray. God will answer prayer because God is gracious.

Seven petitions follow (vv. 31–32, 33–34, 35–36, 37–40, 41–43, 44–45, 46–50). They anticipate virtually every possible future prayer situation that could be faced by the people. Retaining the theological tension noted above, the prayers are directed to God "in" or "toward"—important for exiles—the temple (or city/land), and ask God to "hear in heaven." A strong emphasis on Israel's God as a God who hears and stands ready to hear animates this text. All petitions but the fifth one (vv. 41–43) focus on the people of Israel. The seventh petition relating to the people still in exile (see Deut. 28:36–37) is the most complete and quotes the confession of sin directly for emphasis (v. 47). The petition to be returned to the land in verse 34 needs to be recalled here. The seventh petition is remarkable within this celebrative context; with a notable theological realism that takes sin and its effects seriously, no romantic claims are made for the temple. The temple does not secure a trouble-free future for the people of God. All but the fifth and sixth petitions focus on sins the people have committed (less clearly in the fourth petition, which covers various matters) and the importance of turning back to God (especially in the seventh petition). With all the emphasis upon sin and forgiveness, it is notable that sacrifice is never mentioned as necessary. While this may recognize the exilic context, the canonical positioning of this text claims that sacrifices were not necessary for forgiveness, even when the temple was fully functioning.

Sin, Judgment, and Salvation

Also stressed in the petitions are the ill effects that the sins have had on the people's daily lives. These adversities include personal, communal, and natural disasters. It is notable that God's action is not often linked explicitly to these disasters (only clearly in the first and seventh petition, vv. 32, 46). And then it is a matter, not of introducing a punishment in a retributive sense, but of "bringing their conduct on their own head" (v. 32; cf. also "according to all their ways" in v. 39 and "give them" in v. 46), that is, mediating the effects of the people's own behaviors.

Note further that the prayers are *never* simply for God to forgive sins, but are also for God to act in other ways to reverse the effects that their sins have had on various aspects of their lives. Salvation, therefore, is understood to comprehend more than forgiveness of sin; it includes also the amelioration of the consequences of sin that have reverberated out into the larger community, including the natural order (vv. 35–37). The prayer for being brought back to the land (v. 34) needs to be linked with the seventh petition, where this petition on the part of the exiles is not made explicit. This broader understanding of salvation is also evident in the sixth petition, where no sin is in view, and its concerns are for the people's cause in a time of battle.

God and the Prayers
of Insiders and Outsiders

The importance of prayer in the life of the people of God is given great prominence in this chapter. It fits well with a great variety of Old Testament texts that speak of the efficacy of prayer, not least many in Kings (see the discussions at 1 Kings 17:17–24; 2 Kings 18:1–20:21). The God to whom prayer is offered is one who *encourages* prayer with respect to every situation that life may bring; no matter how difficult the predicament, prayer can be efficacious in bringing life and well-being to the community. The God of Israel *receives* prayer, *evaluates* prayer in terms of the people's repentance, *transforms* prayer in view of the divine promises, and *uses* prayer as a means in and through which to act in the lives of those who pray. This prayer presents itself as exemplary for the worshipers' approach to God for all possible contingencies, whether they be in exile or in any other life situation.

The fifth petition in Solomon's prayer (vv. 41–43) is unusual in that it relates to foreigners who pray and does not focus on a particular situation in life, whether of sin or adversity. The petition relates to anything concerning which the foreigner may offer prayer to God. The call for God is to hear and to act in response. Even such outsiders are understood to have access to God; they do not have to be integrated into the chosen community in order for their prayers to be heard and answered. Given the verses that enclose the entire prayer (see above), this petition on behalf of foreigners is also grounded in God's promises to *Israel* and God's presence in Israel's temple. The faith of Israel is "ecumenical" in that it understands its God not only to be active in lives of such outsiders but also eager to attend to their prayers (see Mal. 1:11). Also to be noted is the reference in the seventh petition that God grant compassion to outsiders—Israel's captors—through whom God may work in response to Israel's prayers in captivity (vv. 46–50). Noteworthy is the absence here of a request to be returned from exile; those in exile are apparently encouraged to pray for what they think is most beneficial for their well-being at that particular moment (see Jer. 29:4–7).

The foreigners of whom Solomon speaks may refer primarily to the numerous travelers who made their way through Israel. They have heard of Israel's God by reputation, namely, the great deeds done on behalf of

Israel. This renown may draw some of these outsiders to Jerusalem and the temple, where they offer prayer. Solomon gives God two good reasons to answer the foreigner's prayer: "so that all the peoples of the earth may know your name and fear you . . . and so that they may know that your name has been invoked on this house" (v. 43). In other words, the way in which *God* responds to these people's prayer is considered a key factor in drawing them into the community of faith; the foreigners would come to fear the Lord and realize that God's presence is indeed associated with this temple now being dedicated. Solomon returns to this missional theme more generally in the conclusion to his prayer (v. 60). The divine objective through Israel is that "all the peoples of the earth may know that the LORD is God and there is no other" (see the discussion at 11:14–25; 20:13, 28; 2 Kings 5:1–27; cf. Deut. 4:35, 39).

Solomon's petition can be related to various texts that focus on foreigners. Prior to this text in Kings, the two Hirams from Tyre (5:1–18; 7:13–14) are portrayed as wise persons whose talents are integral to the preparation, design, and building of the temple. The evaluative witness of the outsiders in 9:8–9 testifies to a theologically mature judgment. The visit of the Queen of Sheba reveals a woman with her own wealth and wisdom, and who is capable of a remarkable and theologically sophisticated witness to Solomon's God. Later, the story of Elisha and Naaman (2 Kings 5; cf. Luke 4:27) speaks of a foreigner who is healed through the mediation of an Israelite prophet. Naaman moves from the healing to a confession of Israel's God as his Lord reminiscent of that of the Queen of Sheba (2 Kings 5:15). This missional impact may well animate Solomon's petition. Among other texts, Isaiah's concern that the temple be "a house of prayer for all peoples" is especially pertinent (Isa. 56:7; cf. 2:3; Ps. 47:9; Mark 11:17).

The Ark, the Temple, and the Presence of God

The centerpiece of the dedication was the procession of the ark of the covenant from the tent David had prepared for it (2 Samuel 6) into the Holy of Holies of the new temple. A copy of the law was kept in the ark of the covenant (vv. 9, 21), which was under the care of the Levites. This function for the ark is central for the Deuteronomic tradition (Deut. 10:1–9; 31:9, 24–26), as is the understanding of temple as both the place of the divine name and as a house of prayer, with God's dwelling place in heaven (8:13, 16–20, 27–30; "hear in heaven" references occur in each petition, but not without reference to the temple). This perspective on the temple would be important for an audience living in exile, whose temple has been destroyed, but whose prayers would still be heard by God, wherever they were thrown. This perspective is reinforced by the stress, in Kings, on the temple as a place of prayer and the virtual absence of the temple as a place of sacrifice (see 9:25), a practice no longer possible for exiles. But even for exiles for whom a temple no longer exists, a temple theology remains important, as they are urged to pray "toward" it (8:48).

At the same time, Kings has integrated this tradition with the (priestly) understanding of the ark as part of a cherubim throne complex, which views the ark, and the temple, as the place where God has deigned to dwell among the people (1 Kings 6:13, 23–27; 8:6–7, 10–13; 2 Kings 19:15). The "cloud" and "the glory of the Lord" (8:10–11; see Exod. 40:34), both symbols of the divine presence, also reflect this understanding. The reference to the poles of the ark being "there to this day" (8:8) may simply indicate that this section of the chapter was written before the destruction of the temple. Yet this language is retained even though Kings was not finally completed until after the destruction of the temple. Perhaps it anticipates a future when such a presence will once again be a reality.

These theological and chronological tensions within the chapter are important to recognize and consider. Keeping these perspectives on the temple together effects a qualification of *both* traditions. That is, whatever traditions lie behind the final form of the text, they no longer function independently of their present context. They no longer speak in isolation; they speak in interaction with each other. One powerful reality from the larger context is that the temple had been destroyed; God had been driven from the temple and had left the city (see Ezek. 8:6; 11:23). So, the theology of presence in this text is presented with the understanding that it comes with no guarantees regarding God's presence in the temple. And so qualifications abound. On the one hand, God's presence could not be confined or localized in the temple (8:27–30; see above) as might be encouraged by the common "house of God" language throughout this section of Kings (22 references). The strange note regarding the carrying poles of the ark (8:7–8) reinforces this point; the ark remains a portable object and, hence, the God who dwelled there was mobile, not static. This suggests that the ark has not been secreted away never to be heard from again (though it is not mentioned again in Kings). The reference to thick darkness (v. 12) also makes clear that the God who is present remains a mystery and cannot be domesticated. On the other hand, God's dwelling among the people in the temple was a reality for Israel in the past, and though God had forsaken that dwelling place (see 9:8–9; 2 Kings 23:27; 25:9), such a divine tabernacling remained a hope for the people in the future.

Keeping these various perspectives together in one's mind may be difficult, but it is also truer to the complex reality of God's presence and more productive of fresh theological insight than simpler formulations. The use of name language is important, not so much because it guards transcendence, but because it shows forth genuine relationship; the name bespeaks availability, being able to be in touch with the one who can be called on by name. Moreover, it is a way of stating the matter so that God is not understood to be confined there, perhaps especially for those who could not be present in Jerusalem (all the more after it had been destroyed). Finally, this text claims that God dwells in *both* temple and heaven, and these claims should be kept in constant interaction with each other so as not to lose the concern that each individually expresses (Ps. 11:4).

The temple and God's dwelling therein is most fundamentally for the sake of the people, as the effects upon the people in 8:66 indicate (see 8:16). This is coupled with the deleterious effects for faith that the high places have by their compromising of the worship of Yahweh. As such, the way in which kings deal with the temple becomes a key evaluative factor on their reigns. This emphasis is not for the sake of the temple per se, but for the sake of the people for whom the temple is integral to their faith and life and for the sake of God who desires to be present among them.

GOD APPEARS AGAIN TO SOLOMON
1 Kings 9:1–9

9:1 **When Solomon had finished building the house of the LORD and the king's house and all that Solomon desired to build,** [2] **the LORD appeared to Solomon a second time, as he had appeared to him at Gibeon.** [3] **The LORD said to him, "I have heard your prayer and your plea, which you made before me; I have consecrated this house that you have built, and put my name there forever; my eyes and my heart will be there for all time.** [4] **As for you, if you will walk before me, as David your father walked, with integrity of heart and uprightness, doing according to all that I have commanded you, and keeping my statutes and my ordinances,** [5] **then I will establish your royal throne over Israel forever, as I promised your father David, saying, 'There shall not fail you a successor on the throne of Israel.'** [6] **"If you turn aside from following me, you or your children, and do not keep my commandments and my statutes that I have set before you, but go and serve other gods and worship them,** [7] **then I will cut Israel off from the land that I have given them;**

and the house that I have consecrated for my name I will cast out of my sight; and Israel will become a proverb and a taunt among all peoples. [8] This house will become a heap of ruins; everyone passing by it will be astonished, and will hiss; and they will say, 'Why has the Lord done such a thing to this land and to this house?' [9] Then they will say, 'Because they have forsaken the Lord their God, who brought their ancestors out of the land of Egypt, and embraced other gods, worshiping them and serving them; therefore the Lord has brought this disaster upon them.'"

Once again God appears to Solomon, apparently in a dream as before (see 3:1–15). At the pinnacle of Solomon's glory, when everything seems to be going right, God appears with a word that is both confirming and a reality check. On the one hand, God responds in a positive way to Solomon's prayer (9:3; see 8:29; 2 Kings 20:5). In fact, God makes promises regarding the divine presence in the temple that do not seem to carry the conditions of 9:6–8 (cf. 6:11–13): "I have . . . put my name there forever; my eyes and my heart will be there for all time" (v. 3). This harks back to the language of God's promise in 8:13 (reiterated in 2 Kings 21:7, though cf. 23:27).

On the other hand, the divine word regarding Solomon's reign is conditionally stated (cf. 2:4). In verses 4–5, God's "if" relates to Solomon's being faithful as David had been. If this happens, then Solomon's throne over Israel will be established forever, just as God had promised David. *All* Israel seems to be in view here in light of what occurs in chapter 11 (see at 2:4). In verses 6–9, God's "if" is extended from Solomon to his descendants (the "you" is plural). A special emphasis is placed on faithfulness, that is, not serving other gods (vv. 6, 9) rather than obedience of an external code (see Introduction). If this happens, then *Israel* will be cut off (that is, excommunicated) from the promised land, will become a "taunt among all peoples," and the temple will be destroyed. Note that the unfaithfulness of the king has deep effects on the people as a whole (a theme common in the narratives that follow), though the people themselves are not excused from their sin (v. 9).

How the eternal promise of verse 3 links to the future possibility of destruction in verses 6–9 is difficult to determine. Perhaps 8:48, with its understanding that God will be related to the place of the temple even for the prayers of the exiles, is in mind. This view would, in turn, provide continuity between the first temple and the second temple. But between the two temples stands a great gulf—Israel's experience of divine judgment. The text does not back off from stating sharply that this God who has been so gracious and has stated promises so clearly can also judge, and this

is judgment against the chosen, the insiders (see Amos 3:2). This judgment does not mean that God's promises have become null and void; they
will always remain for the believing to cling to, even in exile. At the same
time, God will honor the decisions of those who choose to remove themselves from the sphere of the promise.

In view of this perspective, the insight of *outsiders* into what has happened is remarkable (vv. 8–9; see Deut. 29:24–25; Jer. 22:8–9; and the positive evaluation by outsiders in Deut. 4:6). This is *theological* insight on
their part, and should be linked to Solomon's statement in 8:60, "so that
all the peoples of the earth may know that the Lord is God." The outsiders
are here said to have knowledge of and insight into God's ways, both of
salvation (recalling the exodus) and of the call to faithfulness. One wonders whether the "knowing" of the outsiders in 8:60 is here understood to
be accomplished by what God has done in *judgment*; God's judgmental actions constitute a witness, too. Judgment can introduce a sharp clarity into
the meaning of events more generally. At the least, this is the narrator's
way of expressing surprise that Israel did not get such elementary theological points straight (see Isa. 1:3; Jer. 8:7).

That Solomon does not respond to this divine oracle may be a way of
introducing an ominous note into the narrative. The rest of Kings will play
out the theme struck in these verses.

God and the Future

It is noteworthy that the conditions are stated in both positive and negative terms (see the "if" and "if not" of Jer. 22:1–5; Lev. 26:3, 14). That is,
God holds out the possibility of both a positive and a negative future (v. 5;
vv. 7–9). It is clear from the entirety of Kings that the negative future
comes to pass, first for the Northern Kingdom (2 Kings 17:7–8) and then
for the Southern Kingdom (2 Kings 21:11–15; 25:8–12), though these
texts *never* state that the Davidic covenant has been set aside.

It is important to note that, from the perspective of this text, the negative future has not been predetermined; verse 5 holds out the possibility of
a positive future (remembering, of course, that the narrator lived in a time
after the negative future had occurred). This way of putting the matter says
something important about both God and Solomon/Israel with respect to
the future. The way in which Solomon and Israel respond to God and
God's ways makes a difference with respect to the shape the future takes.
What they do and say actually counts in determining what will happen.
Moreover, both of these futures must be considered genuine possibilities

for God as well. For God to hold out the possibility of a positive future, when it was not in fact a possibility, would be an act of deception (and there is no warrant in the text for such an interpretation). If *both* futures are possible for God, then not only has God not determined which future shall come to be, God does not finally *know* for certain which one shall occur (again, unless God is being deceptive). God knows these futures as genuine *possibilities*, though God may be said to know which future is more probable (perhaps shown in the detail given to the negative possibility). But God's knowledge of future *human* responses is not absolute. At the same time, God knows what *God* will do in view of the human response and proceeds to specify those futures.

Texts such as these do not call divine omniscience into question, only an understanding of divine foreknowledge as absolute. God knows all there is to know (omniscience), but there is a future that is not yet available for knowing, even for God. See the Introduction for a consideration of the understandings of the word of God in the Deuteronomistic History, which leaves room for future contingencies. (For further Old Testament texts and a discussion of divine foreknowledge, see Fretheim, *The Suffering of God*, 45–59).

The modern reader can recognize that the exile is in view in this text, but too much can be made of that, as if that future were a certainty at this point in the text. These words of God, in which Solomon's and Israel's faithfulness are said to be decisive for the shaping the future, show that what people do makes a difference. This word, addressed to a very powerful king at the pinnacle of his reign is remarkable; not even such persons are free from a critical and prophetic word from God. Yet, finally, this word is a gracious word, for God speaks of the future in a way that clearly lays out the real possibilities of blessing or judgment.

SOLOMON'S WISDOM AND WEALTH, ONE MORE TIME
1 KINGS 9:10–10:29

This section of Kings consists of various reports about Solomon from the middle of his reign (9:10). They are designed to depict his incredible wealth and wide-ranging wisdom, particularly on the international scene. This portrayal is presented as a series of snapshots, a kind of royal picture album (in rich colors!), rather than a developing story. Consequently, the movement from one portrait to the next is at times abrupt, though an overall image of opulence is certainly conveyed. The extent of the references to wealth—especially gold—in chapter 10 is truly remarkable; silver and cedar were so common they became everyday items (vv. 21, 27). The story of the queen of Sheba stands in the middle of these snapshots and provides a personal, on-site testimony by a royal outsider, cast in theological terms, to the reality of Solomonic splendor. The narrator's summary statement, "Solomon excelled all the kings of the earth in riches and in wisdom" (10:23), reports a fulfillment of God's promise that Solomon would be given "riches and honor all your life; no other king shall compare with you" (3:13). With this kind of divine beneficence one wonders how anything could go wrong (see below).

The reports in 9:10–14, 26–28 and 10:11–12, 22 speak of Solomon's continuing relations with Hiram, the king of Tyre, who had supplied materials for the temple. This relationship was not always so positive (9:10–14). Perhaps to replenish his treasuries, Solomon sold to Hiram twenty (unnamed) cities in Galilee (geographically near Tyre). Hiram was not pleased with the cities, but apparently he had already paid for them and so couldn't cancel the sale. But the commercial relationships between Hiram and Solomon continue. According to 9:26–28, Solomon launched a shipping industry (from a port on the Gulf of Aqaba); Hiram sent his sailors to travel with Israelites in their search for wood, gold, and precious stones, which Solomon used for his building projects and making musical instruments (see also 10:22; Hiram is said to function alone in 10:11–12).

Various actions of Solomon are reported in 9:15–25, including further details of Solomon's building projects in various parts of the land, some of which have been verified by archaeology (e.g., Hazor; Megiddo). The comments about forced labor (vv. 20–22) seek to clarify that Solomon did not enslave Israelites (see 5:13–18), only the descendants of those peoples left from the original inhabitants of the land (perhaps seen as fulfillment of the law in Deut. 20:11?). The Israelites served as officers and overseers.

Chapter 10 is devoted especially to Solomon's international activities and reputation (returning to the theme struck in 4:29–34). The net effect of Solomon's commercial activity was that he "excelled all the kings of the earth in riches" (v. 23). He also excelled them "in wisdom," which in turn became the source of further wealth (vv. 24–25). The reader can understand why the queen of Sheba was enthralled by her visit. The story of this visit, though perhaps adapted from a more commercially oriented encounter, conveys a fundamental truth about the splendor of Solomon's reign.

The queen of Sheba was a wise and wealthy woman (vv. 2, 10), who came with her own and her country's reputation (see Ps. 72:10; Isa. 60:6).

This image in turn enhanced Solomon's standing. Sheba is probably Saba in the Arabian peninsula (modern Yemen), down the gulf from the port where Solomon's fleet was based (9:26). When Solomon's (and God's!) reputation reached her land, the queen determined to test personally what she had heard—with gifts in hand and questions in mind. But none of her questions stumped Solomon, and it "took her breath away" (v. 5); this impression was enhanced by the wisdom evident in everything to which Solomon had put his hand, even his piety (v. 5).

The queen's response is a paean of praise (v. 8), and its length indicates that it is key to the story. How happy must be Solomon's wives and servants! But the climactic word of praise is reserved for God (v. 9), and her use of the name Yahweh for God is striking. The queen's hymnic language is a straightforward and exemplary witness to God's work; it would be remarkable even for a faithful Israelite. In some way, the word of Solomon about "all peoples" knowing God is seen to be exemplified in her (8:60; see at 8:1–66 on the prayers of outsiders in Kings). These blessings are grounded in God's delight in Solomon (see 3:10) and God's love for Israel. Moreover, and striking in the mouth of ancient Near Eastern royalty, God has accomplished these things for a purpose, namely, to execute justice and righteousness, the very realities that Solomon's father in the faith, Abraham, was charged to teach his children (Gen. 18:19) and to which Amos would call Israel to account (5:24). The royal charge in this regard is summarized well in Psalm 72, and the concern for the poor and the needy is central to what justice and righteousness are all about (note Jesus' juxtaposition of Solomon's glory and righteousness in Matt. 6:25–33).

After a typical exchange of gifts, she returns to her own country (vv. 10, 13; vv. 11–12 may make clear that Solomon is not especially dependent upon her). One cannot but wonder what happened to her and whether she really meant what she said.

Solomon's Dealings and the Narrator's Ideology

In this picture album of Solomon's wealth and wisdom, the narrator has been careful to pick out portraits that cast the king in a good light; indeed, the whole seems like a eulogy, centered in the queen's speech. Even more, some texts seem downright apologetic, designed to ensure that Solomon's actions will not be misinterpreted by later generations. For example, in the depiction of the forced labor (9:15–23), the narrator emphasizes that Israelites were not enslaved, though the natives were. Or, in his relations with Hiram in 9:10–14, what might be considered an underhanded commercial transaction wherein Hiram gets cheated out of 9,000 pounds of gold (!) seems to be left standing as an example of Solomonic wisdom (note how 2 Chron. 8:2 "clarifies" this by having Hiram give the land to Solomon). The modern reader might well claim that an unacceptable ideology of wealth has taken control of the narrative (see the discussion of ideology at 1:1–2:46). Should not the narrator have been (more) critical of the king and his various dealings to gain wealth and fame? No doubt some such evaluation is in order. At the same time, there may be more critical material here than first meets the eye.

The notes provided in 9:24–25 introduce into this section devoted to Solomon's wealth and wisdom a certain ambiguity. On the one hand, Solomon carries on his worship of the Lord in apparently appropriate ways (the sacrificial practice of 3:3–4 is discontinued now that the temple is ready). This stands in seeming contrast to his later practice in 11:4–7, but the strictly formal reference to worship in 9:25 may anticipate it (see Amos 5:21–23). Moreover, his building of a house for his wife, Pharaoh's daughter, anticipates the religious problems he faces in 11:1–8 in honoring the worship commitments of his foreign wives (see 3:1). In addition, the defense of Solomon's forced labor is not fully supported by 5:13–18 and 12:4, unless one draws a fine distinction between forced labor and slavery. Many Israelites (like many readers) were not prepared to do this, and the seeds of rebellion were thereby sown (12:4).

The witness of the queen of Sheba may also contain an implicit critique, particularly her statement about the divine purpose in making Solomon king: to execute justice and righteousness. The point of God's giving wealth to Solomon, the queen makes clear, is not the wealth—which she doesn't explicitly mention!—and the wisdom in and of themselves, but the use to which they could be put (see above at 5:1–18 on the use and abuse of wisdom). It is remarkable to have an outsider be so on target regarding the divine purpose; is this really the narrator speaking in a subversive way about the absence of justice and righteousness in the rule of Solomon (note that v. 8 mentions only his wives and servants, not the people generally)? The narrator may well prepare for the queen's words in a not so subtle way by prefacing the reports about Solomon's wealth with the divine word in 9:1–9 about walking in "integrity and uprightness" and obeying the commandments (so concerned with justice and righteousness).

Chapter 10 concludes on a note (vv. 26–29) that seems to be tacked on to the summary in verses 23–25. It may seem just to add more to the list of Solomonic goodies. Yet Solomon's traffic in (Egyptian) horses and chariots is in explicit violation of the Deuteronomic statute regarding such royal behavior (Deut. 17:16) and hence may provide a critical transition into the negative portrayal of Solomon that emerges in chapter 11 (see also the warnings of Samuel in 1 Sam. 8:10–18). If this law is in mind here, and the law about many wives in Deuteronomy 17:17a seems to inform chapter 11, might it be also that the law in Deuteronomy 17:17b that the king not acquire for himself much silver and gold hangs over the entire Solomonic narrative? The divine promise of riches and honor in 3:13 does give pause to this direction of thought; yet the distinction between gift and use is crucial (see at 5:1–18). And does the divine promise really mean the kind of incredible extravagance one sees here, especially in chapter 10?

At the least, keeping Deuteronomy 17:17 and this narrative together (even if the author of Kings is not entirely in agreement with Deut. 17:16–17) should raise many questions about Solomon for the reader who does not want to read the Bible in piecemeal fashion. The Bible has the capacity to be critical of itself, and indeed often is. But in order to grasp and use well that inner-biblical warrant for self-criticism, the reader cannot be content with studying texts in isolation from one another. And perhaps this narrator was not content either. At least he did not do as the Chronicler, who provided no counterpart to 11:1–40! This portrayal of Solomon, for all of its splendor and extravagance, sets up his downfall as all the more precipitous. To that "fall narrative" the text turns.

THE FALL OF SOLOMON
AND THE DIVISION OF HIS KINGDOM
1 Kings 11:1–43

Any reader who has been caught up in all the wealth and the wisdom of chapters 3–10 is brought up short by what follows here. This chapter narrates the "fall" of Solomon and the breakup of his kingdom. The effect of what happens will reverberate in negative ways throughout the rest of Kings. That Solomon's reign is repeatedly evaluated in terms of his relationship to Yahweh reveals the fundamental religious concern of the narrator. At the same time, the sharp contrast between this chapter and chapters 3–10 would seem to say something fundamentally positive about the reign of Solomon, even with the subversive elements present.

The opening segment (11:1–13) describes how Solomon becomes unfaithful to the covenant in repeated, evaluative language. God responds directly to Solomon with an announcement of judgment. Verses 14–25 expand upon this divine response as God takes an active stance against Solomon by raising up external adversaries. Verses 26–40 move to internal rebellion, as Jeroboam, with the encouragement of the prophet Ahijah, moves toward the division of the kingdom. The chapter concludes with the death of Solomon and the succession of his son Rehoboam (vv. 41–43).

Solomon's Sins and God's Response (1 Kings 11:1–13)

> 11:1. **King Solomon loved many foreign women along with the daughter of Pharaoh: Moabite, Ammonite, Edomite, Sidonian, and Hittite women, [2] from the nations concerning which the LORD had said to the Israelites, "You shall not enter into marriage with them, neither shall they with you; for they will surely incline your heart to follow their gods"; Solomon clung to these in love. [3] Among his wives were seven hundred princesses and three hundred concubines; and his wives turned away his heart. [4] For when Solomon was old, his wives turned away his heart after other gods; and his heart was not true to the LORD his God, as was the heart of his father David. [5] For Solomon followed Astarte the goddess of the Sidonians, and Milcom the abomination of the Ammonites. [6] So Solomon did what was evil in the sight of the LORD, and did not completely follow the LORD, as his father David had done. [7] Then Solomon built a high place for Chemosh the abomination of Moab, and for Molech the abomination of the Ammonites, on the mountain east of Jerusalem. [8] He did the same for all his foreign wives, who offered incense and sacrificed to their gods. [9] Then the LORD was angry with Solomon, because his heart had turned away from the LORD, the God of Israel, who had appeared to him twice, [10] and had commanded him concerning this matter, that he should not follow other gods; but he did not observe what the LORD commanded. [11] Therefore the LORD said to Solomon, "Since this has been your mind and you have not kept my covenant and my statutes that I have commanded you, I will surely tear the kingdom from you and give it to your servant. [12] Yet for the sake of your father David I will not do it in your lifetime; I will tear it out of the hand of your son. [13] I will not, however, tear away the entire kingdom; I will give one tribe to your son, for the sake of my servant David and for the sake of Jerusalem, which I have chosen."**

The narrative turns from Solomon's love for the Lord (3:3; see Deut. 6:5), as God had loved him (2 Sam. 12:24), to his love for his foreign wives (vv. 1–2); these two references bracket the reign of Solomon. This is a love story gone awry. God's continuing love does not overwhelm Solomon's decision to turn his love toward that which is not God, to violate his own call for complete devotion to God (8:61).

Solomon's many foreign wives (over 1,000!) provide the focus for the description of his unfaithfulness (vv. 1–8). But it is not Solomon's polygamy per se that centers the account, but disloyalty to God that follows therefrom. Deuteronomic law had prohibited marriage with the peoples of Canaan because of the danger of being led astray to serve other gods (Deut. 7:3–4; see Exod. 34:16; Josh. 23:12–13). Such intermarriage, in fact, had taken place early in Israel's life in the land (Judg. 3:5–6). That law, paraphrased here (v. 2), is interpreted to apply to other non-Israelite peoples as well. Solomon's marriages to women from these peoples had no doubt often occurred in order to cement political alliances, a fact mentioned with respect to Egypt in 3:1. Though the latter is mentioned without explicit evaluation (see 9:24), the reader is here invited to go back to 3:1 and note that the seeds of the problem were planted early on, and earlier decisions have a disastrous, if not inevitable, effect over time.

The narrator may lay more blame on the wives than on Solomon himself ("when he was old," v. 4) for his turning away from Yahweh. But Solomon does more than tolerate his wives' worship and build high places for them. The text repeatedly states the apostasy in personal terms and repeats the evaluation in a variety of ways, as if to make the point crystal clear: "his heart was not true to [or turned away from] the Lord his God" (vv. 4, 9), he has "not kept my covenant" (v. 11), and he "follows" (vv. 5–6, 10) not Yahweh, but these other goddesses or gods. This evaluation is reinforced by God through the prophet Ahijah in 11:33. They include Astarte and Milcom (both are associated with Baal) as well as Chemosh and Molech (though Milcom may be intended here, cf. v. 5). Solomon is in effect portrayed as a polytheist, though no doubt Yahweh is included within the pantheon (as will be the case in the time of Elijah; see 1 Kings 17–19).

This language of (un)faithfulness will be repeated often in the evaluation of the kings (e.g., 14:22–24; 15:11–15; 2 Kings 10:28–31; 14:3–6; 16:2–4; 17:7–18; 18:3–6; 21:2–15; 23:13), including the problem of the religious allegiance of foreign wives (1 Kings 15:13; 16:31). To this theme will be added that of worshiping Yahweh in idolatrous ways at high places throughout the land (see 12:26–33). The effect that royal behavior has on the populace as a whole will be especially noted. Given the repetition of the language from this text, the apostasy of Solomon is understood to be foundational for all subsequent unfaithfulness by Israel's leaders. The difference that one prominent person can have on the history of a people is remarkable. Solomon's reign is, finally, a tragic one. This difference is set off sharply by the reference to David, whose heart was true to the Lord his God (11:4; see 15:4). This seems an overstatement, except that the sin-repentance rhythm of 8:31–50 was exercised by David in a way that was not the case with Solomon (see 2 Sam. 12:13).

Yahweh's angry response is predictable (as Solomon himself had suggested, 8:46); the narrator makes clear that God's anger is not arbitrary, but has been provoked by Solomon's apostasy. Solomon had received ample divine warning about such a possibility. God had even appeared personally to him—twice!—to convey this word (3:5–14; 9:1–9). Moreover, David had reported such a word from God (2:4), and God had spoken to him on still another occasion (6:11–13). In view of Solomon's unfaithfulness, God announces a judgment that picks up on these prior warnings (vv. 11–13). This is the last time that God will speak directly to a king; from this point on, God will speak through the prophets.

Divine Judgment and Its Amelioration

God in judgment does not introduce anything new into the Solomonic situation; rather, God mediates the effects of Solomon's own sins, bringing them back upon his own head. As God puts it in Ezekiel 7:27, "according to their own judgments I will judge them." Solomon reaps what he sows, and the beginnings of the sowing are placed at the head of his story (3:1–3). If those seeds are not dealt with properly (and they were only intensified in his life over time), not even Solomon is rich enough or wise enough to escape from the effects of their growth (for further reflections on judgment, see at 21:1–29; 2 Kings 17:1–41; on divine anger, see at 14:21–16:34).

This judgment is first announced in terms that pertain specifically to Solomon (v. 11): the entire kingdom will be taken away from him and given to "your servant" (Jeroboam, v. 26, but the narrator leaves it open-ended at this point; see Saul and David in 1 Sam. 15:28–29). Then God immediately moves to delay its effect and to demonstrate that the judgment does not pertain to the dynasty, for two closely related reasons. First, the judgment will not occur during Solomon's lifetime, "for the sake of your father David," but during the reign of his son (Rehoboam, 12:1–19). Second, the entire kingdom will not be torn away; one tribe (Judah) will be left for his son, "for the sake of David *and* for the sake of Jerusalem," which God has chosen. The promises of God to David in 2 Samuel 7:14–15 are basic to both of the reasons given; the promise regarding Jerusalem (and its temple; 6:13 seems to be in mind, cf. 11:36) is added to the second reason.

The amelioration of the divine judgment is characteristic of several other texts in Kings (see Introduction), with Ahab (1 Kings 21:27–29), Jehu (2 Kings 10:30), and Hezekiah (2 Kings 20:1–7). In those cases, however, actions on the part of the individuals prompted the amelioration of judgment. In the case of Solomon, the qualification is grounded solely in the divine promise (see 15:4; 2 Kings 8:19). This will also be the case in 2 Kings 13:23, though the covenant with Abraham becomes the grounds at that point.

This theme is to be related to that of divine repentance, wherein God reverses an announcement of judgment so that it does not proceed to its completion. Here, however, the judgment is not reversed, though the delay makes it less severe than initially formulated. Moreover, the judgment does not include the entire dynasty. In a few texts, divine repentance language can be used for the delay or qualification of judgment as well (see Amos 7:1–9; Jer. 42:10). This theme is remarkable in what it reveals about God. God is not one who has set the future in concrete in a kind of "take it or leave it, like it or lump it" perspective. God takes into account the dynamic character of individual and communal relationships and responds in interactive ways that shape the future in ever new directions. At the same time, such divine adjustments in ways and means will always be consonant with God's basic character (e.g., Exod. 34:6–7) and fundamental saving purposes for Israel and the world (see further at 21:1–29; 2 Kings 20:1–7; 23:31–25:30).

God Raises Up Adversaries
(1 Kings 11:14–25)

God's response now turns to external affairs, and that divine move together with Solomonic weakness begins to erode the edges of the empire. Though the connection to Solomon's unfaithfulness is not made explicit, the juxtaposition of this segment with 11:1–13 invites it. God "raises up" Hadad from Edom and Rezon from Zobah (Aram/Syria), who (threaten to) lead rebellions that begin the process of the breakup of the Solomonic empire. While these persons are not much of a threat at this point in the narrative (Solomon wages no known wars), the Arameans will become major troublers later (see 1 Kings 20–22; 2 Kings 6–13), as will the Edomites (see Psalm 137; Obadiah).

God's Activity among Outsiders

Once again in Kings (see the discussion at 8:1–66) God is portrayed as active among peoples who are not Israelites, who have no allegiance to Yahweh (as will also be the case with Assyria and Babylonia). It is commonly noted that these stories bear a striking resemblance to the stories of Moses, Joseph (Hadad), and David (Rezon). As God has been at work to deliver Israelites through Joseph, Moses, and David, so God is at work in comparable ways among other peoples (see Amos 9:7 for a witness to God's exodus-like work among non-Israelites). God's work is as wide as the world. Though the peoples experience this work of God, they are not (yet) able to name the God who is active among them (see Isa. 45:4 on God's working through Cyrus).

What does it mean for God to "raise up" (vv. 14, 23)? It is important to remember, in each of these cases, that God's raising up is linked to situations that are already in process. The text explicitly roots them in the time of David, not Solomon (see 2 Sam. 8:3–8; 11–14; 10:15–19). David's deeds come home to roost here. In other words, for God to "raise up" does not mean that God initiates the activities of these troublemakers. Rather, God taps into already existing situations of discontent and *makes use* of them for specific purposes at this time in the reign of Solomon.

Jeroboam and the Prophet Ahijah
(1 Kings 11:26–43)

11:26 **Jeroboam son of Nebat, an Ephraimite of Zeredah, a servant of Solomon, whose mother's name was Zeruah, a widow, rebelled against the king.** [27] **The following was the reason he rebelled against the king. Solomon built the Millo, and closed up the gap in the wall of the city of his father David.** [28] **The man Jeroboam was very able, and when Solomon saw that the young man was industrious he gave him charge over all the forced labor of the house of Joseph.** [29] **About that time, when Jeroboam was leaving Jerusalem, the prophet Ahijah the Shilonite found him on the road. Ahijah had clothed himself with a new garment. The two of them were alone in the open country** [30] **when Ahijah laid hold of the new garment he was wearing and tore it into twelve pieces.** [31] **He then said to Jeroboam: Take for yourself ten pieces; for thus says the LORD, the God of Israel, "See, I am about to tear the kingdom from the hand of Solomon, and will give you ten tribes.** [32] **One tribe will remain his, for the sake of my servant David and for the sake of Jerusalem, the city that I have chosen out of all the tribes of Israel.** [33] **This is because he has forsaken me, worshiped Astarte the goddess of the Sidonians, Chemosh the god of Moab, and Milcom the god of the Ammonites, and has not walked in my ways, doing what is right in my sight and keeping my statutes and my ordinances, as his father David did.** [34] **Nevertheless I will not take the whole kingdom away from him but will make him ruler all the days of his life, for the sake of my servant David whom I chose and who did keep my commandments and my statutes;** [35] **but I will take the kingdom away from** his son and give it to you—that is, the ten tribes. [36] Yet to his son I will give one tribe, so that my servant David may always have a lamp before me in Jerusalem, the city where I have chosen to put my name. [37] I will take you, and you shall reign over all that your soul desires; you shall be king over Israel. [38] If you will listen to all that I command you, walk in my ways, and do what is right in my sight by keeping my statutes and my commandments, as David my servant did, I will be with you, and will build you an enduring house, as I built for David, and I will give Israel to you. [39] For this reason I will punish the descendants of David, but not forever." [40] Solomon sought therefore to kill Jeroboam; but Jeroboam promptly fled to Egypt, to King Shishak of Egypt, and remained in Egypt until the death of Solomon. [41] Now the rest of the acts of Solomon, all that he did as well as his wisdom, are they not written in the Book of the Acts of Solomon? [42] The time that Solomon reigned in Jerusalem over all Israel was forty years. [43] Solomon slept with his ancestors and was buried in the city of his father David; and his son Rehoboam succeeded him.

The textual move to Jeroboam is not explicitly linked to God's action, but the prior verses suggest that this is another individual that God has raised up against Solomon. This basically positive narrative regarding Jeroboam's rise to power clarifies the dynamics to be associated with the divine announcement in 11:11–13 (see especially "your servant" in v. 11).

Jeroboam was a servant whose industriousness caught the attention of Solomon, who placed him in charge of the forced labor (the contrast with Solomon's actions in v. 40 is especially sharp). His encounter with the prophet Ahijah—from the old sanctuary at Shiloh (see 1 Sam. 1:3)—elicits a word that draws out God's earlier judgmental word *and* articulates a clear direction for his own future. The tearing of Ahijah's new garment into twelve pieces is a prophetic symbolic act (cf. 1 Sam. 15:27–29) that vividly portrays the division of the kingdom. At the same time, the word that follows gives a particular interpretation of the symbolic act. Act and word together give shape to the future, but not magically or inevitably so in just these terms (see below).

The twelve pieces refer to the twelve tribes, the isolated piece to Judah and Jerusalem, and the newness of the garment to the recent establishment of the United Monarchy. Jeroboam is to be the ruler of ten tribes (see 2 Sam. 19:43) and the Davidic dynasty will retain one (as in v. 13). Actually two (see 12:21), but Benjamin is soon absorbed into Judah, and this number makes the correspondence with 2 Kings 17:18 exact, when the Northern Kingdom is destroyed and only Judah remains. The reasons given for this division (v. 33, "he has forsaken me") and for the delay and the limitation are the same as those God gave to Solomon (see at vv. 11–13)—for the sake of David and Jerusalem. In fact, the Davidic promise is repeatedly stated here in unconditional terms (as in 2 Sam. 7:14–16)— so that David may *always* have a lamp (=descendant, see 2 Sam. 21:17) in Jerusalem (v. 36), for God has built David an "enduring" house (v. 38) and, while David's descendants are to be judged, that will not be permanent (v. 39). The "reason" expressed in verse 39 goes back to pick up verse 33, is implicit in verse 38, and pushes forward into the narratives that follow. God's faithfulness to David will perdure in the face of human faithlessness (see the discussion at 2 Kings 23:31–25:30).

As for Jeroboam, though only "a young man," he shall be king, and this prophetic word legitimates him in that position (as was the case with David and Solomon). God's concern for the future of the ten tribes and their leadership is as prominent as that for Judah and the Davidic house; these people remain God's people as much as does Judah. God desires that the North be as perduring as the South. But conditions of faithfulness are attached to his house, if it is to be "enduring" like that of David (v. 38). The reader is given no reason at this point to believe that it could not be so (see below; remembering, of course, that the narrator speaks from the far side of the fall of the North).

The narrator does not make clear how Solomon discovered the identity of "your servant" (v. 11), but his efforts to kill Jeroboam fail when he flees to Egypt, as did Hadad (v. 40; contrast v. 28). Even though God's word about his future is still ringing in his ears (vv. 9–13), Solomon understands it as less than final and seeks to eliminate the threat Jeroboam presents. He seeks to protect all that he has gained at whatever cost, even if it means ignoring the word of God. Solomon's final act is a sign of his unfaithfulness. Solomon's kingdom has come to an end, for reasons that are most fundamentally religious in character, and Israel's identity is about to be reconfigured. The death of Solomon after a forty-year reign and the succession of his son Rehoboam is abruptly announced (vv. 41–43). The reader is informed that more information can be found in the Book of the Acts of Solomon, an otherwise unknown book; its content is not known beyond being the likely source for much of what has preceded. This record shows that the narrator's interpretive moves—choosing what to report and how—have been considerable.

The Prophetic Word and Jeroboam's Future

The reference to Jeroboam's rebellion (v. 27) is not inconsequential; causation in this situation is not ascribed only to God and God's word. Though this part of the story is delayed until chapter 12 and God's powerful word through the prophet fills this scene, the word "rebel" stands at the beginning of this narrative and has important content (as will be evident in chap. 12). This point finds its parallel in verses 14–25, where Hadad and Rezon are rebellious figures *before* God raises them up. To recognize this is important for how one thinks about the prophetic word and what follows.

For one thing, God works in and through what people do and say. This has just been made clear regarding Solomon's external adversaries (see at 11:14–25). What Jeroboam has done and will now do counts in charting a future course, not simply what God does or what God's prophet says. Both Jeroboam and God's word are effective agents. And Jeroboam's faithfulness (v. 38) is seen to be crucial for the course which that future takes. Moreover, the future possibility that God's word gives to Jeroboam in verse 38 is real; it has not been "closed off by prophetic foreknowledge" (contra Nelson, 73). The text gives us no reason to believe that God is being deceptive here, as if God knows for sure that this future will not come to pass but lays it out anyway. (See at 9:1–9 for God's knowledge of the future not being absolute; see also at 22:1–53 for divine deception.) This word to Jeroboam is *a genuine possibility* for the future, for *both* Jeroboam and God. God here treats Jeroboam *with integrity* in the outline of possible futures.

In fact, God uses important theological language for this word to Jeroboam; God will "take" him and he shall reign and be king; and "I will be with you" and "build" you a house, that is, an enduring dynasty. God sees a potential in Jeroboam's rule comparable to David's, as was the case with Solomon. All of this theologically loaded language certainly shows that God is sincere here. More generally, God cares about the future of the North as much as of the South; God's chosen people extend across both kingdoms, as will be evident in the narratives that follow. And, notably, there is no indication that the people of the North should not continue to regard the temple as central to their life of faith; the northern tribes remain a part of the Mosaic covenant and its obligations.

For another thing, God's will may not get worked out precisely in the way sketched by the word of Ahijah. As we have seen (see Introduction and at 9:1–9; 11:1–13), a prophetic word about the future does not set that future in stone (e.g., 2 Kings 20:1–7). One cannot argue from the perspective of fulfillment that that would inevitably have occurred just so at the time the word was spoken. That some prophetic words do not come to precise fulfillment in Kings means that *all* such words must be understood as having that *potential*. God does not leave a word to function on its own; God goes with the word and, in interaction with the community's everchanging history, may make a variety of adjustments in that word, or cut the word off altogether (on God's "control" of history, see at 1:1–2:46).

2. The Division of the Kingdom
1 Kings 12:1–16:34

Unfortunately, Israel did not have an Abraham Lincoln. If such a person had lived at the time Israel became a divided country, its history might have been different. When the American South seceded from the Union over the issue of slavery, the personality and policies of Lincoln were instrumental in keeping the country intact. In Israel's history, the North seceded from the South, but slavery (in a different form) was still involved. No Lincolnesque personalities emerged who could resolve the dilemma of division, either politically or militarily. Divided, Israel fell. First there were two (in 922 B.C.), then there was one (721 B.C.), and finally there were none (587 B.C.).

Amid all the military and political maneuvering of this period of time, the texts claim that the most acute issue for Israel was a spiritual sickness that slowly but surely consumed the heart of its people. And so, while a coherent history of the divided kingdoms is sketched, the narrator is interested most fundamentally in religious and theological matters. Prophets will play a particularly prominent role in what follows.

The bulk of this section focuses on Jeroboam, the first king of the North; some attention is given to his southern counterpart, Rehoboam (12–14). The last two chapters (15–16) alternate in treating the North and the South. The extensiveness of the treatment of the division of the kingdom (and the references back to it in later narratives) indicates the importance it has for shaping the subsequent history of both Israel and Judah. What happens here is decisive for the interpretation of the later history of God's people.

A division between chapters 11 and 12 is traditional; yet chapter 11 functions in a way comparable to chapters 1–2 in providing important transitional material for the narrative to come. The word of God to Solomon and to the prophet Ahijah (11:9–13, 31–39) decisively shapes the story that follows.

THE NORTHERN TRIBES SECEDE
1 Kings 12:1–24

12:1 Rehoboam went to Shechem, for all Israel had come to Shechem to make him king. ² When Jeroboam son of Nebat heard of it (for he was still in Egypt, where he had fled from King Solomon), then Jeroboam returned from Egypt. ³ And they sent and called him; and Jeroboam and all the assembly of Israel came and said to Rehoboam, ⁴ "Your father made our yoke heavy. Now therefore lighten the hard service of your father and his heavy yoke that he placed on us, and we will serve you." ⁵ He said to them, "Go away for three days, then come again to me." So the people went away. ⁶ Then King Rehoboam took counsel with the older men who had attended his father Solomon while he was still alive, saying, "How do you advise me to answer this people?" ⁷ They answered him, "If you will be a servant to this people today and serve them, and speak good words to them when you answer them, then they will be your servants forever." ⁸ But he disregarded the advice that the older men gave him, and consulted with the young men who had grown up with him and now attended him. ⁹ He said to them, "What do you advise that we answer this people who have said to me, 'Lighten the yoke that your father put on us'?" ¹⁰ The young men who had grown up with him said to him, "Thus you should say to this people who spoke to you, 'Your father made our yoke heavy, but you must lighten it for us'; thus you should say to them, 'My little finger is thicker than my father's loins. 11 Now, whereas my father laid on you a heavy yoke, I will add to your yoke. My father disciplined you with whips, but I will discipline you with scorpions.'" ¹² So Jeroboam and all the people came to Rehoboam the third day, as the king had said, "Come to me again the third day." ¹³ The king answered the people harshly. He disregarded the advice that the older men had given him ¹⁴ and spoke to them according to the advice of the young men, "My father made your yoke heavy, but I will add to your yoke; my father disciplined you with whips, but I will discipline you with scorpions." ¹⁵ So the king did not listen to the people, because it was a turn of affairs brought about by the LORD that he might fulfill his word, which the LORD had spoken by Ahijah the Shilonite to Jeroboam son of Nebat. ¹⁶ When all Israel saw that the king would not listen to them, the people answered the king,

"What share do we have in David?
We have no inheritance in the son of Jesse.
To your tents, O Israel!
Look now to your own house, O David."

So Israel went away to their tents. ¹⁷ But Rehoboam reigned over the Israelites who were living in the towns of Judah. ¹⁸ When King Rehoboam sent Adoram, who was taskmaster over the forced labor, all Israel stoned him to death. King Rehoboam then hurriedly mounted his chariot to flee to Jerusalem. ¹⁹ So

Israel has been in rebellion against the house of David to this day. [20] When all Israel heard that Jeroboam had returned, they sent and called him to the assembly and made him king over all Israel. There was no one who followed the house of David, except the tribe of Judah alone.

Verses 1–4 set the issues between Jeroboam and Rehoboam; only in verses 20–24 are they resolved. Reports regarding Rehoboam and Jeroboam thus bracket the section.

Upon the death of Solomon, an assembly of the people is held in the strategic city of Shechem (about forty miles north of Jerusalem) for the purpose of making Rehoboam king over "all Israel" (cf. David in 2 Sam. 5:1–3); in contrast to 11:42, this phrase now refers to the northern tribes (see vv. 20, 24). Rehoboam probably chose Shechem for this occasion because it was an important center for northern tribes (see Deut. 31:9–13; Joshua 24); he may have hoped thereby to mollify northerners who had become weary of burdens imposed upon them by Solomon (see 5:13–18). Meanwhile, Jeroboam heard about this occasion and returned from Egypt. Moses-like, he was called upon to lead a delegation to Rehoboam to request relief from the crown's forced labor policies, language reminiscent of Israel's life in Egypt (see Exod. 1:14; 2:23; the Hebrew and Greek texts disagree on the timing of Jeroboam's return; v. 20 functions as a summary statement in the present text, not as a report of his return).

Rehoboam asks for time to consult with his advisors, a delay that creates some suspense. He first inquires of those who had been his father's advisors, who counsel him to grant the request; if he will serve the people in this way, and speak good words to them, they will serve him (vv. 6–7). This seems to be a remarkably wise understanding of kingship, a kindness that generates a response of serving—a mutuality of serving. This "serving" language for the kingship is unparalleled, though its essential content is conveyed in Psalm 72 and messianic texts (see Isa. 11:1–6), and in the Isaianic servant songs (52:13–53:12).

One can understand why Rehoboam (or most kings!) would not be satisfied with this counsel, but he seems especially bullheaded and politically naive. And so, with his mind essentially made up (v. 8), he turns to his peers, "young bucks," newly appointed minions of the crown (note the "we" and "what" in v. 9 in contrast to the "you" and "how" of v. 6). These persons are portrayed as remarkably foolish and even obscene (Rehoboam's "little finger" [literally, "little one"] is probably contrasted with his father's penis). They advise him, not only to ignore the request, but to intensify the burden, promising even more painful whips (for which "scorpions" is a metaphor). In this way he will demonstrate that he has more strength than his father had.

Rehoboam follows the advice of his peers, even naively conveying to Jeroboam and the people their harsh words (vv. 12–14). When "all Israel" (the northern tribes) hear this, they reject the kingship of Rehoboam in language reminiscent of earlier taunts by rebellious northern tribes in the time of David (v. 16; cf. 2 Sam. 20:1–2). The name "David" is here used for the southern tribes; the contrast between "tents" and "house" suggests a distinction between the Davidic dynasty (house) and a more traditional understanding of leadership, harking back to premonarchical structures. When Rehoboam seeks to impose his harsh policies on the northerners, his representative is stoned to death and Rehoboam flees to the South, whose tribes remain loyal to him (Judah and Benjamin and Israelites living in the South, v. 17; see at 11:26–40 for the problem of one tribe or two in vv. 20–21). The narrator's "editorial" comment in verse 19 signals both the intensity and the length of the break, extending even to his own time. This suggests that the break is not seen to be finally permanent.

When Rehoboam prepares to resolve the issue militarily (v. 21, continuing from v. 18), God moves the man of God (=prophet) Shemaiah to speak. He is to tell Rehoboam (and his people, here confined to Judah and Benjamin and "the rest," v. 17) the divine will regarding the northern tribes, namely, that they be allowed to secede (the speaking of the word is not reported). The word "kindred" (v. 24; literally, "brothers") indicates that for God the two parts of the country remain one family. Rehoboam and his people heed the prophetic word and the secession occurs without incident (vv. 22–24). Though Rehoboam's foolishness stands out in vv. 6–18; here his response to the word of God contrasts with the following actions of Jeroboam. At the same time, the narrator gives him a mixed evaluation overall. Rehoboam's obedience regarding northern secession does not pertain to his entire reign (14:30), and 14:22–24 recounts that he did not lead his people very well (though he himself is not judged for it).

In the meantime, the northern tribes had made Jeroboam their king (v. 20), which ironically reverses the "all Israel" efforts of Rehoboam in verse 1. Given the events of verses 21–24, he is now free to rule without threat from the South. Yet he does not accept that state of affairs, and the rest of the portrayal of Jeroboam is entirely negative.

The Division of the Kingdom and Divine Action

In 11:31–39, the prophet Ahijah had conveyed the word of the Lord to Jeroboam regarding the division of the Solomonic kingdom and his own accession to the kingship of the northern tribes. Chapter 12 recalls this word in two ways. First of all, in verses 22–24 the prophet Shemaiah conveys to Rehoboam (and the two southern tribes) the essence of God's word to Jeroboam. They are not to fight against the North because the division of the kingdom is the will and work of God ("this thing is from me"). It is important to note that Rehoboam and his people heed (*šāmaʿ*) the word of the Lord and return to their homes (v. 24). In other words, the word of the Lord is not something that is effected apart from the human response of obedience. As elsewhere in Kings, the prophetic word will not necessarily or fully or precisely come to be. What occurs subsequent to the word of God counts toward the shape of the fulfillment. Von Rad betrays a magical understanding of word when he says that once Yahweh "has spoken, his word always and invariably achieves its purpose in history by virtue of its own inherent power" (*Problem of the Hexateuch*, 208).

Second, verse 15 is an assessment by the narrator as to why Rehoboam followed the advice of his younger advisors and did not "listen" to the people's request for relief from oppression. He did not listen "because it was a turn of affairs brought about by the LORD that he might fulfill his word" (NRSV; literally, however: "for it was a turning by [*or* away from] the LORD that he might fulfill his word.") Again, Rehoboam is the subject of the verb "listen"; that he did not listen is something that he himself did. It is not clear what the "turning" means or even who the subject is (this word occurs only here in the Hebrew Bible), but it does not imply that God micromanaged his mind. At the same time, the claim is clear that Rehoboam did not act alone. God was at work in this situation on behalf of the future outlined by Ahijah, even through the bumbling efforts of Rehoboam's listening and not listening, and that work of God was effective in this instance toward that end (on divine work through human intrigue, see at 1:1–2:46). But God's will as articulated through the word of the prophet Ahijah is clearly resistible, as evident in the actions of Jeroboam (see the discussion at 12:25–33).

JEROBOAM'S SIN
1 Kings 12:25–33

> 12:25 **Then Jeroboam built Shechem in the hill country of Ephraim, and resided there; he went out from there and built Penuel.** 26 **Then Jeroboam said to himself, "Now the kingdom may well revert to the house of David.** 27 **If this people continues to go up to offer sacrifices in the house of the LORD at Jerusalem, the heart of this people will turn again to their master, King Re-**

hoboam of Judah; they will kill me and return to King Rehoboam of Judah." ²⁸ So the king took counsel, and made two calves of gold. He said to the people, "You have gone up to Jerusalem long enough. Here are your gods, O Israel, who brought you up out of the land of Egypt." ²⁹ He set one in Bethel, and the other he put in Dan. ³⁰ And this thing became a sin, for the people went to worship before the one at Bethel and before the other as far as Dan. ³¹ He also made houses on high places, and appointed priests from among all the people, who were not Levites. ³² Jeroboam appointed a festival on the fifteenth day of the eighth month like the festival that was in Judah, and he offered sacrifices on the altar; so he did in Bethel, sacrificing to the calves that he had made. And he placed in Bethel the priests of the high places that he had made. ³³ He went up to the altar that he had made in Bethel on the fifteenth day in the eighth month, in the month that he alone had devised; he appointed a festival for the people of Israel, and he went up to the altar to offer incense.

In response to perceived threats from the South, Jeroboam establishes new centers of power. He builds several cities, including his political capital at Shechem, later moving it to Tirzah (14:17; King Omri will move it to Samaria). Jeroboam also establishes two religious capitals, at Bethel and Dan (in the far south and far north of the country)—a move typical of ancient Near Eastern monarchs. The rationale given by the narrator for Jeroboam's move, however, was fear for his life at the hands of his own people (v. 27). These shrines would help break connections with the Jerusalem temple (still "the house of the Lord" for both North and South) and continuing (or renewed) allegiance his people might have to Rehoboam. The narrator considers this a lack of trust by Jeroboam in the word of God that he would be king over the ten tribes (11:35–37), also evident in the fact that, unlike Rehoboam in verse 24, he takes counsel only with himself (vv. 26, 28, 33). Note also his reference to Rehoboam as the people's "master" (v. 27).

At each shrine (though Bethel is the more important) Jeroboam sets up a golden calf (actually bull) and recalls the exodus and Aaron's words in Exodus 32:4 (v. 28). These objects were probably not intended to be idolatrous (the plural "gods"—with plural verb—represents the narrator's perspective); otherwise, they would hardly have been accepted by the religiously conservative northerners. They were likely pedestals on which the invisible Yahweh was thought to stand. They would thus be parallel to the cherubim throne (including the ark of the covenant) in the Jerusalem temple. Generally, these and other moves by Jeroboam could be considered an effort to reinstate older Israelite worship practice. They were, however, at least dangerous, given the connections that the bull had with the Canaanite god Baal. From the narrator's perspective, they were deeply problematic from the beginning; they "became" a sin and led Israel into sin (12:30; 13:34; 14:15–16). Jeroboam becomes, in effect, a new Aaron.

Jeroboam's actions are presented most fundamentally as apostasy. The veritable litany of sins includes the use of images for Yahweh (see Deut. 5:8–10), the confusion of the one God and "gods" (see the prophetic condemnation in 14:9), and the establishment of "a house" (or houses; and further "high places") with its own altar other than the Jerusalem temple. The links to Exodus suggest that Jeroboam seeks to appropriate Israel's foundational event as the actions of his own "gods." But even more, Jeroboam appoints priests who are not Levites (contrary to Deut. 18:1–8), initiates a celebration of the feast of Tabernacles (in the eighth month rather than the seventh; see Num. 29:12) to rival that of Jerusalem, and functions as a priest at this festival (compare Solomon in 9:25). This litany provides the introduction to a further castigation of Jeroboam in chapters 13–14. Jeroboam's priestly service (v. 33) forms an introduction to chapter 13.

Jeroboam and the Will of God

God held out high hopes for Jeroboam and his reign. Indeed, God's will spoken through the prophetic word was clearly on record; God wanted Jeroboam to be king, and God anticipated a Jeroboam dynasty similar to that of David (11:37–38). This was no divine deception (see discussion at 11:26–43); God's desire for his kingship was real, and the conditions stated were actual conditions. In fact, 12:15 and 24 indicate that God has been at work to fulfill the prophet's word. God no doubt sees the potential in Jeroboam, that he has the strength to resist the oppressive forces at work under Solomon and Rehoboam. God raises him up as, in effect, a savior figure.

But God's will for Jeroboam does not get done. Not because God has failed, but because Jeroboam has. Jeroboam's sins are of such a magnitude that they successfully resist the will of God for him and his dynasty. The only other interpretive option for understanding Jeroboam is to view the litany of his sins in 12:28–32 as the will of God. But, whatever historical judgments one might make, the narrative in chapters 12–14 is critical of his actions in uncompromising terms. The will of God is evident in the *condemnation* of his actions. These were idolatrous acts standing in the tradition of the golden calf of Exodus 32 (32:4; see also Hos. 8:5–6; 10:5–6). These innovations of Jeroboam initiated a process whereby Baalized worship practices increasingly made significant inroads into Israel's life (already in 14:15). The book of Kings will pass a theological judgment on subsequent Israelite kings in terms of how they relate to Jeroboam's apostasy (over twenty times; first in 1 Kings 15:26; finally in 2 Kings 17:22–23). The assumption is that Jeroboam's successors could have reversed this state of affairs, but none of them did (2 Chron. 28:9–15 and 30:6–11 cite exceptions), and it no doubt became more difficult to do as time passed.

It is important to note that all of Jeroboam's sins are connected to worship in some way. There are no signs that he violated the principles of justice for the oppressed upon which his rebellion was grounded (with God's approval). In that regard, from both political and theological perspectives, Jeroboam's work is commended. Jeroboam's religious violations, however, which are used to serve personal and political ends (a universal way of using religion), subvert the positive political effect. Political liberation cannot stand by itself if the worship of God is not in order. This seems exactly opposite the problem addressed by later prophets, where the worship was appropriate, but justice was absent (Amos 5:21–24; Isa. 1:10–15). Neither religion nor justice can go it alone; both are necessary for life and well-being. The temptation will be to fall off the horse on one side or the other.

Jeroboam, who started out as a savior, ends up as such a sinner that the last state of affairs for Israel is worse than the first. God's hopes for him are dashed and God's will for Israel is frustrated.

GOD'S WORD AGAINST BETHEL
1 Kings 13:1–34

This chapter consists of two originally independent stories about prophets (vv. 1–10; 11–32) that have been integrated to provide a dual prophetic judgment on Jeroboam's religious activity; the chapter ends with a Deuteronomic judgment of indictment and disaster for his house (vv. 33–34). This narrative also provides an occasion to refer prophetically to Josiah (v. 2), whose reform three hundred years later reversed these actions of Jeroboam (2 Kings 23:15–20). As such, this chapter anticipates Josiah's reign and is concerned to establish his reforms as a God-given corrective to Jeroboam's condemned idolatrous religion.

This integrated story is legendary in character (for example, the account of the lion's behavior), has a complex, puzzling, even bizarre plot that does not become clear until the end (and even then one has to read back to figure it out), and there are many repeated words and phrases (way; turn/return). It seems likely that the narrator understood himself to be writing, not a straightforward historical account, but rather a story about prophets that could be adapted to sharpen the judgment on Jeroboam. The smashing of the altar (if it happened at this time), the withering of the hand, and the lion's behavior are interpreted as signs of God being at work (on symbolic narrative, see at 2 Kings 2:1–25; on miracle, see at 2 Kings 4:1–44). The narrator probably inserted the *specific* reference to Josiah to make the parallels between situations clear (2 Kings 23:15–20), but not to make it any less a prophetic word; it is not a testimony to a prophet's ability to make long-term forecasts (a rare phenomenon in the Old Testament). This prophecy unites 1 Kings and 2 Kings. (The study of Long, *1 Kings*, 145–52, is especially well expressed.)

13:1–10. The end of chapter 12 focused on Jeroboam's visit to Bethel, one of the two religious centers he established to be a rival to the Jerusalem temple. An unnamed man of God (=prophet, v. 18) from Judah (v. 14), moved by the word of God, interrupts Jeroboam at the altar (the scene of the crime) and issues an announcement of divine judgment on Bethel's altar (implying the entire sanctuary), addressing it directly (rather than the false priest Jeroboam). Burning disinterred human bones on the altar would desecrate the sanctuary. The sacrifice of priests anticipates Jeroboam's loose practice of verse 33 (and includes the king!). This prophetic word is reported as fulfilled in 2 Kings 23:15–20, and Josiah honors the publicly marked burial place of this man of God.

The man of God proceeds to give a God-given sign, the function of which is to authenticate the truthfulness of the prophecy (see Isa. 7:11–17); yet signs do not unequivocally do so, as Deuteronomy 13:1–3 makes clear. The altar at which Jeroboam is presiding is to be torn down and the sacrificial ashes on it strewn about (rather than carefully disposed of), thereby invalidating Jeroboam's sacrifice. Jeroboam reacts with anger and commands that the man of God be seized, failing to recognize that this was a true prophet. But the hand (a symbol of royal power) he had stretched out in command immediately withers. While prophetic signs do not always take place immediately, in this case it does (v. 5; this verse could be an aside by the narrator that the sign was fulfilled in his own day by Josiah). The altar collapses and the ashes of Jeroboam's sacrifice are scattered (no agent is specified). The sign prefigures the real event. The withering of the king's hand is also a sign of God's judgment and a sign of prophetic power over royal power.

Upon being personally affected, Jeroboam turns on a dime; he entreats the man of God to pray for the restoration of his hand. Inasmuch as prophets are often associated with intercession (1 Sam. 12:19, 23), Jeroboam may ironically acknowledge that the man is a prophet. The man of God proceeds to do so and Jeroboam's hand is healed (another sign that this is an authentic prophet—cf. Elijah in chap. 17—which Jeroboam fails to recognize). The man of God sharply resists Jeroboam's uncertainly motivated invitation to dine with him and receive a gift (see vv. 14–17), and he recalls a word from God that he was not to eat or drink "in this place" (a sign of participation in its rituals) or return by the way he came (a sign of an unfulfilled mission, cf. 2 Kings 19:33). This he proceeds to do, in an exemplary way. The prohibition and the refusal reinforce the word as a public renunciation of the ritual activity at Bethel. The prophet's authority in word and deed stands against that of the king. Whether it can stand against the word of other prophets is another question.

13:11–34. This segment of the story introduces us to a second "prophet" and is most fundamentally concerned to get a *second* prophetic word in place regarding the future of Bethel. It turns on a *specific case* of true and false prophecy, that is, on the identification of the truth of the word of the man of God on the part of the prophet from Bethel. The explicit reference to Bethel may mean that he is associated with Jeroboam's religious leadership. It is important to remember here that the word "prophet" is used indiscriminately for true and false prophets throughout the Old Testament (e.g., Deut. 13:1–6; 18:20–22) and that prophets can move back and forth between truth and falsehood.

The prophet is informed of the words and deeds of the man of God by one of his "sons" (probably a reference to a disciple of the prophet; cf. vv. 26–27). Having inquired of the "way" taken by the man of God, the prophet pursues him on a donkey. Having found him, he inquires as to whether he is the man of God, and invites the man of God home to dine (just as Jeroboam had done) and receives the same divinely directed negative response. But the prophet persists, identifying himself as a prophet and claiming that an angel spoke to him "by the word of the Lord," commanding him to invite the man back to dine. The narrator, surprisingly, interrupts the story to make clear that this word was a deception and not a true word from God (on deception, see at 1 Kings 22:1–53), and hence he is a false prophet, at least in this instance. His motivation is not made clear, but if he is a sympathizer of Jeroboam, he may have wanted to negate the word of judgment against Bethel by showing up the man of God as false.

But the man of God doesn't see the deception. Without hesitation, he interprets that word of God from an angel as having superseded the word he had received directly from God (or as calling into question the authenticity of his own word). In any case, he accepts the invitation (he had resisted the invitation of a *king* in v. 9!). He will suffer for incorrectly and uncritically interpreting this as a word from God (should the reference to an angel and the absence of "Thus says the Lord" have clued him in?). Because the narrator emphasizes the deception, this disobedience does not call the word of the man of God against Jeroboam into question for the reader (all the signs of vv. 1–10 have put that firmly in place, and v. 32 pounds it home, as does 2 Kings 23:15–20). Interestingly, the prophet does not suffer the effects of his false prophecy (no retributionary scheme here).

While the two are eating, the prophet speaks a word from the Lord (it is a genuine word, but it is not yet clear that it is) to the man of God—with the appropriate messenger formula ("Thus says the LORD"); it is an indictment and an announcement of judgment. Because he had disobeyed the divine command, he would not be buried in his ancestral tomb. The man of God has no response, leaves on the prophet's donkey, and is killed by a lion on the road (see a similar story in 20:35–36). Both the lion and the donkey remain standing by the dead man; remarkably, the lion neither attacks the donkey nor eats the man, as if (emblematically) to guard the point the dead man of God will now "speak" (v. 28).

When passersby report this unusual situation, the prophet interprets the death as God having "given him" over to the effects of his disobedience (he overinterprets in the reference to his being torn by the lion). The prophet adds (v. 26) that this potential judgment had been spoken to "the man of God" (implied, but not reported in vv. 8–9, 16–17, 22). And so, ironically, the death of the man of God confirms that his prophecy was true. The prophet then goes to the scene (cf. vv. 12–13), carries the body of the prophet home, mourns for him, and buries him in his own grave (he himself thus fulfills the word of God in v. 22)—and the monument remains until the time of Josiah as a sign of his authentic word (2 Kings 23:17–18). He tells his "sons" to bury him in the same place at his death, saying that the message of the man of God about the destruction of Bethel (and he adds his own word, that other high places will be destroyed as well!) will surely come to pass.

In spite of the prophetic warning to Jeroboam (and he does not know of the events of vv. 11–32), he persists in his "evil ways" and appoints to the priesthood not only non-Levites (see 12:31) but any who may be interested. The narrator's judgment in v. 34 is final: the house (=dynasty) of

Jeroboam will be cut off. But the future of his kingdom remains hanging in the air, if by a thread.

The Prophets and the Word of God

The false prophet from Bethel is convinced by a remarkable series of events (including a prophet's death and God's use of him to utter a genuine word, vv. 21–22) that the man of God from Judah was indeed a true prophet and, by implication, that he himself had been a deceiver. By asking to be buried next to the man of God, he identifies with him and publicly repeats his announcement of judgment. In effect, a false prophet has been convinced by events that the man of God was a true prophet and he himself becomes a true prophet, first by mediating the word to the man of God (vv. 21–22) and then by reiterating his word about Jeroboam. Moreover, inasmuch as this prophet was from Bethel, and probably a Jeroboam sympathizer, the testimony against Jeroboam comes not only from Judah (the man of God) but from within Israel itself and from its leadership.

The focus of the story must not be placed on the obedience or disobedience of the man of God or prophet. The story is not centered on these men, but on the word of God they speak about Jeroboam. The key effect of the story is a *double* prophetic witness against Jeroboam, from the leadership of *both* kingdoms, and so forceful that even a false prophet has seen the light though the true prophet has failed.

This story does *not* claim, however, that the word of God will inevitably be fulfilled or that no one can frustrate its workings (see the discussion at 11:26–43). Even the explicit mention of Josiah (a rare prophetic specification) does not suggest this, for this is also the case with other specifics that are not fulfilled (e.g., 2 Kings 20:1–7). The narrator, of course, lives with the fulfillment as past event. The amount of attention given in the following narrative to continued nonrepentance by northern kings indicates that the future of the North is not closed off and remains a matter of divine concern. Rather, the story shows the *tenacity* of the word of God to work in and through deceptions, disobedience, and death—even of prophets— to accomplish God's purposes. But what the prophets do, even if only— especially?—in death, is integral to the working of that word (on tenacity, see also at 19:1–21).

Given the interest of Deuteronomy in false prophets (especially Deut. 13:1–3), a more general point may be of interest here: do not be uncritical of words that people claim to have received from God (or angels); it can lead you astray or cost you your life. Such persons may be consciously (or unconsciously!) deceitful; actual defenders of Jeroboam (including from the narrator's own time) may be in view here, given the prophet's Bethel connections. The man of God could have used the good advice from 1 John 4:1: "Do not believe every spirit, but test the spirits to see if they are from God."

The notice in v. 34 about Jeroboam's "matter" (Hebrew: *dābār*) becoming a sin (better, the *effect* of the sin or judgment on the dynasty) relates back to the "word" (Hebrew: *dābār*) of Yahweh (v. 32 and often). God's *dābār* of judgment flows from, correlates with Jeroboam's *dābār* of sin (on judgment, see at 21:1–29; 2 Kings 17:1–41). Once again, God's judgment introduces nothing new into the situation.

GOD'S WORD AGAINST JEROBOAM
1 Kings 14:1–20

14:1 At that time Abijah son of Jeroboam fell sick. [2] Jeroboam said to his wife, "Go, disguise yourself, so that it will not be known that you are the wife of Jeroboam, and go to Shiloh; for the prophet Ahijah is there, who said of me that I should be king over this people. [3] Take with you ten loaves, some cakes, and a jar of honey, and go to him; he will tell you what shall happen to the child." [4] Jeroboam's wife did so; she set out and went to Shiloh, and came to the house of Ahijah. Now Ahijah could not see, for his eyes were dim because of his age. [5] But the LORD said to Ahijah, "The wife of Jeroboam is coming to inquire of you concerning her son; for he is sick. Thus and thus you shall say to her." When she came, she pretended to be another woman. [6] But when Ahijah heard the sound of her feet, as she came in at the door, he said, "Come in, wife of Jeroboam; why do you pretend to be another? For I am charged with heavy tidings for you. [7] Go, tell Jeroboam, 'Thus says the LORD, the God of Israel: Because I exalted you from among the people, made you leader over my people Israel, [8] and tore the kingdom away from the house of David to give it to you; yet you have not been like my servant David, who kept my commandments and followed me with all his heart, doing only that which was right in my sight, [9] but you have done evil above all those who were before you and have gone and made for yourself other gods, and cast images, provoking me to anger, and have thrust me behind your back; [10] therefore, I will bring evil upon the house of Jeroboam. I will cut off from Jeroboam every male, both bond and free in Israel, and will consume the house of Jeroboam, just as one burns up dung until it is all gone. [11] Anyone belonging to Jeroboam who dies in the city, the dogs shall eat; and anyone who dies in the open country, the birds of the air shall eat; for the LORD has spoken.' [12] Therefore set out, go to your house. When your feet enter the city, the child shall die. ^{13} All Israel shall mourn for him and bury him; for he alone of Jeroboam's family shall come to the grave, because in him there is found something pleasing to the LORD, the God of Israel, in the house of Jeroboam. ^{14} Moreover the LORD will raise up for himself a king over Israel, who shall cut off the house of Jeroboam today, even right now! ^{15} "The LORD will strike Israel, as a reed is shaken in the water; he will root up Israel out of this good land that he gave to their ancestors, and scatter them beyond the Euphrates, because they have made their sacred poles, provoking the LORD to anger. ^{16} He will give Israel up because of the sins of Jeroboam, which he sinned and which he caused Israel to commit." ^{17} Then Jeroboam's wife got up and went away, and she came to Tirzah. As she came to the threshold of the house, the child died. ^{18} All Israel buried him and mourned for him, according to the word of the LORD, which he spoke by his servant the prophet Ahijah. ^{19} Now the rest of the acts of Jeroboam, how he warred and how he reigned, are written in the Book of the Annals of the Kings of Israel. ^{20} The time that Jeroboam reigned was twenty-two years; then he slept with his ancestors, and his son Nadab succeeded him.

As in chapter 13, a story becomes the vehicle for a prophetic word. The focus is a third prophetic word against Jeroboam, which reinforces and more closely specifies the prophetic judgments of chapter 13. At the same time, the story elements are not so much fluff; the sickness within the royal household and the deceptive attempt at a cover-up enhance the point of the oracle. Even the name of the dying child (Abijah means "Yahweh is my father") signals the death of genuine Yahwism in Israel. The "bad news" is spoken to Jeroboam's unnamed wife by an aged Ahijah, who had earlier brought a positive word from the Lord to Jeroboam (11:31–39).

The narrator now needs to go back and make clear that this original word to Jeroboam does not continue to stand, because the conditions for his reign (specified in 11:38) have been violated. Jeroboam has not walked in God's way and done what is right in God's sight. The sharply contrasting words of Ahijah to Jeroboam bracket the account of his reign. In a typical prophetic speech pattern, Ahijah specifies the nature of Jeroboam's sins (vv. 8–9), announces God's judgment both on his house (vv. 9–13) and on all of Israel because of him (vv. 15–16), and specifies that God will raise up a king who will undo what Jeroboam has done (v. 14). The section ends with a typical notice of kingly transition (vv. 19–20; cf. 11:41–43).

The movement of this narrative from beginning to end is carefully orchestrated. It begins slowly, with a mother, a father, and a sick child and a possible prophetic healing; it picks up steam with disguises, a nearly blind prophet, and God's word of uncertain content. It increases in intensity as the prophet moves through indictment to judgment and delivers a block-buster at the end with the destruction and exiling of all Israel.

The narrative begins with a notice of sickness in the house of Jeroboam (both a literal and metaphorical reference, cf. 2 Kings 1:2–4). Jeroboam is no doubt concerned about issues of succession (the only prophetic word spoken to him directly since Ahijah's original word is 13:2–3; the reader knows far more than he does). Remembering Ahijah's good word, yet fearful of what he might now say, he asks his wife to inquire of Ahijah regarding Abijah's future, hoping for healing. He asks her to keep her identity secret and bring a payment for services appropriate to her supposed station in life (cf. 2 Kings 8:7–9); after all, prophets were known for their healing powers (see 1 Kings 17; 2 Kings 4–5; 20). A nearly blind Ahijah, who may not have recognized her in any case, is forewarned by God—who sees through every disguise (see 8:39)—of her coming and her reasons for doing so and gives him a message (not yet revealed to the reader) for direct delivery.

Ahijah immediately unmasks her and announces that he has only "bad news" for her. Ahijah recalls his former word to Jeroboam (11:31–39) and testifies that God had indeed acted to make him king as had been promised (note that "tearing the kingdom away" from the house of David does not mean the entire kingdom). The implication is clear that God's actions were genuine; they were not an effort to set him up for a fall but a provision for a future that God wanted for him (see below and the discussion at 11:26–43). He then proceeds to recall the original conditions, contrasting him (uniquely among northern kings) with David, "who did only what is right in my sight" (this evaluation is qualified in 15:5 and hence cannot stand alone as the reason). And he even outdoes (apparently) Solomon in the evil done—a galling reference, given the fact that Jeroboam was elevated by God because of that evil (yet even he is outdone by Omri and Ahab, 16:25, 33). The continuing reiteration of the Davidic ideal over the course of Kings implies that a life like that of David remains a possibility; but that is now beyond the pale for Jeroboam. The indictment specifies *making* other gods (not just serving them, an unparalleled indictment) and casting images, provoking God to anger, and "thrusting me behind your back."

The announcement of judgment, with its shift to the more impersonal third person (vv. 10–11), is very sharp and graphic, even vulgar. God will bring "evil" (see the discussion at 21:1–29; 2 Kings 17:1–41) on Jeroboam's "evil" house and consume it. In crude language, this means that every male (literally, "he who urinates against a wall," see KJV) of his household will be cut off (the meaning of the phrase translated as "bond and free" is uncertain; it may continue the coarse language, "decently and openly") and burned as dung (perhaps the sense both of stench—urine and dung—and worthlessness). Moreover, they shall not be given a proper burial but shall be eaten by dogs and birds (a terrible fate in that culture, see 2 Sam. 21:10–14). The language used for the fate of some later kings shows that this prophetic word continues to work itself out (16:2–4; 21:21–24; 2 Kings 9:8–9).

Shifting gears, and now speaking directly to Jeroboam's wife in less formal terms (v. 12), Ahijah announces that only Jeroboam's sick son, Abijah, who shall die when his mother reenters the city (not literally fulfilled, v. 17), will receive a proper wake and burial (see v. 18 for the fulfillment). He is graciously singled out because in Jeroboam's household only he was found pleasing to God (for reasons unstated). This positive word about the son signals the word in verse 14 that there are still positive forces at work in Israel. Ahijah announces that God is raising up a king "over Israel" who will accomplish this deed, "even right now" (an obscure phrase, perhaps referring to Josiah from the narrator's own time, see 13:2).

Ahijah concludes by casting the net beyond Jeroboam's house to the entire Northern Kingdom (vv. 15–16). The judgment will be the uprooting of the people and scattering them into exile beyond the Euphrates (Assyria)—the first clear reference since Deuteronomy. This anticipates what does in fact happen to Israel in the fall of Samaria (see 2 Kings 17), but at this point in the narrative does not represent an inevitable future (see the discussion at 11:26–43), though the readers know it as fulfilled. The reason for the judgment—they have made their Asherim ("sacred poles," see Deut. 16:21) and provoked the Lord to anger. Asherim are objects associated with Canaanite worship, particularly the goddess Asherah, consort of Baal. Israelite worship had probably become syncretistic (this anticipates the ministry of Elijah). This specific sin is probably representative of the wide range of apostasies committed by the people; they were led by Jeroboam into sin. Yet while Jeroboam's "sins which he sinned" were the root of the problem, specifying the sins of the people means that they bore direct responsibility for following in their leader's train.

The narrator concludes the story with the return of the mother, the death of the child, and the small comfort of the fulfillment of the word of Ahijah about his wake and burial (v. 13). The framing of the narrative with the mother (who has borne the brunt of the prophet's words) and the sick child gives a certain pathos and poignancy to the whole, a microcosm of their larger world. She who had begun as the king's messenger, hoping for good news, becomes the prophet's messenger, a bearer of bad news. What did she tell Jeroboam when she got home? And how did Jeroboam receive it? By leaving such questions unaddressed, the narrator in effect says that the answers don't matter; Jeroboam is done.

The regnal summary of Jeroboam's reign concludes his sad story, and, remarkably, he escapes the judgment of verses 10–11 and is buried in the family tomb. He reigned for 22 years (922–901 B.C.) and his son Nadab succeeded him; the judgment announced in verses 10–11 is delayed (15:28–30). The narrator gives credit to a source for his work in a "footnote," the otherwise unknown Book of the Annals of the Kings of Israel (see also 15:31; 16:5, 14).

The Coarse Language of God and Prophet

The coarse language used in the prophetic word may be troubling to some readers, but perhaps for the wrong reasons. Such language is revealing of God's *intense feeling* about what has happened; the twice-stated report about God being provoked to anger by all that has happened makes the deep effects upon God's emotional life clear (vv. 9, 15; on God's anger, see at 14:21–16:34). God had staked a great deal on Jeroboam (see discussion at 11:26–43) and now that had all gone down the tubes. It is remarkable that God lets that divine frustration, disappointment, and disillusionment with Jeroboam be visible through the prophet's words. One is reminded of Heschel's definition of a prophet as one who "feels the feelings of God" (Heschel, *The Prophets*, 26). The prophet, of course, puts those feelings into words that he thinks best capture the depth of those emotions.

These negative divine emotions over what has happened, however, are not the only feelings of God revealed in this text. They are contrasted with God's "pleasing" feeling toward the child Abijah (v. 13). This report reveals that God's anger has not taken control of the divine life, shaping everything that God is about in that world. A moment of divine pleasure is revealed to the reader in the midst of all the displeasure. And the mourning of "all Israel" over the death of the child (vv. 13, 18) mirrors God's own response to all that has happened. This signals the positive word of verse 14 that God will raise up a king who shall undo this mess. God's anger is not God's last word.

Jeroboam's family suffers because of his sins. This sounds reprehensible, particularly when announced by the word of God. Yet we know only too well the effects of "the sins of the fathers" on others in our own time, and God's judgment should not be understood in forensic terms (see at 21:1–19; 2 Kings 17:1–41). The singling out of Abijah from suffering the fate of the other members of the family introduces some differences in the effects of the father's sins. The death of the child signals the death of the dynasty; the mourning at his death signals the divine graciousness still at work among the people of God.

The twice-noted provoking of God to anger (vv. 9, 15) is also important for what it reveals about God's original word to Jeroboam; it demonstrates that God's word to Jeroboam about establishing his throne was not a sham (see the discussion at 11:26–43). If God absolutely knew in advance that these things would happen to Jeroboam, it makes no sense for God to be provoked to anger at this point; God should, indeed would, have been angry at the point of the divine knowledge of it. God certainly knew that these developments were possible, but the extent of the divine disillusionment suggests that they were not viewed as probable at the time of their original formulation.

THE EARLY YEARS OF JUDAH AND ISRAEL
1 Kings 14:21–16:34

From this point on, the narrator works through the story of North and South in synchronistic fashion, first one and then the other, with overlaps and resumptions as necessary (for detail and ancient Near Eastern parallels, see Long, *1 Kings*, 159–64). This reveals an understanding that North and South, while divided, are both part of the story of the one people of God. Major "interruptions" (e.g., the Elijah stories) and transitional materials interweave this rhythmic retelling, particularly in view of the theological issues presented. Introductory and concluding royal résumés, typically structured (see 14:21–24, 29–31), punctuate the narrative. The repeated basic evaluation of the royal regimes will be cast in religious terms regardless of their political and military success. Sin, particularly in the form of apostasy, becomes a dominant theme. Faithfulness to God is what finally counts over the long haul. The interwoven references to prophets will bring the word of God to bear at key points in the story; indeed, when the prophets do become involved the story is commonly expanded and theological interpretation is much more in play. In the final analysis, what God is about in this story drives the narrative and determines what is important to consider.

A victor-to-victim pattern often characterizes the North, as a relentless spiral downward consumes king after king, with only occasional respites on the way to doom for the community. An apostasy-reform rhythm is common in the South, though infidelity will finally bring the South to ruin as it had the North. The repeated drumming of this cadence throughout the chapters to follow not only sketch a pattern for interpreting this history, but also provide the readers with a word of warning and a call for ongoing reform. The narrator is not fundamentally concerned with historiographical matters, reconstructing the past for the sake of writing history. The concern is to bring a word of God to the readers and to learn from the past in such a way as to chart a course for the future of the community.

Jeroboam will live on in a striking way; he often becomes the measure for what other kings do. Unfortunately for Israel, the directions he set will prevail. Rehoboam is not given the same notoriety as his northern counterpart, but directions he set, following his father Solomon, will finally not be overcome and in time will also bring the South to ruin.

This section quickly covers the reigns of nine kings, three of Judah and six of Israel, covering about half a century (922–869 B.C.). The succinct entries may reflect the available information and/or the level of importance to the narrator. The number of kings evidences greater stability in the South. As with the kings of Israel (14:19), the narrator references a source for further reading (and perhaps for checking his accuracy), namely, The Book of the Annals of the Kings of Judah (14:29; 15:7, 23; 22:45). The title suggests a more "historical" source than Kings, with its overriding theological interests, proves to be. Some additional details about the history of the South are given in 2 Chronicles 11–36; the Chronicler passes over the northern apostates. The chronological framework of the 200 years of the divided monarchy presents problems that have not yet been resolved.

Judah's Early Years
(1 Kings 14:21–15:24)

The overall assessment of the southern kings is something of a mixed bag, with apostasy followed by reform (Asa), but no major breakthrough in a positive direction occurs.

14:21–31. The reign of Rehoboam (922–915 B.C.). The narrator's treatment of Rehoboam began with his accession (11:43) and continued with his naive and arrogant policies that significantly contributed to the division of the kingdom (12:1–24). At the same time, a solitary positive word about him is included in his response to the prophetic word (12:24). This brief coverage of his reign is sharply negative. Though he himself is not named as the problem at this point (he will be in 15:3), the reader is invited to think of 14:16 and the negative effect that Jeroboam's sins had on the people as a whole.

The typical report (v. 21) includes a striking contrast. Jerusalem is named as the city of the temple, the place of God's dwelling among the people. This is followed by a religious evaluation of the people of Judah in uncompromisingly negative terms: "they did what was evil in the sight of the Lord"—in fact, "more than all their ancestors had done" (v. 22). The narrator proceeds to specify their sins and focuses entirely on worship or, more precisely, on the First Commandment (see Introduction). As had happened in the North, they had built high places, had introduced into their worship certain sacred objects associated with Baal (see 14:15), and had engaged in rituals involving male prostitution to promote fertility (see Deut. 15:18; Hos. 4:14). Such a sweeping analysis may be anachronistic at this point, but it is put in place here for future reference. Reforming kings will later be active against such rituals (15:12; 22:46; 2 Kings 23:7), but they will finally not be successful. Judah, too, will be swept away.

The summary comment of the narrator is stunning (v. 24): the situation in Judah was no different from what had been the case under the Canaanites, the previous inhabitants of Canaan. While Judah's queen mothers are regularly noted in the royal summaries, the repeated reference to Rehoboam's Ammonite mother, Naamah (vv. 21, 31), one of Solomon's many foreign wives, may signal some connection with the idolatry here (see 11:1–8). The specifics of Judah's sins outdistance those of Israel in 14:15, and the reader is prepared for a comparable judgment. But the reference is more indirect: God's driving the Canaanites out suggests that the same could well happen to Judah; God will be consistent.

The brief reference to Judah's troubles with Egypt under the Pharaoh Shishak (Shoshenq I, 931–910 B.C.) is not specifically linked to what precedes (as in 2 Chron. 12:5). The reader is invited to make the connection. Though Shishak's own description suggests otherwise, he is said to have taken *all* of the Solomonic treasures out of the temple and the palace, including shields of gold. It is almost as if it took a foreigner to cleanse the temple! And gold becomes bronze. The protective measures that Rehoboam needed to take (vv. 27–28) suggest that Shishak presented a continuing threat to him and his reign.

The summary of rule (vv. 29–31) includes a jarring reference to continual wars with Jeroboam (cf. 12:24); yet, conflict between the North and South was so common during the early years of division that it becomes a refrain in this section (14:30; 15:6–7, 16, 32).

15:1–8. The reign of Abijam (915–913 B.C.). Abijam's reign is negatively

evaluated; evil and war seem to say it all, though the fuller account given
in 2 Chronicles 13 assesses him more positively. The "nevertheless" of
verse 4 stands out; in spite of his evil way, God would remain true to the
promises to David (2 Sam. 7:1–17) and keep a "lamp" (descendant; 11:36)
on the throne. The qualification of David's obedience in the Bathsheba af-
fair (2 Samuel 11–12) is unusual (and more honest than other such notices,
see 14:8), but does not undercut the positive assessment of David.

 15:9–24. The reign of Asa (913–873 B.C.). Asa's long reign is given a positive evaluation, even though the high places remain. He instituted various
reforms, including removing his mother (grandmother?) Maacah (Abijam's mother, 15:2, though see 2 Chron. 13:2) from being queen mother
because of an abominable image for Asherah (see 14:15, 23), perhaps
pornographic. Maacah, Absalom's daughter, was able to wield considerable power as queen mother across three generations of kings. The war between North and South continues, with king Baasha of Israel pushing to
within five miles of Jerusalem (Ramah). But king Asa completes an expen-
sive treaty (clearing out the valuables in the temple, v. 18; cf. v. 15) with
Aram (modern Syria) and its king Ben-hadad (several kings have this
name), who breaks a treaty with Israel, subjects several of its cities, and re-
lieves the pressure on Asa and the South. When Baasha withdraws from
Ramah, Asa commissions all Israel to carry the stones to build two cities in
the South. For such building Asa is remembered, as well as for his diseased
feet, which killed him according to 2 Chronicles 16:11–14; the Chronicler
assesses his reign more negatively, reporting a conflict between him and
the prophet Hanani (16:7–10).

Israel's Early Years
(1 Kings 15:25–16:34)

16:29 In the thirty-eighth year of King Asa of Judah, Ahab son of Omri began
to reign over Israel; Ahab son of Omri reigned over Israel in Samaria twenty-
two years. [30] Ahab son of Omri did evil in the sight of the LORD more than all
who were before him. [31] And as if it had been a light thing for him to walk in
the sins of Jeroboam son of Nebat, he took as his wife Jezebel daughter of King
Ethbaal of the Sidonians, and went and served Baal, and worshiped him. [32] He
erected an altar for Baal in the house of Baal, which he built in Samaria. [33]
Ahab also made a sacred pole. Ahab did more to provoke the anger of the
LORD, the God of Israel, than had all the kings of Israel who were before him.
[34] In his days Hiel of Bethel built Jericho; he laid its foundation at the cost of
Abiram his firstborn, and set up its gates at the cost of his youngest son Segub,
according to the word of the LORD, which he spoke by Joshua son of Nun.

The narrator's judgment of these northern kings is unrelenting and un-ambiguous; as the years go by they become politically more successful, but religiously more apostate—climaxing in the most evil kings of all, first Omri and then Ahab. Their renown as politicians and military strategists will finally count for nothing in view of their violation of the First Commandment—unfaithfulness to Yahweh in spite of all the warnings from the prophets (2 Kings 17:13–14).

15:25–16:7. The reigns of Nadab (901–900 B.C.) and Baasha (900–877). Nadab walked in the evil ways of his father, Jeroboam; when trying to extend his territory to the southwest, he is assassinated by Baasha. Upon becoming king, Baasha proceeds to kill the entire house of Jeroboam, in fulfillment of the prophetic word of Ahijah (14:10–11), the reasons for which are repeated (v. 30). Yet Baasha does not change things for the better, and the prophet Jehu (who was also critical of king Jehoshaphat and wrote a book about him, 2 Chron. 19:2–3; 20:34) delivers an oracle using language that recalls Ahijah against Jeroboam (compare 16:2–4 with 14:11, 15–16). Note that, for God, Israel is still "my people" (v. 2). Another oracle of Jehu (v. 7) strikingly condemns Baasha for destroying the house of Jeroboam when he managed no better himself, even though God raised him up and he fulfilled a prophetic word (15:29).

16:8–20. The reigns of Elah (877–876 B.C.) and Zimri (one week, 876 B.C.). The typical negative evaluation, missing in the summary of Elah's rule, is picked up in verse 13. The focus of the account is his assassination by his servant, Zimri, who also eliminates all of Baasha's family and friends (remembered as a traitor in 2 Kings 9:31). This is interpreted as a fulfillment of the prophet Jehu's word against Elah's father Baasha (the delay in fulfillment until the next generation was also true of Jeroboam and Nadab). When the army heard about the assassination, they (and "all Israel") made Omri, the commander of the army, king. When their siege of the capital city (Tirzah) was clearly successful, Zimri committed suicide (a rarity in Israel) by burning the king's house down over himself. It is hard to understand how Zimri, who had successfully eliminated the house of Baasha according to the prophetic word, and who reigned for only seven days, deserved the narrator's typical judgment of verse 19.

16:21–28. The reign of Omri (876–869 B.C.). After an initial civil war (16:21–22), Omri becomes king and is established as a person of renown even in extrabiblical sources (Assyrians called Israel "the land of Omri"). Yet the report of his reign is very brief. He is remembered by the narrator only for his building of a new capital (Samaria) that unified the country, and for doing "more evil that all who were before him." Even Jeroboam!

The narrator passes by all of his political success (his was the first northern dynasty to last beyond the first generation) in view of his faithlessness to Yahweh. Without fidelity, worldly achievement is finally of little import. As with his son Ahab, his chosen priorities count against him, and he is judged for that.

16:29–34. The beginning of the reign of Ahab (869–850 B.C.). In contrast to Omri, the narrator treats the reign of Ahab at length (16:29–22:40). As with Omri, we know from extrabiblical sources that he was considered a great political leader. But the narrator sums up his reign with a repeated judgment (vv. 30, 33); his evil doings were incomparable, seen fundamentally in terms of a violation of the First Commandment (see Introduction). This evaluation sets up the narratives about Elijah. Ahab also follows in the footsteps of Solomon; he marries a foreign woman (Jezebel), builds a temple for her god in the capital city, and follows her in worshiping Baal (see 11:1–8). The archival note regarding the building of Jericho (v. 34) reports the working out of Joshua's curse on a builder of Jericho (Josh. 6:26). The link to Ahab, who may have sponsored the building, may suggest that he, too, will fulfill ancient prophecies of doom by his apostate dealings. With the reference to the driving out of the Canaanites (14:24), this may suggest an undoing of God's gift of the land.

The Jealousy and Anger of God

Throughout this section, we are again told of the feelings of God, first jealousy and then, in a more sustained way, anger (see at 14:1–20; see also 2 Kings 3:1–27).

In one text, God has been "provoked to jealousy" (14:22) over Judah's worship of other gods. This language for God is rooted in the Decalogue (Exod. 20:5; Deut. 5:9; cf. 32:16, 21; Ps. 78:58) and is first "activated" in connection with the golden calf debacle (Exod. 34:14). It is no doubt picked up here because of the connections with Jeroboam's calf images. Warnings regarding apostasy are laid out at various points in the Pentateuch (e.g., Exod. 23:24, 32–33; Deuteronomy). In this context, verse 24 explicitly refers to the issue of driving out the inhabitants of the land because of the temptations to apostasy they present.

The jealousy of God is a metaphor drawn from the sphere of marriage and focuses on faithfulness within the relationship and the importance of undivided loyalty for the health of the relationship. The language of jealousy indicates that this relationship is more than a formal matter (as covenant is often conceived by scholars), but a matter of divine inwardness, indeed touching the deepest divine feelings. Jealousy by definition has both an inner and an outer reference, but the inner reference is the prior one. God cares deeply about this relationship with Israel, and *because of that*, cares about what Israel does with its allegiances. The divine jealousy is a sign that God is not unmoved by Israel's unfaithfulness. Jealousy is a complex emotion, entailing (at least) pain, sorrow, disappointment, and anger.

Anger is the most common of these divine emotions expressed here, and punctuates the apostasies reported in these chapters (14:9, 15; 15:30; 16:2, 7, 13, 26, 33). In every case, the anger is provoked by the idolatrous practices of the kings of the *North*. The issue is always the First Commandment, faithfulness to God alone within a committed relationship. The dominant metaphor assumed, as with jealousy, is marital, and assumes an intimacy that the parental metaphor does not (so anger by parents is not as helpful an analogy here). In "unpacking" the metaphor, the anger (mixed with other emotions) felt by a spouse at the unfaithfulness of the partner may begin to approximate the feelings of God here. The divine anger reflects the seriousness with which God takes the relationship, the intimacy that has been violated, and the inevitably negative "fallout" that comes from such a breakdown.

It is important to note that God is not imaged as a wrathful God, as if anger were a divine attribute. God is *provoked* to anger. Anger is a divine response to a specific human situation. If there were no sin, there would be no divine anger. (The most helpful treatment of divine anger is in Heschel, *The Prophets*.)

3. Prophets and Kings I
1 Kings 17:1–22:53

The stylized notices regarding the kings in the previous section are here "interrupted" by a return to narratives. The change in style signals a change in content; Elijah is an interruption! The narratives take the form of spirited stories about Elijah, focused on his confrontation with Baal and his advocates. These stories address directly issues of idolatry that have been raised in the preceding chapters, but the narrator with whom we have become familiar (the Deuteronomist) is less visible; the stories themselves carry the freight of his concerns.

Structuring this confrontation, this section may be divided into two major segments (17:1–19:21; 20:1–22:53). In the first, the centering chapter (18) focuses on Yahweh's rival, Baal; it is bracketed by chapters focused more on Yahweh's advocate himself, Elijah (17; 19). Individual chapters are structured in such a way as to climax in a witness to Israel's God as the giver of life (17:24; 18:39; 19:19–21). In the second segment, the interest is more focused on King Ahab and his confrontations with various prophets. These chapters explore some of the implications of life lived in unfaithfulness to Yahweh. The effect on issues of justice centers the section (21), in connection with which Elijah's announcement of doom on the house of Ahab occurs (21:21–24); this chapter is bracketed by stories that speak of the effects of infidelity on broader relationships with other nations, particularly military conflict (20; 22).

These structures and rhythms serve to emphasize these basic purposes: to resist the policies and practices of the evil rulers of Israel; to oppose the idolatrous worship of Baal (most blatantly introduced into Israel's worship by King Ahab in 16:31–33); to enhance the role of the prophets and the word they speak in charting Israel's course through dangerous times; and to magnify the God of Israel. The witness of these stories is that *Israel's* God makes life possible in every sphere. Even more, there can be no compromise on this point; Yahweh and Baal cannot live together in an easy syncretism.

ELIJAH AND AHAB; YAHWEH AND BAAL
1 Kings 17:1–19:21

The conflict between Baal and Yahweh takes on historical and bodily form in the figures of Ahab (and Jezebel) and Elijah, a newly configured embodiment of the conflict between Pharoah and Moses. Elijah is a towering figure, a new Moses, who bursts upon the scene from outside normal channels (Gilead is east of the Jordan, away from the centers of power) and confronts the power structures in uncompromising terms. But Elijah's journey is not depicted simply in heroic terms; a deep questioning of self, of vocation, and of God characterizes his journey. No doubt because of this complexity, Elijah lives deeply embedded in Israel's memory, so much so that the last words of the Old Testament (Mal. 3:5–6) are expectant of his return to usher in the day of the Lord. At the same time, these chapters are not simply a story about a prophet's life; they are also a story about the divine life, and the interaction between the two. God's future with this people is on the line, and neither God nor prophet remain unaffected by that struggle.

Stories of Elijah
(1 Kings 17:1–24)

17:1 Now Elijah the Tishbite, of Tishbe in Gilead, said to Ahab, "As the LORD the God of Israel lives, before whom I stand, there shall be neither dew nor rain these years, except by my word." 2 The word of the LORD came to him, saying, 3 "Go from here and turn eastward, and hide yourself by the Wadi Cherith, which is east of the Jordan. 4 You shall drink from the wadi, and I have commanded the ravens to feed you there." 5 So he went and did according to the word of the LORD; he went and lived by the Wadi Cherith, which is east of the Jordan. 6 The ravens brought him bread and meat in the morning, and bread and meat in the evening; and he drank from the wadi. 7 But after a while the wadi dried up, because there was no rain in the land. 8 Then the word of the LORD came to him, saying, 9 "Go now to Zarephath, which belongs to Sidon, and live there; for I have commanded a widow there to feed you." 10 So he set out and went to Zarephath. When he came to the gate of the town, a widow was there gathering sticks; he called to her and said, "Bring me a little water in a vessel, so that I may drink." 11 As she was going to bring it, he called to her and said, "Bring me a morsel of bread in your hand." 12 But she said, "As the LORD your God lives, I have nothing baked, only a handful of meal in a jar, and a little oil in a jug; I am now gathering a couple of sticks, so that I may go home and prepare it for myself and my son, that we may eat it, and die." 13 Elijah said to her, "Do not be afraid;

go and do as you have said; but first make me a little cake of it and bring it to me, and afterwards make something for yourself and your son. [14] For thus says the LORD the God of Israel: The jar of meal will not be emptied and the jug of oil will not fail until the day that the LORD sends rain on the earth." [15] She went and did as Elijah said, so that she as well as he and her household ate for many days. [16] The jar of meal was not emptied, neither did the jug of oil fail, according to the word of the LORD that he spoke by Elijah. [17] After this the son of the woman, the mistress of the house, became ill; his illness was so severe that there was no breath left in him. [18] She then said to Elijah, "What have you against me, O man of God? You have come to me to bring my sin to remembrance, and to cause the death of my son!" [19] But he said to her, "Give me your son." He took him from her bosom, carried him up into the upper chamber where he was lodging, and laid him on his own bed. [20] He cried out to the LORD, "O LORD my God, have you brought calamity even upon the widow with whom I am staying, by killing her son?" [21] Then he stretched himself upon the child three times, and cried out to the LORD, "O LORD my God, let this child's life come into him again." [22] The LORD listened to the voice of Elijah; the life of the child came into him again, and he revived. [23] Elijah took the child, brought him down from the upper chamber into the house, and gave him to his mother; then Elijah said, "See, your son is alive." [24] So the woman said to Elijah, "Now I know that you are a man of God, and that the word of the LORD in your mouth is truth."

The three stories in chapter 17 have been crafted from older legends to speak to the above-stated purposes. They challenge the belief that Baal (though never mentioned in this chapter) controlled life and death, whether in the human or the natural order; Yahweh alone makes life possible and Yahweh alone brings judgment. This portrayal of Elijah should not be reduced to preparatory work for the major event of chapter 18. Elijah's ministry at this point is key to the continued life and well-being of a family—in Baal's home territory and in more private contexts as well as public ones. These stories have their own integrity and provide a richer and deeper witness to Israel's God.

Following upon Ahab's idolatrous actions of 16:31–33, the stories are prefaced with an abrupt appearance of Elijah before Ahab with a crisp, ominous announcement of an oath (cf. the oath in v. 12): there will be no dew (summer) or rain (winter) until it is sent by God through his own word—an audacious claim (v. 1). No suggestion is made that this is a divine judgment. Elijah draws his authority from Yahweh, not Baal ("before whom I stand"; his name means "My God is Yahweh"). This God lives and all of life is dependent upon that divine life; this God's word will be decisive, not fertility rituals. The theme of life and death centers on the drought, which provides the focus for the next two chapters, as the conflict between Yahweh and Baal comes to a head, climaxing in the end of the drought (18:46).

Following the announcement to Ahab (v. 1, picked up again at 18:1), God commands Elijah to "hide" from growing opposition (see 18:4, 10). Two of the three stories in chapter 17 begin with a word from God prompting actions from Elijah that sustain his life (vv. 2, 8); the third story continues from the second, where Elijah's life is extended beyond himself to the widow's son. The chapter as a whole is bracketed by the word of the Lord (vv. 1–2, 24).

In the first story (vv. 1–7), Elijah is commanded by God to hide himself east of the Jordan by a certain wadi (or seasonal stream), otherwise unknown, but probably outside Ahab's jurisdiction. This seems almost as risky as staying near Ahab; he is to drink from a wadi and be fed with food provided by ravens. Ravens are not known as providers but as scavengers (cf. also the woman in v. 10). Elijah obeys (as does the woman in v. 15) and God provides—in an extravagant way for that culture (meat twice a day!)—through unlikely sources (links to Israel's being fed in the wilderness are evident, see Exod. 16:8–12). The wadi soon dries up for lack of rain; the natural order cannot sustain itself. But God, unlike Baal, is not dead during the dry season; God can be relied upon even for such times.

In the second story (vv. 8–16; cf. a comparable story about Elisha in 2 Kings 4:1–7), with the drought and its effects still in place (v. 14), Elijah is commanded to go to Zarephath, on the Mediterranean coast near the capital of Baal worship (Sidon, see 16:31). There he is to demonstrate in the very center of the opposition that the God of Israel is the only true God. There—outside Israelite channels, among the poorest of the poor, another risky place—God will provide for the prophet through a widow. Elijah will provide for her need, too, but only through what she first provides and only after interaction between them. Elijah encounters the widow, from whom he requests food and water. The widow objects with an oath comparable to Elijah's own (v. 1), lamenting that she was scavenging (as ravens do) for sticks in order to cook a final meal for her son and herself (might she be exaggerating, given her social status in vv. 17, 19?).

Elijah assures the widow in the name of the God of Israel that food will be provided for him as well as for them until the drought is ended. God acts through both the word of the prophet and the food and deed of a widow (those pursued and neglected by the political power structures) to provide life-giving food for both prophet and widow. Note Jesus' appeal to this story in a context of opposition (Luke 4:25–26).

The third story (vv. 17–24; see the similar story of Elisha in 2 Kings 4:18–37) continues with the same characters in the same opposition-filled setting, though the drought is not in view. This time the issue of life and death is more sharply raised. The story begins with a report that the widow's son is no longer breathing (if not actually dead, as good as dead). She accuses Elijah of deception with respect to his visit; he has really come to mediate the effects of her own sin, that is, her son's death. This response to tragedy is generic to the human race and is here set aside by the prophet's actions. Without defending himself, Elijah takes the son, lays him on his own bed (away from his mother), and prays to God, demanding to know whether the widow is right in saying what she did about God. In so doing, Elijah questions the common theology, and God's life-giving actions through him show this common theology to be bankrupt.

God responds to the prophet; in fact, God "listened" to Elijah! The child's life returns, and he is restored. The prophet himself, like the ravens and the poor widow, mediates the power of God for life by raising the widow's son from the dead. Elijah brings the boy back to his mother, speaking only the word the mother most wanted to hear: Your son is alive! The mother's evaluation of the prophet is transformed. She speaks a confession that witnesses both to the power of the word of the Lord and to its mediation through the "man of God." "Now I know" represents clarity regarding who Elijah is and "the word is . . . truth" probably refers back to the word of verse 14 about provisions. This testimony sets the stage for the major confrontations of Elijah with the powers that be—both divine and human—in chapter 18. This prophet is "God's man" for this moment in a dangerous time for Israel and God's mission in the world.

God's Use of Means and Issues of Life and Death

In each of these stories, God through the word (vv. 1, 4, 9, 16, 24) mediates life—to both prophet and those to whom the prophet relates—in and through various less than royal creatures: nonhumans, a poor widow, and the prophet himself. Note that the agency issue is important; the activities of *both* God and creature are considered crucial in bringing life at each step. Israel's God works for life in and through that which is not God. Regardless of the creatures' place in God's creation, God's effective word is at work through them to serve life (on miracle, see the discussion at 2 Kings 4:1–44).

The text moves at three levels in relating to the opposition to Baal. First, in its movement from death to life, the life-giving power of God is acclaimed. Israel's God is the God of life, in the world of nature, in the provision of life-giving food and water by the poor, and even at the point where physical death itself has intruded upon human life. Wherever in all creation life and death issues are raised, there the God of Israel is shown to be the source of life. It should be stressed that these stories are not basically about spiritual life, but about physical life. God's providing and healing work has to do with the whole person. In fact, God's work is about more than healing; it is finally about resurrection from the dead, from actual death to actual life.

Second, in the movement of the woman's fear, hesitation, and accusation to her affirmation, a public witness is made to this God and to God's prophet by a resident within Baal's own land. The questions raised by the woman are not dismissed or considered irrelevant; they are integral to the development of faith and a solidly grounded public witness. The climactic note in the chapter lies not in the restoration of the boy as much as in the testimony of the woman (parallel to the acclamation in 18:39). One small healing act here and there, and more testifying women like her, and the word about this life-giving God will get around!

Third, God's work in the world is always mediated, and God's use of means in this struggle is varied and, according to the usual standards, of little account. Initially, rain comes by means of the word of God (v. 1), a reference to Genesis 1 and God's continuing work in creation through the prophet. This passage does not reductionistically consider rain to be an issue of the divine micromanagement of nature. Rather it stakes a claim regarding the identity of the Creator; it is Yahweh, not Baal, who sees to the cycle of the dry and rainy seasons.

As for the ravens, communication between God and the nonhuman is not an uncommon Old Testament theme (even for ravens, Ps. 147:9). But the point, again, is not miracle or micromanagement. Rather, it stakes a claim that Israel's God, not Baal, is the Creator, who provides water and who works through nonhuman creatures that are not usually among the animals who provide food in order to sustain the faithful.

As for the woman's meal and oil, no specifics are given regarding how the food will be provided. But no unmediated action of God is claimed; God works through the word of the prophet *and* through the food provided by the widow and her positive response to the word (vv. 12, 15; cf. v. 5). As with the ravens, the prophet is finally dependent, not only upon God but also upon such a lowly one, for his basic needs. Without her and her food (which never fails; there is no creation out of nothing in this action), Elijah would have had no food; the word of God works with what *she* makes available. And, interestingly, no dramatic moment is announced and no marvel is expressed at what happens.

As for the raising of the boy back to life, the prophet is not a passive agent and uses more than one means. Elijah not only prays but uses an existing healing ritual, which combines stretching his body over the boy (to communicate some of his own life to the boy) and, then, a further prayer to God to restore his life (this time with an imperative!). God works through what Elijah wants done and does. It is noteworthy here (as also in 2 Kings 20:1–7) that prayer is not considered sufficient for the healing process. Certain rituals, no doubt familiar in that culture, are closely followed and integral to the healing that takes place. Not only is the boy removed from the mother's presence into a more private space, but the prophet makes use of a specific rite. And God "listened" to Elijah (v. 22)! God has chosen not to act alone.

God and his agents enter into enemy territory and begin to conquer the powers of death *from within*. No military, political, or ecclesiastical powers are active here. Indeed, the sources of life in this chapter are not normally associated with power. Here we have no imposition of strength from without, no exercise of power as it is normally conceived. Rather, effective power is exercised through the birds of the air, small gestures, meager resources, feeble words, human obedience, and the witness of a poor woman. Through such lowly means, God's work gets done, even in the most hostile of places. This theme will balance the fire of chapter 18 and link up with the "still small voice" to Elijah in chapter 19.

Yahweh and Baal and Their Prophets (1 Kings 18:1–46)

> 18:1 **After many days the word of the LORD came to Elijah, in the third year of the drought, saying, "Go, present yourself to Ahab; I will send rain on the earth."** [2] **So Elijah went to present himself to Ahab. The famine was severe in Samaria.** [3] **Ahab summoned Obadiah, who was in charge of the palace. (Now Obadiah revered the LORD greatly;** [4] **when Jezebel was killing off the prophets of the LORD, Obadiah took a hundred prophets, hid them fifty to a cave, and provided them with bread and water.)** [5] **Then Ahab said to Obadiah, "Go through the land to all the springs of water and to all the wadis; perhaps we may find grass to keep the horses and mules alive, and not lose some of the animals."** [6] **So they divided the land between them to pass through it; Ahab went in one direction by himself, and Obadiah went in another direction by himself.** [7] **As Obadiah was on the way, Elijah met him;**

Obadiah recognized him, fell on his face, and said, "Is it you, my lord Elijah?" [8] He answered him, "It is I. Go, tell your lord that Elijah is here." [9] And he said, "How have I sinned, that you would hand your servant over to Ahab, to kill me? [10] As the LORD your God lives, there is no nation or kingdom to which my lord has not sent to seek you; and when they would say, 'He is not here,' he would require an oath of the kingdom or nation, that they had not found you. [11] But now you say, 'Go, tell your lord that Elijah is here.' [12] As soon as I have gone from you, the spirit of the LORD will carry you I know not where; so, when I come and tell Ahab and he cannot find you, he will kill me, although I your servant have revered the LORD from my youth. [13] Has it not been told my lord what I did when Jezebel killed the prophets of the LORD, how I hid a hundred of the LORD's prophets fifty to a cave, and provided them with bread and water? [14] Yet now you say, 'Go, tell your lord that Elijah is here'; he will surely kill me." [15] Elijah said, "As the LORD of hosts lives, before whom I stand, I will surely show myself to him today." [16] So Obadiah went to meet Ahab, and told him; and Ahab went to meet Elijah. [17] When Ahab saw Elijah, Ahab said to him, "Is it you, you troubler of Israel?" [18] He answered, "I have not troubled Israel; but you have, and your father's house, because you have forsaken the commandments of the LORD and followed the Baals. [19] Now therefore have all Israel assemble for me at Mount Carmel, with the four hundred fifty prophets of Baal and the four hundred prophets of Asherah, who eat at Jezebel's table." [20] So Ahab sent to all the Israelites, and assembled the prophets at Mount Carmel. [21] Elijah then came near to all the people, and said, "How long will you go limping with two different opinions? If the LORD is God, follow him; but if Baal, then follow him." The people did not answer him a word. [22] Then Elijah said to the people, "I, even I only, am left a prophet of the LORD; but Baal's prophets number four hundred fifty. [23] Let two bulls be given to us; let them choose one bull for themselves, cut it in pieces, and lay it on the wood, but put no fire to it; I will prepare the other bull and lay it on the wood, but put no fire to it. [24] Then you call on the name of your god and I will call on the name of the LORD; the god who answers by fire is indeed God." All the people answered, "Well spoken!" [25] Then Elijah said to the prophets of Baal, "Choose for yourselves one bull and prepare it first, for you are many; then call on the name of your god, but put no fire to it." [26] So they took the bull that was given them, prepared it, and called on the name of Baal from morning until noon, crying, "O Baal, answer us!" But there was no voice, and no answer. They limped about the altar that they had made. [27] At noon Elijah mocked them, saying, "Cry aloud! Surely he is a god; either he is meditating, or he has wandered away, or he is on a journey, or perhaps he is asleep and must be awakened." [28] Then they cried aloud and, as was their custom, they cut themselves with swords and lances until the blood gushed out over them. [29] As midday passed, they raved on until the time of the offering of the oblation, but there was no voice, no answer, and no response. ^{30} Then Elijah said to all the people, "Come closer to me"; and all the people came closer to him. First he repaired the altar of the LORD that had been thrown down; ^{31} Elijah took twelve stones, according to the number of the tribes of the sons of Jacob, to whom the word of the LORD came, saying, "Israel shall be your name"; ^{32} with the stones he built an altar in the name of the LORD. Then he made a trench around the altar, large enough to contain two measures of seed. ^{33} Next he put the wood in order, cut the bull in pieces, and laid it on the wood. He said, "Fill four jars with water and pour it on the burnt offering and on the wood." ^{34} Then he said, "Do it a second time"; and they did it a second time. Again he said, "Do it a third time"; and they did it a third time, ^{35} so that the water ran all around the altar, and filled the trench also with water. ^{36} At the time of the offering of the oblation, the prophet Elijah came near and said, "O LORD, God of Abraham, Isaac, and Israel, let it be known this day that you are God in Israel, that I am your servant, and that I have done all these things at your bidding. ^{37} Answer me, O LORD, answer me, so that this people may know that you, O LORD, are God, and that you have turned their hearts back." ^{38} Then the fire of the LORD fell and consumed the burnt offering, the wood, the stones, and the dust, and even licked up the water that was in the trench. ^{39} When all the people saw it, they fell on their faces and said, "The LORD indeed is God; the LORD indeed is God." ^{40} Elijah said to them, "Seize the prophets of Baal; do not let one of them escape." Then they seized them; and Elijah brought them down to the Wadi Kishon, and killed them there. ^{41} Elijah said to Ahab, "Go up, eat and drink; for there is a sound of rushing rain." ^{42} So Ahab went up to eat and to drink. Elijah went up to the top of Carmel; there he bowed himself down upon the earth and put his face between his knees. ^{43} He said to his servant, "Go up now, look toward the sea." He went up and looked, and said, "There is nothing." Then he said, "Go again seven times." ^{44} At the seventh time he said, "Look, a little cloud no bigger than a person's hand is rising out of the sea." Then he said, "Go say to Ahab, 'Harness your chariot and go down before the rain stops you.'" ^{45} In a little while the heavens grew black with clouds and wind; there was a heavy rain. Ahab rode off and went to Jezreel. ^{46} But the hand of the LORD was on Elijah; he girded up his loins and ran in front of Ahab to the entrance of Jezreel.

This chapter, a story with a complex history of transmission, brings the issue of the drought to a head, with a direct confrontation between Yahweh and Baal: who would be able to break the drought and provide the rains needed for fields and flocks? Baal was supposedly the "expert" in such areas; but Elijah enters into the heart of Baal's very domain and goes for the jugular. The dramatic character of the ensuing contest has few biblical peers. This story might be called a dramatized form of the First Com-

mandment, with special attention to the risk that prophets play on its behalf in the face of royal opposition and apostasy.

God commands Elijah to announce to Ahab that the God of Israel will
send rain. This encounter is delayed as verses 2–16 create suspense by
showing how dangerous the situation has become for Yahweh's prophets.
Ahab, desperate for food for his animals, calls his servant Obadiah to help
him search for areas where grass could still grow. As it turns out, Obadiah
was a faithful Yahweh worshiper (living up to his name, "servant of
Yahweh") and had hidden 100 prophets from Jezebel's "prophetic cleansing." When Elijah encounters him and asks him to report his presence to
Ahab, however, Obadiah gives a frenetic rationale (vv. 9–14) as to why he
ought not be asked to do this; he will be killed if he tells Ahab and Elijah disappears (see 2 Kings 2:11). His hesitancy is another instance of less than full
commitment (see v. 21). This is the first we learn of Elijah being the object
of a manhunt; that Jezebel is twice named as the antagonist (vv. 4, 13)
and the prophets of Baal are her functionaries (v. 19) tends to soften the
presentation of Ahab, as does his somewhat passive demeanor. This means
that this chapter is more a contest between gods and their prophets. Obadiah's reasoning about the relation between sin and death approximates
that of the widow in 17:18. Elijah ought not to put him at risk, because he
has been faithful to the cause of Yahweh's prophets. Elijah promises that
he will appear (strangely, Obadiah drops out of the story), and Ahab and
Elijah meet (for the first time since 17:1). Trading insults, Ahab identifies
Elijah as "a troubler [a disaster-bringer; see 17:1] of Israel" (v. 17) and Elijah's fearless reply pinpoints Ahab as the true source of trouble and charges
him directly with apostasy—that of personally following Baal and institut-
ing Baal worship throughout the land, though Jezebel seems to be in control (vv. 4, 13, 19; the plural "Baals" refers to local manifestations of Baal
at various high places).

Elijah's strategy is to set up a contest between himself (and Yahweh)
and 450 prophets of Baal (also 400 prophets of Asherah, his consort, who
drop out of the story—as does Jezebel—but intensify the odds; they may
return in 22:6) to resolve the matter of the identity of the true God of Israel. Ahab accepts the challenge and summons "all Israel" to watch. Elijah begins with a challenge to the people to choose between Yahweh and
Baal; they are the true object of Elijah's actions (see vv. 24, 30, 37, 39).
They cannot go on "limping," attempting to hedge their bets by keeping
one foot in each camp (v. 21), that is, they cannot join the "limping" of
Baal's prophets (v. 26). Finally, this is actually no neutral or indifferent
position; Baal, not Yahweh, has become "your god" (v. 24). Initially

greeted with silence, Elijah uses hyperbole to sharpen the stance of one against the many (contrast 18:4, 13) and sets up the challenge, to which "all the people" agree. The challenge is to find out which "god" will respond to the request to bring fire (=lightning, associated with rain) upon the prepared sacrifice.

The prophets of Baal, given every advantage and the entire day (vv. 26, 27, 29), repeatedly try to rouse their god; finally, they resort to ecstatic behaviors (not necessarily inappropriate, see 1 Sam. 19:18–24) and self-lacerating rituals. But to no avail; there is "no voice and no answer" (vv. 26, 29). Baal neither speaks nor acts; the silence speaks volumes. Elijah's goading response (vv. 27–29) is filled with satire, mocking such efforts as futile. Baal must be asleep or meditating or on a journey or going to the bathroom (so TEV)! Then Elijah, bringing the witnesses up close (v. 30), slowly and methodically proceeds with his own game plan. He prepares an appropriate Yahwistic sacrifice on a restored altar of twelve stones, invokes God's birthing of the twelve tribes (v. 31, cf. v. 36; note that a unified people is here presupposed), and cuts a deep trench around it. He then soaks (!) the altar and fills the trenches with water (making the sacrifice harder to burn, the better to make the point).

Showing the centrality of prayer (cf. v. 42; 17:20–21), Elijah calls upon Yahweh, using traditional names, to demonstrate who is truly God. His focus is on the community, "that this people may know" and that God's action would prompt their repentance (v. 37; 17:24), and on God's power not his; he is a "servant" (like Moses). The "fire of the LORD" (a resounding lightning bolt, often associated with Baal and also a typical accompaniment of Yahwistic theophanies, see Exod. 19:18) falls from heaven like a laser beam and, following levitical guidelines, consumes the burnt offering and the entire sacrificial structure, including the water. The people fall on their faces and respond with a traditional confession (see Ps. 95:7) that Yahweh is *the* God (v. 39), notably saying nothing about his prophet. Remarkably, the confession occurs before the rain comes. The people seize the prophets of Baal at Elijah's command, and Elijah singlehandedly kills them all at a local stream (Deut. 13:1–5 calls for the death penalty for false prophets; cf. 2 Kings 10:7).

Elijah then withdraws (cf. 17:19) and proceeds with an intense prayer ritual in response to which God breaks the drought (vv. 41–46; cf. 17:1), completing the demonstration that Yahweh, not Baal, is God of life and fertility. Anticipating (even hearing!) rain, he urges Ahab, now vanquished and compliant, first to celebrate (v. 41; food and water will be plenteous again) and then to flee from the rains (to his palace in Jezreel, 21:1, about

17 miles from Mount Carmel). When the rains come, Elijah is filled with the Spirit and dashes ahead of Ahab all the way to Jezreel.

What Kind of God Is This?

The reader might be tempted to suggest that this story is most basically concerned to demonstrate God's transcendent power. But such language can be misleading. The problem with Baal (as with idols more generally; see Ps. 115:3–8; Isa. 44:10, 17; Jer. 10:5) is not that he is distant and removed (he does that well!), but that he does not listen or speak or feel or act or care: "There was no voice, no answer, and no response" (vv. 26, 29). The concern here is more to protect Yahweh's immanence than to demonstrate divine transcendence. Yahweh listens to Elijah's prayers and responds to them (also strongly emphasized in 17:22).

One might also be tempted to think that this story, in contrasting Yahweh with idols, emphasizes Yahweh's freedom. But more to the point here is the concern for God's commitment, which by definition entails a self-limitation of freedom. God has promised to send rain (v. 1); God honors the relationship with the prophet; God remembers commitments made to Abraham, Isaac, and Israel (v. 36; cf. v. 31) by responding to that particular formulation in the prophetic prayer. This commitment is also sharply evident in God's responding to Elijah's basic and repeated rationale for acting in this situation, namely, the knowledge of God (vv. 36, 37). God acts so that their hearts might be turned back to him, "so that his people may know" that Yahweh is indeed God alone. For God to respond to a prayer with this basic motivation is for God to remember commitments made, most fundamentally to Abraham, Isaac, and Jacob. God has named this people Israel (v. 31; all twelve tribes), has called them his own, and acts in faithfulness to that relationship.

The concern of the text, then, is not simply to show that Yahweh alone is God, as important as that is. The concern is also to reveal something about the basic character of this God. Yahweh is one who is active in human affairs, who listens, speaks, and acts, and who honors commitments made to chosen representatives and to the people with whom a special relationship has been established. It is precisely *this kind of God* that is to be the only God for Israel. Even more, it is this kind of God who is the only God, period.

Yahweh is the only God for Israel, and divided allegiances are as unfaithful as abandonment of Yahweh altogether. Israel's limping with two different opinions needs to be named for what it is: It is not neutrality, tolerance, apathy, indecision, indifference, or lukewarmness. It is apostasy, pure and simple.

This story ought not be used to suggest that "God cannot lose in any contest" (Nelson, *First and Second Kings*, 122). To be consistent, such a perspective would have to claim that there was no loss for God in the apostasies of Solomon or Jeroboam or anyone else in this spiraling downfall of Israel. The alternative is for apostasy to be considered the will of God. And, if that, God has no business being jealous or angry at what happens (see the discussion at 14:21–16:34). Apostasy such as we encounter in these texts means that the will of God is resistible. And if it is resisted, that is a loss for God and the occasion for divine grief (see Ps. 78:40; Eph. 4:30).

We might speak in a more qualified way and say that in *this* particular contest God could not lose. It is certainly true to say that God *does* not lose here. But the divine action is not unrelated to prior human activity, and that human action is not irrelevant to God's action. The list is considerable: Elijah's boldness in standing before Ahab and all the false prophets; his conviction that Baal is nothing and Yahweh is God and his speaking and acting on that conviction; the care and confidence with which he sets the scene in terms of a perfectly executed sacrificial act; his prayer with its fine historical sense and proper communal motivations, to which God listens (see 17:22); and his ritual actions to prepare for the coming of the rain. These human activities count; they make a difference to the situation and to God. The stress we have placed on God's actions as *mediated* (see the discussion at 17:1–24) is continued here in great depth and breadth. The possibilities for God in this contested moment are sharply enhanced by the prophet's words and deeds.

One might also consider that this human reality has effects on the natural order. Unfaithfulness has a negative impact upon the natural order (Deut. 11:13–17), and faithful confession leads to a restoration of nature's gifts; the rain does not precede the confession. Those of us who live in a more ecologically sensitive age have come to see this link between human faithfulness and the functioning of the world of nature. The fulfillment of the word of God through the prophet (17:1) is testimony most fundamentally to God's word and work, but what people do makes a difference to God.

Yet human violence is in evidence here as well (v. 40). This should not be explained away, but neither should it be considered necessarily just, even if it is understood to obey the law (Deut. 13:1–5). Once again (see the discussion at 1:1–2:46; 17:1–24), God does not act alone; but God works in and through that which is available, with human beings as they are, with all of their flaws and foibles. God does not perfect people before deciding to work through them. Moreover, this divine action does not necessarily confer a positive value on the specific human means through which God chooses to work, nor does that divine involvement allow one to say that the end necessarily justifies the means.

A Still Small Voice?
(1 Kings 19:1–21)

19:1 **Ahab told Jezebel all that Elijah had done, and how he had killed all the prophets with the sword.** [2] **Then Jezebel sent a messenger to Elijah, saying, "So may the gods do to me, and more also, if I do not make your life like the life of one of them by this time tomorrow."** [3] **Then he was afraid; he got up and fled for his life, and came to Beer-sheba, which belongs to Judah; he left his servant there.** [4] **But he himself went a day's journey into the wilderness, and came and sat down under a solitary broom tree. He asked that he might die: "It is enough; now, O LORD, take away my life, for I am no better than my ancestors."** [5] **Then he lay down under the broom tree and fell asleep. Suddenly an angel touched him and said to him, "Get up and eat."** [6] **He looked, and there at his head was a cake baked on hot stones, and a jar of water. He ate and drank, and lay down again.** [7] **The angel of the LORD came a second time, touched him, and said, "Get up and eat, otherwise the journey will be too much for you."** [8] **He got up, and ate and drank; then he went in the strength of that food forty days and forty nights to Horeb the mount of God.** [9] **At that place he came to a cave, and spent the night there. Then the word of the LORD came to him, saying, "What are you doing here, Elijah?"** [10] **He answered, "I have been very zealous for the LORD, the God of hosts; for the Israelites have forsaken your covenant, thrown down your altars, and killed your prophets with the sword. I alone am left, and they are seeking my life, to take it away."** [11] **He said, "Go out and stand on the mountain before the LORD, for the LORD is about to pass by." Now there was a great wind, so strong that it was splitting mountains and breaking rocks in pieces before the LORD, but the LORD was not in the wind; and after the wind an earthquake, but the LORD was not in the earthquake;** [12] **and after the earthquake a fire, but the LORD was not in the fire; and after the fire a sound of sheer silence.** [13] **When Elijah heard it, he wrapped his face in his mantle and went out and stood at the entrance of the cave. Then there came a voice to him that said, "What are you doing here, Elijah?"** [14] **He answered, "I have been very zealous for the LORD, the God of hosts; for the Israelites have forsaken your covenant, thrown down your altars, and killed your prophets with the sword. I alone am left, and they are seeking my life, to take it away."** [15] **Then the LORD said to him, "Go, return on your way to the wilderness of Damascus; when you arrive, you shall anoint Hazael as king over Aram.**

[16] Also you shall anoint Jehu son of Nimshi as king over Israel; and you shall anoint Elisha son of Shaphat of Abel-meholah as prophet in your place. [17] Whoever escapes from the sword of Hazael, Jehu shall kill; and whoever escapes from the sword of Jehu, Elisha shall kill. [18] Yet I will leave seven thousand in Israel, all the knees that have not bowed to Baal, and every mouth that has not kissed him." [19] So he set out from there, and found Elisha son of Shaphat, who was plowing. There were twelve yoke of oxen ahead of him, and he was with the twelfth. Elijah passed by him and threw his mantle over him. [20] He left the oxen, ran after Elijah, and said, "Let me kiss my father and my mother, and then I will follow you." Then Elijah said to him, "Go back again; for what have I done to you?" [21] He returned from following him, took the yoke of oxen, and slaughtered them; using the equipment from the oxen, he boiled their flesh, and gave it to the people, and they ate. Then he set out and followed Elijah, and became his servant.

This chapter has long captured the imagination of biblical interpreters, especially the "still small voice." The move from Mount Carmel to Mount Horeb (Sinai), with the differences and similarities in these mountaintop experiences, is indeed striking. But the chapter seems not to signal an interest in the nature of the prophetic role per se. Rather, in the face of the threat posed by Jezebel, coupled with Elijah's despondent response, the chapter centers upon a direct encounter with a God who refuses to let him off the hook regarding his calling and renews the prophetic commission (vv. 15–18), which Elijah fulfills in part (vv. 19–21).

The narrative is carried along by a journey motif and is punctuated with several divine appearances and communications. As such, the portrayal of Elijah is constructed in such a way as to parallel the story of Moses, evidencing both similarity and difference. Connections with the wilderness journeys, Moses' lamenting, God's appearances to him (especially at Mount Sinai), and his commissioning are especially to be noted.

In a sharp reversal, Elijah moves from the triumph at Mount Carmel to Jezebel's most wanted list (unlike Ahab, she was not around for the display in chap. 18). Elijah flees for his life (as in 17:1), heading south toward Sinai, the traditional site of divine revelation. Jezebel sends a messenger with a message of death (to scare him away?); God will send another messenger (=angel) with a gift that enables life (vv. 5–7). During his flight, Elijah relives some of Israel's experiences in the wilderness, both negative and positive. Negatively, he complains because he has apparently failed to turn the apostasy around (his "ancestors" may be predecessor prophets) and (from vv. 10, 14, 18) the confession of the people has been short-lived. Despairing of his vocation, he demands that God take his life (this is an issue for God, not Jezebel; cf. Moses, in Num. 11:15, and Jonah, in 4:3, who wishes to die for the opposite reason!). The effect, of course, would be the end of Elijah's mission. What follows is God's refusal to accept this decision; God has more work for him to do. Positively, God (as in 17:1–7) provides both for his life and for his continued vocation: Through a messenger (see Gen. 21:16–19) who, initially, leaves him food and water and, later, provides counsel regarding the long journey—to Sinai, it turns out (forty days and nights, a period with wilderness and Sinai connections, Exod. 16:35; 24:18). While God will question his presence there, God leads him there for the sake of the right context for the confrontation.

Having arrived at Sinai, he spends the night in a cave (see Exod. 33:12–23, a divine appearance in response to Moses' complaint). The word of the Lord comes to Elijah and two remarkably similar exchanges occur. The word of God twice (vv. 9, 13) rebukes Elijah, asking what he is doing in *this* place (yet note that God had encouraged the journey in v. 7). The implication is that Elijah should be someplace else (to be specified in vv. 15–18). Elijah, focusing on himself (note the repeated "I") and perhaps expecting divine commiseration, twice replies in identical terms (vv. 10, 14), in effect: I've been working my head off to no effect; all Israelites have proved unfaithful, and now my life is in danger. Elijah's zeal has matched God's jealousy (14:22). In this state, he had come to believe his own hyperbole of 18:22 (see 18:4). Interestingly, no reference is made to Jezebel's threat to his life (unless she is included among the "Israelites" as one who "killed prophets with the sword," v. 1). Both of the responses are followed by a divine commmand (vv. 11, 15).

What in fact happens between the questions is a much disputed matter. The word of God tells Elijah to go out of the cave and stand on the mountain "before the Lord," for God is about to pass by (v. 11; compare his standing in 17:1; Exod. 33:19–22; 34:6). This command is not immediately obeyed (see v. 13), because of an ear-splitting, multimedia "interruption" (vv. 11b–12). The wind, and presumably the fire and earthquake, occur "before the Lord" (v. 11); they are the *vanguard* for God's passing; God is not "in" them (as Baal was thought to be). These are upheavals in nature associated with an appearance of Yahweh (for example, Exod. 19:18; Psalm 29). After the noisy demonstration there was only a "sound of sheer silence," an absence of sound, but palpable after all the noise. With these phenomena having passed "before" God, God *now* stands before the emergent Elijah, a presence he acknowledges by hiding his face (see Exod. 3:6; 34:8). God has appeared directly for the sake of moving Elijah beyond his despondency and refusal to continue his commission. Some translations (for example, "still small voice") imply that a verbal communication occurred. In either case, Elijah "heard" it, and he responds by hiding his face.

Then God (now "a voice") speaks (v. 13). The "sound of silence" is a pregnant moment of calm before the directly spoken (face-to-face) voice of God (see Num. 12:8; Job 4:16).

Why does Elijah simply repeat his reply? Elijah understands that the first question he heard (v. 9) came from the angel (vv. 5–7), or at least more indirectly; v. 11 implies that the first exchange did *not* take place "before the Lord." Now, given the signs of God's presence, he knows the question comes directly from God, and hence he repeats the answer. All of this is preparatory to a renewed commission directly from God (cf. Exod. 3:6 with 3:8–10). God responds (vv. 15–18), in effect: Quit the pity party, go back home, much work remains to be done, and here are a few starters; besides, you are not alone. God's word is essentially the same old word: God will continue to be working to rid Israel of its apostasy, judgment will be visited against Baal worshipers (though a faithful remnant shall be delivered), and Elijah's commission is to set that in motion. God will continue to act in decisive ways through human agents, though those agents are now drawn from a larger group in God's creation. Elijah's commission is enfleshed with some new particulars and the promise of help to carry out his responsibilities. Hazael and Jehu will be instruments of God's purposes, and a successor prophet will be raised up to continue his work—along with 7,000 others.

The purpose for making Hazael king of Aram (2 Kings 10:32–33) is to cut back Israel's territory and mediate God's judgment on Israel for its idolatry (as God will later use the Assyrians and the Babylonians). The second case (2 Kings 9:1–13) also relates to divine judgment as Jehu puts an end to Omri's dynasty and initiates reforms that begin to turn back the inroads of Baal on Israel's life. In effect, Baal's adherents will be eliminated; even more, a faithful remnant will continue. Both promises are a response to Elijah's despair associated with seeming failure and isolation.

But what happens to these commands and promises? God's commands to anoint two kings are not actually carried out by Elijah, but by Elisha and one of Elisha's followers (2 Kings 8:7–15; 9:1–13). Elijah leaves for heaven before it is possible for him to do so (2 Kings 2:11)! Even more, Elisha does not literally anoint Hazael, but engages in political cunning that enables Hazael to assume the throne of Aram. Nor does Elisha actually kill anyone. Moreover, Hazael's judgment occurred *after* Jehu's purge (v. 17; 2 Kings 9:14–10:27). Finally, the one command that Elijah carries out (19:19–21) is not literally an anointing of Elisha, though his act of throwing his mantle over Elisha symbolically accomplishes that. These changes do not signal disobedience, but recognize that God's word regarding the future may have to be adjusted in view of new circumstances, and prophets are given freedom in the shaping of the divine word (see at 1 Kings 21:1–29; 2 Kings 20:1–7; 22:20 with 23:29). While Elijah did not see the fulfillment of this word—just as Moses did not enter the promised land— the essence of the word was fulfilled.

Elisha, however, is not eager to pick up Elijah's mantle and begs for a delay to say his good-byes. Whether Elijah rebukes him is unclear; he appears to tell Elisha (a rich man) to return to what he was doing as if the call had not occurred. Elisha is too indecisive to serve the calling Elijah has in mind. But when Elisha returns home he slaughters his oxen (rather than, say, selling them) and provides a feast for the community; he is given a second chance (unlike the would-be disciple in Luke 9:61). Elisha's act is a sign that he has made the decision, and that it is irrevocable; he no longer has a vocation to which he can return. Having burned his bridges, he leaves the farm and follows Elijah, becoming fully his successor in 2 Kings 2:13–14.

This is not the usual way in which prophets are raised up in Israel. Succession is the means God uses in this instance because of Elijah's concerns and the severity of the crisis for Yahwism in Israel at this time. This crisis calls for continuity in having a "man of God" on the scene who can address the issues forthrightly. This stress on continuity shows that the calling of the prophet is the central concern of this narrative.

On the Tenacity of God's Call

What kind of God is this? The God portrayed here is a God who does not leave Elijah to wallow in his despondency. This God is one who is faithful to the prophet, providing for his needs as in 17:2–16 (vv. 4–8). This God is one who refuses to allow the prophet to stew in his feelings of dejection, but rather comes to him through a messenger, gets him going, and then sharply confronts him with questions. This God is one who, having encountered Elijah's initial response of self-pity, refuses to be content with that interpretation of the situation and finds a way to confront him more directly with the divine presence. And then, allowing him to state his self-pity in the very presence of God, recommissions him to his vocation, assures him that God is still at work through him, and promises him successors, through whom this mission will ultimately be successful. Once again, God becomes involved in violent human activities, whereby judgment is mediated upon Israel for its unfaithfulness within relationship (see at 1:1–2:46). But the last word is one of promise that God will not leave himself without witnesses.

What kind of prophet is this? Elijah and Elisha exhibit two different responses to God's call. For Elijah, it is deep discouragement. The work seems to be nothing more than failure and dangerous to his health, occasioning a retreat into self-pity or a mountaintop hideaway. But God's response moves him back to center. For Elisha, it is hesitation about becoming involved in the first place. And Elijah's response leads him to take up the task.

A primary image in the texts is movement. Elijah's long and torturous journey includes threat to life, despondency regarding call, remarkable provision, an encounter with God's questions, commands, and promises that refuse to let him go, and a call to Elisha to take up the same journey (cf. Luke 9:57–62). The walk behind the plow is arduous, the heat makes the sweat run down the face, and the disciple will keep running into boulders. The way is narrow, steep, filled with bandits and hangers-on; it moves through many a wilderness, with long distances between oases, and no autobahns; it moves through "fast-food strips," with numerous temptations to detour. The food will become scarce, the water will barely slake the thirst, and on many a night there will be no place to sleep. A stable may have to do.

The interpreter should not soften the claim these texts place upon those servants who take this journey in response to God's call. No detours or side roads, just straight ahead. No excuses, indecisiveness, self-pity, or looking back once begun. Even second thoughts seem to be ruled out, and failures are no excuse. God may come with sharp questions and refuse to back off from the calling. The call is to faithfulness and responsibility. This is a call to stay the course, come what may.

But in this walk, the servant of God is not alone. There is the promise of God's presence (maybe even a memorable moment on some mountaintop or in some valley), remarkable supplies that provide for new energies and encouragement along the way, and a recognition that others have this same calling and will share the load. This way may seem restrictive, with too many constraints on behavior and too many disappointments and frustrations; it may seem too rigorous, with too few "rest areas." But it is a way of remarkable freedom, uncommon joy, and an incredible sense of fulfillment.

AHAB, ARAM, AND PROPHETS
1 Kings 20:1–22:53

Ahab's War with Aram
(1 Kings 20:1–43)

This narrative moves to Ahab's foreign policy; stories of two battles focus on his relations with Aram (Syria). Long a nemesis (11:23–25; 15:18–21),

Aram will continue to harass Israel through 2 Kings 10. At the same time, insufficient detail is provided to set these episodes historically. Ben-hadad is the name of several Aramean kings, but he becomes here a type of royal arrogance that leads, finally, to the undoing of Ahab.

This chapter may have been inserted into the Elijah stories at this point because of the reference to Aram in 19:15–17 and its demonstration that (unnamed) prophets beside Elijah are at work in Israel (vv. 13, 22, 28, 35; contrast 18:22; 19:10, 14). Prophets, who take the initiative with Ahab again and again, shape how this narrative develops. Yet it only gradually becomes clear that the issue at stake is the proper execution of a holy war; the reader may be as surprised as Ahab. Once this is recognized, one has to read back and see where the twists and turns of the narrative lie (cf. 1 Kings 13). Seemingly nonreligious details come to have theological import.

The story begins as Ben-hadad amasses his army, puts together a coalition of kings (of cities), and attacks Israel. Laying siege to Samaria, he makes two demands of Ahab. The first—Ahab's wealth and his wives and children—is agreed to by Ahab, without hesitation! The second demand delivers a timed ultimatum: free reign for his servants in Ahab's palace—to take whatever they want (vv. 5–6). After consultation with less pliant elders, Ahab refuses the request (v. 9). Trading proverbial boasts (vv. 10–11), Ben-hadad claims he has more soldiers than Israel has handfuls of dust, while Ahab warns that Ben-hadad is confident before he has good reason. Ben-hadad's response (while in his cups) is to command his soldiers to ready themselves for attack against Samaria.

At this high danger point, an unnamed prophet appears to Ahab with a word from the Lord (compare David in 2 Sam. 5:19). Given the story of Elijah, the reader is prepared to hear a word of judgment. But the word from God speaks of deliverance: In spite of the odds, God will give the Aramaeans, "a great multitude," into his hand and "you shall know that I am the LORD" (v. 13; the "you" is singular, a reference to Ahab; connections are again made to Exodus—7:17; 8:10; the theme is common in Ezekiel). That is, the victory against a superior force will be a witness to God's work among them. Requesting further tactical information, Ahab follows the prophet's word from God and musters 232 young men (perhaps untrained; cf. Gideon's 300 in Judg. 7:7) and 7,000 regulars (see 19:18). When Ben-hadad's scouts report the advance of this elite corps, he (still drunk) miscalculates and sends careless orders. The Israelites, led by Ahab himself and the young men (vv. 14, 20–21; the trained soldiers seem not to have been so engaged), win a decisive victory, though Ben-hadad escapes. The word of God has been fulfilled, though the narrative does not give a theological report either regarding God's action or that, because of this victory, Israel now "knows that I am the LORD" (v. 13).

The prophet warns Ahab (v. 22) to prepare for another campaign in the spring (a common season for war, see 2 Sam. 11:1). Before attacking Israel again, Ben-hadad's advisors recommend several personnel and tactical changes, including attacking Israel in the plains because "their gods" are associated with the hills (Carmel, Sinai). The Aramaeans attack Israel at Aphek (near the Sea of Galilee). Their army, which "fills the country," is met by a small Israelite force, likened to "two little flocks of goats" (v. 27). Once again, a prophet speaks a word of God to Ahab: Ahab will be victorious because Aram's knowledge of Israel's God must be challenged; God's power cannot be localized or tied to specific military tactics. The effect will be: "you shall know that I am the LORD" (v. 28; the "you" is plural, probably all involved; cf. v. 13). The result was a second quick victory and the slaughter of Ben-hadad's entire army (127,000 strong; for the seven days and falling walls and connections to holy war, see Josh. 6:3–5). Again, the narrative does not speak of God in association with the victory, nor report its religious effect on Israel as had been promised (vv. 13, 28; contrast 18:39).

Ben-hadad's servants advise him to ask for clemency, wearing apparel that symbolizes submission (cf. the armor in v. 11), for their kings are "merciful" (or loyal; an ironic comment, given Ahab's lack of loyalty to Yahweh!). When the servants approach Ahab, he responds by calling Ben-hadad his "brother" (treaty language expressing equality). This provides an opening for a meeting between Ahab and Ben-hadad. When Ben-hadad promises to restore the Israelite towns taken earlier (see 15:20) and to give Ahab commercial opportunities in Damascus (the capital of Aram), Ahab agrees and spares him (v. 34). The tables have been turned (contrast vv. 1–12); Ahab and Ben-hadad have changed places; Israel now has the decisive edge over Syria. Ahab no doubt thought that God was on Israel's side—and his. But what seemed to be good politics and humane considerations will be evaluated as disobedience.

Verses 35–43 describe the prophetic response, and it surprises both Ahab and readers. At God's command, a prophet (from a guild) sets a stage, designed (we shortly learn) to reveal that Ahab has disobeyed the law regarding holy war (Deut. 20:10–18; see 1 Sam. 15:17–24). He asks another prophet to strike him, so that he will look as if he has been wounded in battle. The ploy to be executed must be as realistic as possible; the bandage also serves as a disguise—Ahab may recognize him (v. 13). When the prophet refuses, he is told he will be killed by a lion, and he is (see 13:24).

This reluctant prophet mirrors Ahab; he should have struck Ben-hadad and because he didn't he will be subject to God's lion-like judgment. When another prophet does strike him, the wounded and bandaged prophet encounters the king. Ahab mirrors this prophet as well (cf. his disguise in 22:29–30). The prophet makes his point by telling a juridical parable, devised to trap the king into declaring his own punishment (for a similar parable, see 2 Sam. 12:1–7). Unlike the mercy shown to Ben-hadad, Ahab declares that the prophet/servant was to be killed for not obeying orders, being "busy here and there," and letting a prisoner escape (no excuses are accepted and the talent of silver would be impossible to pay). The prophet reveals his identity and announces God's judgment in comparable terms: just like the prophet, Ahab is to be killed (and his people) because he let Ben-hadad, the one "devoted to destruction," go free.

God and Ahab's Future

This indictment against Ahab adds to the case against him that has been building up over the course of the Elijah narratives. Yet there have been signs of a different Ahab (e.g., 18:41–46), and Jezebel seems more the culprit at times than he (e.g., 18:19; 19:1–2). This narrative is not anti-Ahab in most respects; only Ahab's merciful treatment of Ben-hadad at the end of the story is evaluated negatively. Up to this point, Ahab receives and follows prophetic counsel and never boasts of his victories. Inasmuch as God works through human activity, what Ahab does is not inconsequential in the success of the battles. The narrative says as much in that it does not return to make a theological point in connection with either victory. While it may simply assume that the reader will draw these conclusions from verses 13 and 28, the lack of explicit theological language suggests that the human factor in these battles was key to God's work. Even what *Ahab* does! Another important factor to remember here is that the prophetic announcement regarding Ahab's future, when combined with the announcement in 1 Kings 21:19–24, will be later qualified because Ahab humbles himself before God (1 Kings 21:27–29).

This varied openness to Ahab demonstrates that his future has not all been blocked out. His relationship to God does not run straight downhill; he is given opportunity to turn the situation around. And here, despite appearances, God does not pull a fast one on Ahab. The assumption is that Ahab should have known about the law regarding holy war; it is set deeply within the tradition and Israel's history to this point (Deuteronomy 20; Joshua 6–7; 1 Samuel 15). Far from being tricked by God, Ahab is implicitly faulted for not steeping himself in the law as a good king would (Deut. 18:18–20).

Given Ahab's choices, even if he should have known the law, modern readers would tend to side with his show of mercy toward Ben-hadad, challenge the law, and resentfully respond just as he did (v. 43). And the reader is probably right to do so in view of the entire biblical perspective on such violence. At the same time, it should be asked whether there may be situations wherein the showing of mercy would be a violation of the will of God. Should one freely pardon the Hitlers of this world? (For the understanding of holy war more generally, see Fretheim, *Deuteronomic History*, 68–75).

Naboth's Vineyard
(1 Kings 21:1–29)

21:1 Later the following events took place: Naboth the Jezreelite had a vineyard in Jezreel, beside the palace of King Ahab of Samaria. 2 And Ahab said to Naboth, "Give me your vineyard, so that I may have it for a vegetable garden, because it is near my house; I will give you a better vineyard for it; or, if it seems good to you, I will give you its value in money." 3 But Naboth said to Ahab, "The LORD forbid that I should give you my ancestral inheritance." 4 Ahab went home resentful and sullen because of what Naboth the Jezreelite had said to him; for he had said, "I will not give you my ancestral inheritance." He lay down on his bed, turned away his face, and would not eat. 5 His wife Jezebel came to him and said, "Why are you so depressed that you will not eat?" 6 He said to her, "Because I spoke to Naboth the Jezreelite and said to him, 'Give me your vineyard for money; or else, if you prefer, I will give you another vineyard for it'; but he answered, 'I will not give you my vineyard.'" 7 His wife Jezebel said to him, "Do you now govern Israel? Get up, eat some food, and be cheerful; I will give you the vineyard of Naboth the Jezreelite." 8 So she wrote letters in Ahab's name and sealed them with his seal; she sent the letters to the elders and the nobles who lived with Naboth in his city. 9 She wrote in the letters, "Proclaim a fast, and seat Naboth at the head of the assembly; 10 seat two scoundrels opposite him, and have them bring a charge against him, saying, 'You have cursed God and the king.' Then take him out, and stone him to death." 11 The men of his city, the elders and the nobles who lived in his city, did as Jezebel had sent word to them. Just as it was written in the letters that she had sent to them, 12 they proclaimed a fast and seated Naboth at the head of the assembly. 13 The two scoundrels came in and sat opposite him; and the scoundrels brought a charge against Naboth, in the presence of the people, saying, "Naboth cursed God and the king." So they took him outside the city, and stoned him to death. 14 Then they sent to Jezebel, saying, "Naboth has been stoned; he is dead." [15] As soon as Jezebel heard that Naboth had been stoned and was dead, Jezebel said to Ahab, "Go, take possession of the vineyard of Naboth the Jezreelite, which he refused to give you for money; for Naboth is not alive, but dead." [16] As soon as Ahab heard that Naboth was dead, Ahab set out to go down to the vineyard of Naboth the Jezreelite, to take possession of it. [17] Then the word of the LORD came to Elijah the Tishbite, saying: [18] Go down to meet King Ahab of Israel, who rules in Samaria; he is now in the vineyard of Naboth, where he has gone to take possession. [19] You shall say to him, "Thus says the LORD: Have you killed, and also taken possession?" You shall say to him, "Thus says the LORD: In the place where dogs licked up the blood of Naboth, dogs will also lick up your blood." [20] Ahab said to Elijah, "Have you found me, O my enemy?" He answered, "I have found you. Because you have sold yourself to do what is evil in the sight of the LORD, [21] I will bring disaster on you; I will consume you, and will cut off from Ahab every male, bond or free, in Israel; [22] and I will make your house like the house of Jeroboam son of Nebat, and like the house of Baasha son of Ahijah, because you have provoked me to anger and have caused Israel to sin. [23] Also concerning Jezebel the LORD said, 'The dogs shall eat Jezebel within the bounds of Jezreel.' [24] Anyone belonging to Ahab who dies in the city the dogs shall eat; and anyone of his who dies in the open country the birds of the air shall eat." [25] (Indeed, there was no one like Ahab, who sold himself to do what was evil in the sight of the LORD, urged on by his wife Jezebel. [26] He acted most abominably in going after idols, as the Amorites had done, whom the LORD drove out before the Israelites.) [27] When Ahab heard those words, he tore his clothes and put sackcloth over his bare flesh; he fasted, lay in the sackcloth, and went about dejectedly. [28] Then the word of the LORD came to Elijah the Tishbite: [29] "Have you seen how Ahab has humbled himself before me? Because he has humbled himself before me, I will not bring the disaster in his days; but in his son's days I will bring the disaster on his house."

The story begins and ends in the vineyard. Ahab's confronting Naboth ends with Elijah confronting Ahab. The story is a dramatic rendering of a typical prophetic word of judgment, focused on justice. The sin leads to the prophetic indictment and announcement of judgment (enhanced by the narrator in vv. 25–26); even the mitigating word (vv. 27–29) is not unlike that spoken by many prophets (see below).

Apostasy was not the only issue Elijah confronted. He also took on the royal practice of injustice and the arrogant use of power against the weaker members of society. God's law was richly and pervasively concerned about the needs of the disadvantaged in Israel's society. The divine origin of such laws meant that injustice was not just an offense against human beings, but against God as well. Israel's royal theology at its best focused on justice and supported it with commitments (see Ps. 72:1–4). Ahab's sin in chapter 20 was failure to know the law; here it is neglect of the broader concern of the law for justice.

The text begins at Ahab's summer palace in Jezreel (see 18:45–46). A peasant farmer named Naboth has a vineyard adjacent to the king's property. Ahab covets the property for a royal vegetable garden (comparable to Egypt; see Deut. 11:10–12); he is willing to buy it or give Naboth a better vineyard. Naboth swears by an oath in the name of Yahweh not to give it up because it is his family's inheritance (and another vineyard would not be). The Torah had no prohibitions against the sale of land as such, so Ahab's request violated no law. From the perspective of priestly law, however, the property could not be sold for any reason or in perpetuity (see Lev. 25:8–17, 23–25). At some point it was to be returned to the original family. Whether or not this law was in effect in this time, Naboth chose not to reduce his family's inheritance (vines take years to develop compared to vegetables), or to put it at future risk. Importantly, Naboth casts this issue as one of family and community rights, not of individual property rights. The issue has to do with the very foundations of Israelite society and social well-being. The repeated phrase "ancestral inheritance" recalls other forms of "inheritance" Ahab is undermining; the "vineyard" may have indirect reference to Israel itself (see Psalm 80; Isa. 5:1–7).

Ahab's displeasure is described in unusual detail (he is resentful, sullen, depressed, sleeps too much, won't eat), perhaps because of the oath (though 20:43 suggests it is habitual). Yet he accepts Naboth's decision. But not Jezebel, though Ahab does not fully report Naboth's reason to her (v. 6). She belittles Ahab for not "governing," which for her is doing whatever he wants and getting whatever he covets. *She* will govern as *he* should, including writing letters in his name, and get the vineyard for him.

Interestingly, she does not simply take the vineyard or kill Naboth outright; she devises a royal cover-up, but completely within the law, whereby Naboth could be framed and condemned for treason and blasphemy. She commands leaders in Naboth's city—no doubt beholden to the crown—to have him prominently seated at a solemn fast next to two scoundrels (two witnesses are needed, Deut. 19:15). This is likely an occasion involving penitence at a time of crisis (1 Sam. 7:6)! Thus, a religious occasion is used for irreligious purposes. The witnesses are (falsely) to accuse Naboth of cursing God and the king, the penalty for which is death (see Lev. 24:15–16; Exod. 22:28). Is this a way for Naboth to be fingered as the cause of the community crisis that necessitated calling the fast? The ruse works, the men do just as Jezebel had ordered, and Naboth (with his sons? see 2 Kings 9:26) is stoned by the two men and his community (and his property forfeited). Jezebel commands Ahab to go and take possession of the vineyard, which he proceeds to do. There he receives a "gift" he had not anticipated!

In response to these developments God commands Elijah to confront Ahab while he is in the vineyard. Ahab's identification of Elijah as enemy shows insight (cf. 18:17), but the prophet's words fill the scene. Two charges are brought (as had been the case with Naboth): murdering Naboth and taking possession of his vineyard (see below). Elijah is to pronounce doom upon Ahab, the second such announcement (see 20:42).

God tells Elijah to speak against Ahab himself (v. 19), and Elijah expands that word of judgment on his own to include, not only Ahab, but Ahab's house (vv. 21–22). Then Elijah reports God's word regarding Jezebel and others who belong to him (vv. 23–24; extended further in Micah 6:16). To be eaten by animals and birds is to be denied a proper burial. Elijah uses language similar to that spoken by Ahijah against Jeroboam (1 Kings 14:10–11; see there for the issue of coarse language) and Jehu against Baasha (16:3–4). He even states that Ahab has "caused Israel to sin," language used before only for apostasy. The narrator picks up this theme in a parenthetical comment (vv. 25–26; cf. 14:24 for another link to the Canaanites), adding that Ahab, urged on by Jezebel, "sold himself to do what was evil" (an act of enslavement [to Jezebel?]; see Deut. 28:68), and that his sin was unparalleled (16:30, 33). That the issue of idolatry is introduced is surprising, but pertinent to the larger context. The connection between injustice and going after other gods is thereby kept in close connection. Idolatry has led to injustice; the latter has deep roots in the former.

Ahab's response to Elijah's word is penitence, demonstrated by public signs of sackcloth, fasting, and dejected behavior. When God sees this response, Elijah is told that the judgment made against Ahab will be qualified. The judgment stands against Ahab's house, but will not be visited during his lifetime, but during the reign of his son (Jehoram as it turns out, not Ahaziah; see 2 Kings 9:25–26; 10:17).

Judgment and Reprieve for Ahab

Several features of the prophetic word in this chapter merit further attention. First, the penalty fits the crime. Ahab's "evil" (Hebrew: ra^c) will be brought back on him by God (vv. 20–21; "disaster" translates ra^c; on judgment, see also at 2 Kings 17:1–41; 22:1–23:30). The correspondence between act and judgment is precise: the double charge (vv. 10, 19) and blood-licking dogs (v. 19). God's judgment does not introduce anything new into the situation. The sins that have been "planted" by Ahab bear fruit in ways that correspond to the deeds (see Jer. 6:19; 21:14). The words against Jezebel and against those who belong to Ahab (vv. 23–24) also correspond, though the behavior of the dogs is extended to eating their flesh (on the harsh metaphors, see at 14:21–16:34).

Second, the language Elijah uses for judgment is developed beyond that given him by God to use (v. 19). Here we observe a prophetic freedom to adapt the word received from God in view of the relationship between them. In this adaptation, words from prophet and God are interwoven (see Jer. 8:18–9:3 where the speakers are difficult to sort out): the "I" of verse 20 is clearly Elijah; the "I" of verses 22–23 does not distinguish between Elijah and God, as Elijah conveys the *divine* anger *he* "feels"; verse 23 is clearly a quote from God (v. 24 may be as well, though NRSV ends the quotation at v. 23). In verses 25–26, the narrator's words join those of God and prophet. This elision of prophetic word and divine word demonstrates the closeness of prophet and God; the prophet is so caught up into the divine life that he becomes a veritable embodiment of the word of God (see 22:19–23). He is thereby given the freedom to reformulate or extend that word or develop new metaphors (see Jer. 23:18–22). When Ahab calls Elijah his "enemy," he (knowingly?, given 18:17–18) recognizes that this is also to say that God has become his enemy. If Elijah and God do not stand together as enemies of the Ahabs and Jezebels of this world, then they participate in the injustice.

Third, these texts demonstrate that the fulfillment of a prophetic word is not mechanical or necessarily precise (see Introduction; and at 19:15–17). This is seen most clearly in Ahab's penitence and God's response to it. God qualifies Elijah's words about his house, saying that the judgment will be delayed a generation, as it was (2 Kings 9:25–26; 10:17; cf. 22:11–20). This qualification shows that the prophetic word about the future retains a certain openness to events, in this case, Ahab's penitence. God has not strait-jacketed himself to fulfill a prophetic word in precise terms. God remains open to change and adjustment in view of how people will respond and what the course of history will present (see also at 2 Kings 20:1–7). This tradition within the Deuteronomistic History (see also 1 Samuel 15) connects with texts regarding divine repentance, particularly in the prophets (for example, Jer. 26:3, 13, 19). The generational delay ought not be explained as an arbitrary divine move, but a recognition that the buildup of the forces of evil have now been extenuated in view of human response.

The judgment against Ahab personally (v. 19) is not qualified in fulfillment; but it is not fully precise either (see 22:37–38, where the "place" of
the dogs is Samaria rather than Jezreel). Moreover, the reference to fulfillment speaks of prostitutes bathing in his blood, not a part of Elijah's
prophecy. Similarly, the word regarding Jezebel (v. 23) is fulfilled in
2 Kings 9:30–37; yet in the quotation Elijah's words are made even more
harsh.

Micaiah and the Death of Ahab
(1 Kings 22:1–53)

22:1 **For three years Aram and Israel continued without war. ² But in the
third year King Jehoshaphat of Judah came down to the king of Israel. ³ The
king of Israel said to his servants, "Do you know that Ramoth-gilead belongs
to us, yet we are doing nothing to take it out of the hand of the king of
Aram?" ⁴ He said to Jehoshaphat, "Will you go with me to battle at Ramoth-
gilead?" Jehoshaphat replied to the king of Israel, "I am as you are; my people are your people, my horses are your horses." ⁵ But Jehoshaphat also said
to the king of Israel, "Inquire first for the word of the LORD." ⁶ Then the king
of Israel gathered the prophets together, about four hundred of them, and
said to them, "Shall I go to battle against Ramoth-gilead, or shall I refrain?"
They said, "Go up; for the LORD will give it into the hand of the king." ⁷ But
Jehoshaphat said, "Is there no other prophet of the LORD here of whom we
may inquire?" ⁸ The king of Israel said to Jehoshaphat, "There is still one
other by whom we may inquire of the LORD, Micaiah son of Imlah; but I hate
him, for he never prophesies anything favorable about me, but only disaster." Jehoshaphat said, "Let the king not say such a thing." ⁹ Then the king
of Israel summoned an officer and said, "Bring quickly Micaiah son of Imlah." ¹⁰ Now the king of Israel and King Jehoshaphat of Judah were sitting on
their thrones, arrayed in their robes, at the threshing floor at the entrance of
the gate of Samaria; and all the prophets were prophesying before them.
¹¹ Zedekiah son of Chenaanah made for himself horns of iron, and he said,
"Thus says the LORD: With these you shall gore the Arameans until they are
destroyed." ¹² All the prophets were prophesying the same and saying, "Go
up to Ramoth-gilead and triumph; the LORD will give it into the hand of the
king." ¹³ The messenger who had gone to summon Micaiah said to him,
"Look, the words of the prophets with one accord are favorable to the king;
let your word be like the word of one of them, and speak favorably." ¹⁴ But
Micaiah said, "As the LORD lives, whatever the LORD says to me, that I will
speak." ¹⁵ When he had come to the king, the king said to him, "Micaiah,
shall we go to Ramoth-gilead to battle, or shall we refrain?" He answered
him, "Go up and triumph; the LORD will give it into the hand of the king."**

[16] But the king said to him, "How many times must I make you swear to tell me nothing but the truth in the name of the LORD?" [17] Then Micaiah said, "I saw all Israel scattered on the mountains, like sheep that have no shepherd; and the LORD said, 'These have no master; let each one go home in peace.'" [18] The king of Israel said to Jehoshaphat, "Did I not tell you that he would not prophesy anything favorable about me, but only disaster?" [19] Then Micaiah said, "Therefore hear the word of the LORD: I saw the LORD sitting on his throne, with all the host of heaven standing beside him to the right and to the left of him. [20] And the LORD said, 'Who will entice Ahab, so that he may go up and fall at Ramoth-gilead?' Then one said one thing, and another said another, [21] until a spirit came forward and stood before the LORD, saying, 'I will entice him.' [22] 'How?' the LORD asked him. He replied, 'I will go out and be a lying spirit in the mouth of all his prophets.' Then the LORD said, 'You are to entice him, and you shall succeed; go out and do it.' [23] So you see, the LORD has put a lying spirit in the mouth of all these your prophets; the LORD has decreed disaster for you." [24] Then Zedekiah son of Chenaanah came up to Micaiah, slapped him on the cheek, and said, "Which way did the spirit of the LORD pass from me to speak to you?" [25] Micaiah replied, "You will find out on that day when you go in to hide in an inner chamber." [26] The king of Israel then ordered, "Take Micaiah, and return him to Amon the governor of the city and to Joash the king's son, [27] and say, 'Thus says the king: Put this fellow in prison, and feed him on reduced rations of bread and water until I come in peace.'" [28] Micaiah said, "If you return in peace, the LORD has not spoken by me." And he said, "Hear, you peoples, all of you!" [29] So the king of Israel and King Jehoshaphat of Judah went up to Ramoth-gilead. [30] The king of Israel said to Jehoshaphat, "I will disguise myself and go into battle, but you wear your robes." So the king of Israel disguised himself and went into battle. [31] Now the king of Aram had commanded the thirty-two captains of his chariots, "Fight with no one small or great, but only with the king of Israel." [32] When the captains of the chariots saw Jehoshaphat, they said, "It is surely the king of Israel." So they turned to fight against him; and Jehoshaphat cried out. [33] When the captains of the chariots saw that it was not the king of Israel, they turned back from pursuing him. [34] But a certain man drew his bow and unknowingly struck the king of Israel between the scale armor and the breastplate; so he said to the driver of his chariot, "Turn around, and carry me out of the battle, for I am wounded." [35] The battle grew hot that day, and the king was propped up in his chariot facing the Arameans, until at evening he died; the blood from the wound had flowed into the bottom of the chariot. [36] Then about sunset a shout went through the army, "Every man to his city, and every man to his country!" [37] So the king died, and was brought to Samaria; they buried the king in Samaria. [38] They washed the chariot by the pool of Samaria; the dogs licked up his blood, and the prostitutes washed themselves in it, according to the

word of the LORD that he had spoken. ³⁹ Now the rest of the acts of Ahab, and all that he did, and the ivory house that he built, and all the cities that he built, are they not written in the Book of the Annals of the Kings of Israel? ⁴⁰ So Ahab slept with his ancestors; and his son Ahaziah succeeded him.

This chapter concludes a series of stories in which Ahab is confronted by God's prophets (see the similar account in 2 Chron. 18:4–34). Elijah has been Ahab's chief antagonist, but other prophets confronted him in chapter 20 and here still another does (Micaiah). The word of 2 Kings 17:13 that God had warned the kings of Israel by "every prophet and every seer" is especially true for Ahab.

Israel's relationships with Aram are the subject of the narrative once again. The story begins with Ahab's peace treaty in jeopardy (20:34) and closes with peace reestablished (promised in v. 17). Ahab is still "the king of Israel" (but mentioned by name only in v. 20!) and consults with king Jehoshaphat of Judah regarding a conflict with Aram. An alliance between them had been sealed when Ahab married his daughter (Athaliah) to Jehoram, Jehoshaphat's son (2 Kings 8:18). The issue centers on the city of Ramoth-gilead; it had been one of Solomon's administrative centers east of the Jordan (4:13) and was likely one of the cities Ben-hadad had promised to return (20:34). Ahab wants to wrest it from Aramean control and easily receives support from Judah, the weaker state.

Before proceeding against Aram, Jehoshaphat asks for a word from the Lord, typical for such situations (see 20:13, 28). Ahab requests the advice of some 400 prophets (cf. 18:19, 40, where only the prophets of Baal are killed) and they counsel him to do battle, for God would give Ramoth-gilead into his hand. But Jehoshaphat is suspicious and asks for another "prophet *of the Lord*." Ahab's reply and the portrayal of the royal setting (vv. 8, 10) are both humorous and pathetic. He knows of a prophet named Micaiah (one wonders where Elijah is) but hates him because he prophesies only disaster (Hebrew: *ra*ʿ; Elijah's language in 21:20–21). Before he is brought, Ahab's prophets continue to dominate the ostentatious royal scene with their antics, symbolic acts (horns of iron, anticipating victory over the Aramaeans), and unanimous counsel.

The narrative about Micaiah (vv. 13–28; his name means "Who is like Yahweh?") is remarkable in several respects. It reveals the depth of prophetic conflict in Israel (a reality that will continue until the fall of Jerusalem; see Jeremiah 28) and provides insight into the prophet's relationship with God. Key to understanding verses 19–23 in particular are texts such as Jeremiah 23:18–22 (cf. Isa. 6:8, "us"). The prophet is invited into the divine council, overhears the divine word, and faithfully conveys that word to the people. The divine council consists of angelic messengers with whom God consults regarding earthly matters. The story Micaiah tells about the workings of the council indicates that there is genuine interaction in that council (v. 20), where disagreement (with God!) is possible. This sets up a contrast between God and Ahab, who wants prophets who only agree with him. Yet by sharing the council's deliberations with Ahab, and even telling him that the prophets are lying (!), God (through Micaiah) gives Ahab an opportunity to repent and reach out for divine mercy.

We return to the story at verse 14. Micaiah is encouraged to support the prophetic majority, and he takes an oath to speak whatever the Lord wants spoken (v. 14). Surprisingly, Micaiah, speaking under oath, simply supports the majority voice, because (as v. 22 shows) he knows that the word they speak is from God (though a lie). But the king (Ahab) objects on the basis of past experience with the prophet; Micaiah never seems to tell him the *truth* ("how many times"), for when he does, he disagrees with the others. Then Micaiah brings a word that does disagree, foreseeing disaster for Ahab (v. 17), with the soldiers scattered like sheep because they have no shepherd (=Ahab, see 2 Sam. 5:2). Yet because Ahab is dead they can go home in peace. Ahab interprets this as a change in the word that Micaiah speaks, that Micaiah disagrees with his prophets after all, and speaks a word that is not *good* ("favorable") for him. But the ironic point is that Micaiah speaks the word of God in *both* instances. Even more, both are "the truth" (which even a deceptive word that has its source in God proves to be) *and* both are *not* "good" for Ahab. But Ahab believes that he has heard "the truth" (v. 16) and what is "not good" for him only in the second speech. But he does not act on what he now knows to be the truth.

Micaiah's appeal to the divine council is an effort to make *both* prophecies as authoritative as possible, but will Ahab believe what he hears? What does Micaiah say? Micaiah claims that *all* that follows is the word of the Lord. God is not the "I" in verse 19, but Micaiah claims the whole to be the word of God. Micaiah claims to have *seen* something (a vision, as in v. 17), which included a hearing of the word of the Lord. Within the council session, God asks for a volunteer to entice Ahab (through his prophets) so that he will do battle against Ramoth-gilead and be killed ("fall"). One spirit volunteers to be a *temporary* "lying spirit" (no satanic thought is present here) in the mouth of *Ahab's* (stressed as "his"; "your") prophets, *not* God's prophets. God commands the spirit to do that and he will succeed. Verse 23 is Micaiah's specific interpretation for Ahab; *both* words he spoke were the word of God: the prophets (and he himself!) lied about Ahab's being successful *and* he will experience disaster (Hebrew: *ra*ᶜ).

Micaiah tells Ahab that the words of his prophets (and by implication, Micaiah's own first word! v. 15) have been God-inspired lies. Micaiah (and God) thereby forewarns him. Ahab (and Jehoshaphat!) now has the opportunity to respond by *not* going to Ramoth-gilead and saving himself! "Deception exposed is no longer deception but something more complicated. It hands over to the person whom one intends to deceive the capacity of choosing whether to be deceived or not. Therefore, despite the strong rhetoric in Micaiah's vision, the *effect* of the vision, once it has become a matter of public knowledge, is just the opposite" (Hamilton, 658, n. 18).

One of Ahab's prophets, Zedekiah, enters the scene (vv. 24–25), contests Micaiah's words, and apparently decides the matter for Ahab. Zedekiah wonders by what way the (lying!) spirit has passed from him and spoken to Micaiah; in effect, he accuses Micaiah of lying about the deception. Micaiah replies (in a way that claims the spirit has spoken to *both* of them): wait and see if you don't seek to hide from the disaster in the innermost parts of your house (the fulfillment of which is not reported). Ahab demands that Micaiah be thrown into prison until he returns from the battle, which he is confident will be successful. Micaiah admits that, if peace comes about, God has not spoken by him, and warns everyone to listen (see Jer. 28:6–9). Micaiah thereby indicates that whether the prophecy is true or false will become evident only in the events that follow; it cannot be demonstrated in advance. The ironic thing about this reply is that Micaiah had predicted that "peace" *would* come, but *not* for Ahab (v. 17). In other words, Ahab's death would bring peace!

The result is that Ahab seeks to heed *both* of Micaiah's words. He goes into battle against Aram and he seeks (ironically, as it turns out) to protect himself from disaster by going as a commoner, deceitfully telling Jehoshaphat to go in full royal regalia. When Ben-hadad commands his soldiers to go after king Ahab, they attack the royal-robed Jehoshaphat; but his cry demonstrates that he is not Ahab (2 Chron. 18:31 attributes his escape to God). In the melee, Ahab is accidentally ("unknowingly," but the human agency is real) but mortally wounded, dying as his soldiers seek to prevent the enemy from discovering that he has fallen by propping him up as an ensign. When he has died, the soldiers scatter to their own cities, but in peace, thus fulfilling Micaiah's word (v. 17). Ahab's death is also seen to have fulfilled Elijah's words, though in ways beyond his own words with the reference to the prostitutes, emblematic of Ahab's infidelity (cf. v. 46;

14:24; 15:12; see the discussion at 21:1–29). The story of Ahab concludes, typically (and ironically?), with a positive summary of his rule (vv. 39–40).

The reader has been introduced to Jehoshaphat, the king of Judah; verses 41–50 comprise a summary account of his reign (873–849 B.C.; a much more complete account is given in 2 Chronicles 19–20). He is portrayed as a good king, as his father Asa was, with mixed military and commercial success; though he did not remove the local high places either (15:14), his reform was more extensive regarding fertility rituals (v. 46; see 14:24). Finally, the regnal summary of Ahaziah, son of Ahab, who ruled for only two years (850–849 B.C.), is presented. He is portrayed as an evil king, following in the steps of his father. This continuing evil activity provokes the Lord to anger (on anger, see at 14:21–16:34).

That 1 and 2 Kings are a single work can be seen in that the account of Ahaziah continues to 2 Kings 1:18. Yet 1 Kings has its own integrity as a book, leaving the reader in some suspense regarding what will happen to the house of Ahab, yet knowing that God is angry at the apostasy of the kings of the Northern Kingdom. 1 Kings concludes with a summary of the reigns of two kings, one from Judah and one from Israel. They are contrasted to some extent, but at the end of 2 Kings their heirs will come together in disaster and exile.

God's Use of Deception

The variety of ways in which interpreters have sought to understand the lying spirit in this chapter is strange. Even notions of causality wherein God is said to cause everything that happens have intruded upon this conversation. But of course, if that were the case there would be nothing remarkable about this text! And despite some claims, such a notion of divine monism cannot be certainly found in any Old Testament text. (A full treatment cannot be provided here; for the finest guide available through these kinds of texts, see F. Lindström, *God and the Origin of Evil*.)

God can indeed use deception for God's own purposes. We have seen in 1 Kings 13 that God makes use of a prophet who speaks both deceitful and truthful words to accomplish an objective, though God is not said to inspire the deceit there. Various texts make clear that false prophets who are explicitly said *not* to have been sent by God speak out over the course of Israel's history (for example, Jer. 23:21; Deut. 18:22); at the same time, God can integrate such prophetic words into God's larger purposes for Israel and the world. Texts like this, where God inspires the deceit (for example, Jer. 20:7; Ezek. 14:9), must be examined in their own contexts.

Several details should be lifted up for attention in trying to sort out this reference. The prophets of Ahab are specifically identified by God and Micaiah as "his prophets" and "all these your prophets" (vv. 22–23); they are contrasted with the "prophet of the Lord" by Jehoshaphat in verse 7. These are hired prophets (see Micah 3:5, 11; the links to Micah are strong; v. 28b opens the book of Micah); they opportunistically speak assuring words to the king in order to assure themselves a living. There is no reason to think that these prophets are any different from the earlier 450 plus 400 prophets who ate "at Jezebel's table" (18:19; only the 450 are slaughtered, 18:40). These are to be identified as false prophets, though their self-understanding might have been that they were true, as was the case with Hananiah (see v. 24; Jer. 28:2).

When the 400 prophets speak what they do, namely, that Ahab and company will defeat the Aramaeans, they are speaking as such opportunists commonly do (e.g., Jer. 8:11; 23:17; Amos 5:18–20; Micah 3). So God does not use them against their natural proclivities or inclinations; the divine action is to encourage or inspire them in the direction they are already apt to go. It would be not unlike God's intensification of already existing human obduracy (e.g., both God and pharaoh are the subject of hardening verbs in Exodus) or God's giving the people up to their own stubbornness (Ps. 81:12). God is not in "total control of events" here; rather, the divine influence has been successful in inspiring them to stay on their opportunistic course.

It is noteworthy that Ahab sees through the lie when it is uttered by Micaiah (vv. 15–16); even more, in verses 19–23 Micaiah confirms to him that it was a lie. As discussed above, God's remarkable sharing of the vision with Ahab gives him the opportunity to change directions. Deception revealed changes the dynamics of the situation; Ahab is given insight into what God is about here. We are not told how Ahab responded, but he apparently believes Zedekiah, who says that Micaiah is lying about the lying (v. 24). Just as earlier, when Ahab recognized that Micaiah did not speak "the good" on his behalf (v. 18), so here, one more "not good" word was something Ahab expected to hear from him and hence it did not prompt him to act.

From another angle, the deception does not serve further deception or a greater evil; rather, it is "a divinely inspired lie in the service of truth" and goodness (Brueggemann, *1 Kings*, 100). God is sharply opposed to Ahab and his apostasy and related policies, not least because they have affected adversely the religious practices of the entire community and hence their life and well-being. And so God will be at work from as many angles as possible to deliver the community of faith from powerful apostates such as Ahab. God, with the help of both true and false prophets and even "un-knowing" Syrian soldiers, is able to achieve that end, which serves the larger purposes of God for Israel. God's judgmental activity is in the service of God's saving work. The Old Testament does not often claim that the death of specific individuals is the will and work of God. Such language is used either when the future of Israel is at stake (for example, pharaoh) or the death is conceived in vicarious terms (for example, Isaiah 53).

Second Kings

4. Prophets and Kings II
2 Kings 1:1–10:36

The stories of interaction between kings and prophets begun in 1 Kings 17 continue here. The focus continues to be on the Northern Kingdom, but the primary figure is now Elisha.

The reign of Ahaziah, the son of Ahab, spans the ending of 1 Kings and the beginning of 2 Kings. The prophetic legend of 2 Kings 1 illustrates the evil summary of 1 Kings 22:52. Though the revolt of Moab is not discussed until 3:5, the reference in 1:1 links that revolt to the evil reign of Ahab and his sons. More generally, 2 Kings 1–2 parallels 1 Kings 1–2 in that both are concerned with issues of succession, royal and prophetic.

ELIJAH DENOUNCES AHAZIAH
2 Kings 1:1–18

1:1 After the death of Ahab, Moab rebelled against Israel. ² Ahaziah had fallen through the lattice in his upper chamber in Samaria, and lay injured; so he sent messengers, telling them, "Go, inquire of Baal-zebub, the god of Ekron, whether I shall recover from this injury." ³ But the angel of the LORD said to Elijah the Tishbite, "Get up, go to meet the messengers of the king of Samaria, and say to them, 'Is it because there is no God in Israel that you are going to inquire of Baal-zebub, the god of Ekron?' ⁴ Now therefore thus says the LORD, 'You shall not leave the bed to which you have gone, but you shall surely die.'" So Elijah went. ⁵ The messengers returned to the king, who said to them, "Why have you returned?" ⁶ They answered him, "There came a man to meet us, who said to us, 'Go back to the king who sent you, and say to him: Thus says the LORD: Is it because there is no God in Israel that you are sending to inquire of Baal-zebub, the god of Ekron? Therefore you shall not leave the bed to which you have gone, but shall surely die.'" ⁷ He said to them, "What sort of man was he who came to meet you and told you these things?" ⁸ They answered him, "A hairy man, with a leather belt around his

131

waist." He said, "It is Elijah the Tishbite." [9] Then the king sent to him a captain of fifty with his fifty men. He went up to Elijah, who was sitting on the top of a hill, and said to him, "O man of God, the king says, 'Come down.'" [10] But Elijah answered the captain of fifty, "If I am a man of God, let fire come down from heaven and consume you and your fifty." Then fire came down from heaven, and consumed him and his fifty. [11] Again the king sent to him another captain of fifty with his fifty. He went up and said to him, "O man of God, this is the king's order: Come down quickly!" [12] But Elijah answered them, "If I am a man of God, let fire come down from heaven and consume you and your fifty." Then the fire of God came down from heaven and consumed him and his fifty. [13] Again the king sent the captain of a third fifty with his fifty. So the third captain of fifty went up, and came and fell on his knees before Elijah, and entreated him, "O man of God, please let my life, and the life of these fifty servants of yours, be precious in your sight. [14] Look, fire came down from heaven and consumed the two former captains of fifty men with their fifties; but now let my life be precious in your sight." [15] Then the angel of the LORD said to Elijah, "Go down with him; do not be afraid of him." So he set out and went down with him to the king, [16] and said to him, "Thus says the LORD: Because you have sent messengers to inquire of Baalzebub, the god of Ekron,—is it because there is no God in Israel to inquire of his word?—therefore you shall not leave the bed to which you have gone, but you shall surely die." [17] So he died according to the word of the LORD that Elijah had spoken. His brother, Jehoram succeeded him as king in the second year of King Jehoram son of Jehoshaphat of Judah, because Ahaziah had no son. [18] Now the rest of the acts of Ahaziah that he did, are they not written in the Book of the Annals of the Kings of Israel?

This chapter presents one last story about Elijah's encounter with the house of Ahab. As heretofore, it consists of indictment and announcement of judgment because of apostasy, in this case an inquiry about healing with a god other than Yahweh. The chapter moves from the king's injury to the king's death; repeated phrases, questions, and actions drum home certain key points.

King Ahaziah was injured by a fall through a latticed window (or other opening). He commands his servants to inquire (the verb occurs five times) of the god Baalzebub about his chances of recovery (see 1 Kings 14:1–18; 2 Kings 8:7–15). Baalzebub is the name of a local manifestation of the god Baal in the Philistine city of Ekron (Ahab introduced Baal worship, 16:31–33). The name means "Lord of the Flies" and may be a satirical corruption of Baalzebul ("Baal the Prince"; cf. Jezebel), a name that survives as Beelzebul (Satan) in the New Testament (Mark 3:22).

The initial reaction comes from God. Elijah is commanded by God's messenger to intercept the king's messengers (the same Hebrew word is used) and ask: "Is it because there is no God [god] in Israel . . . ?" (see below), and to announce that the king will not recover. "So Elijah went." The king's messengers return, ironically speaking a word for the king from Yahweh, not Baalzebub; the question of "whether I shall recover from this injury" (v. 2) is sharply answered, but not by the god that Ahaziah sought! Having ascertained that it was Elijah who answered (his strange appearance was well known), the king makes three attempts to bring him from the top of a hill (Carmel?) down to the palace (ironically, the king has to go *up* to the prophet). His purpose is not clear, but it was probably to placate him (and get the prediction of the king's death removed) or see what healing he might have to offer. Ironically, the king confronts not simply Elijah, but Elijah's God, and the question of whether there is a god in Israel is directly answered.

In the wake of the first two attempts to force Elijah (the language of vv. 9–10 and vv. 11–12 is virtually identical, though the second more urgent), a company of soldiers is consumed by fire called down from heaven by Elijah, a "man of God" (=prophet; see 1 Kings 13:1). In each case, God responds to Elijah's condition, "If I am a man of God," and thereby publicly verifies (the words are addressed to the captain, not God) that Elijah is a "man of [this] God." Fire from heaven (probably lightning) was also used as a means of divine demonstration in the contest at Mount Carmel (18:24; cf. 19:11–12) and informs this text. The fire is less a divine means to protect the prophet than a public demonstration of the power of Israel's God in a situation where that power (to heal) has been called into question and a public verification of Elijah as mediator of this power (and links up with Elisha in 2:11). It is almost as if in approaching Elijah (on a hill) they approach the reality of God himself (see Exod. 19:18).

In the third attempt, this power is publicly recognized by Ahaziah's own officers. The captain, abandoning the king's order, eloquently pleads with Elijah not to repeat the firestorm and to preserve his life and that of his company. The plea contrasts with the earlier efforts to force Elijah. But all this does not change the result. Upon receiving a safe sign from God's messenger, Elijah goes to the palace and announces the word of judgment to the king face to face. The word is fulfilled and Ahaziah dies. Being childless, he is succeeded by his brother Jehoram, whose reign (849–842 B.C.) almost exactly overlaps that of another Jehoram, son of Jehoshaphat, king of Judah.

Is It Because There Is
No God in Israel?

This key question of chapter 1 is a theological question, repeated three times (vv. 3, 6, 16) and spoken by three different subjects. In search of healing, Ahaziah sends his servants to inquire of a god in a city outside of Israel. Elijah confronts them with God's question: Is it because there is no God (Hebrew: *’elohim*) in Israel that you are going to inquire of Baalzebub the god (*’elohim*) of Ekron? Should the first *’elohim* be translated "God" (following most interpreters) or "god"? I submit that the word is purposely ambiguous and should be translated with something like "G(g)od." Another issue is the nature of the question. It is commonly considered a rhetorical question, with the implied answer that because they think there is no such God, they are unfaithful to Yahweh. But the question seems more complex. Either a "yes" or "no" response would concede the insufficiency of Baal. And by not addressing the question at all, they admit its force. The purpose of the question is not simply to make a claim for the Lord, but to get these individuals themselves explicity or implicitly to downgrade the godness of Baal.

To answer the question in the affirmative would mean they are going outside Israel because there is a divine vacancy or vacuum in Israel. Ahab's policy had meant the establishment of numerous shrines for the god Baal within Israel. To say "yes" to the question would be to declare this Baal a nonentity. It would also mean the same for Yahweh, the Lord of Israel, whatever standing they gave to Yahweh in a syncretistic system. To answer in the negative would be to admit that the Baals (or Yahweh) were not (as) effective with regard to matters of healing as they believed the god of Ekron to be. It would be to admit that the neither the Baals in Israel nor the Lord were up to healing the king.

The third statement of the question adds a phrase, "to inquire of his word" (that is, through the prophet; see the similar formulation by Jehoshaphat in 3:11). This may turn the question into a Yahweh question and stress the royal infidelity to the God of Israel. Only in the word of the Lord through the prophet can healing and true life be found. Ahaziah has forfeited that source of healing by looking elsewhere and hence cannot live.

In 2 Kings 5, another healing story, Naaman is healed and testifies, "Now I know there is no God in all the earth except in Israel" (5:15). This becomes the proper response to the question of chapter 1; only Israel's Yahweh is God anywhere and only this God can bring life and healing. To follow in the ways of other gods, whether within Israel or without, leads only to death.

FROM ELIJAH TO ELISHA
2 Kings 2:1–25

2:1 Now when the LORD was about to take Elijah up to heaven by a whirlwind, Elijah and Elisha were on their way from Gilgal. 2 Elijah said to Elisha, "Stay here; for the LORD has sent me as far as Bethel." But Elisha said, "As the LORD lives, and as you yourself live, I will not leave you." So they went down to Bethel. 3 The company of prophets who were in Bethel came out to Elisha, and said to him, "Do you know that today the LORD will take your master away from you?" And he said, "Yes, I know; keep silent." 4 Elijah said to him, "Elisha, stay here; for the LORD has sent me to Jericho." But he said, "As the LORD lives, and as you yourself live, I will not leave you." So they came to Jericho. 5 The company of prophets who were at Jericho drew near to Elisha, and said to him, "Do you know that today the LORD will take your master away from you?" And he answered, "Yes, I know; be silent." 6 Then Elijah said to him, "Stay here; for the LORD has sent me to the Jordan." But he said, "As the LORD lives, and as you yourself live, I will not leave you." So the two of them went on. 7 Fifty men of the company of prophets also went, and stood at some distance from them, as they both were standing by the Jordan. 8 Then Elijah took his mantle and rolled it up, and struck the water; the water was parted to the one side and to the other, until the two of them crossed on dry ground. 9 When they had crossed, Elijah said to Elisha, "Tell me what I may do for you, before I am taken from you." Elisha said, "Please let me inherit a double share of your spirit." 10 He responded, "You have asked a hard thing; yet, if you see me as I am being taken from you, it will be granted you; if not, it will not." 11 As they continued walking and talking, a chariot of fire and horses of fire separated the two of them, and Elijah ascended in a whirlwind into heaven. 12 Elisha kept watching and crying out, "Father, father! The chariots of Israel and its horsemen!" But when he could no longer see him, he grasped his own clothes and tore them in two pieces. 13 He picked up the mantle of Elijah that had fallen from him, and went back and stood on the bank of the Jordan. 14 He took the mantle of Elijah that had fallen from him, and struck the water, saying, "Where is the LORD, the God of Elijah?" When he had struck the water, the water was parted to the one side and to the other, and Elisha went over. 15 When the company of prophets who were at Jericho saw him at a distance, they declared, "The spirit of Elijah rests on Elisha." They came to meet him and bowed to the ground before him. 16 They said to him, "See now, we have fifty strong men among your servants; please let them go and seek your master; it may be that the spirit of the LORD has caught him up and thrown him down on some mountain or into some valley." He responded, "No, do not send them." [17] But when they urged him until he was ashamed, he said, "Send them." So they sent fifty men who searched for three days but did not find him. [18] When they came back to him (he had remained at Jericho), he said to them, "Did I not say to you, Do not go?" [19] Now the people of the city said to Elisha, "The location of this city is good, as my lord sees; but the water is bad, and the land is unfruitful." [20] He said, "Bring me a new bowl, and put salt in it." So they brought it to him. [21] Then he went to the spring of water and threw the salt into it, and said, "Thus says the LORD, I have made this water wholesome; from now on neither death nor miscarriage shall come from it." [22] So the water has been wholesome to this day, according to the word that Elisha spoke. [23] He went up from there to Bethel; and while he was going up on the way, some small boys came out of the city and jeered at him, saying, "Go away, baldhead! Go away, baldhead!" [24] When he turned around and saw them, he cursed them in the name of the LORD. Then two she-bears came out of the woods and mauled forty-two of the boys. [25] From there he went on to Mount Carmel, and then returned to Samaria.

This story of Elijah's ascent into heaven (rather than dying a normal death) has long captured the imagination of readers. It has generated a variety of speculations, including the notion that he would return to earth to presage the coming of the day of the Lord or the messianic age. This began already in the Old Testament period itself (Mal. 4:5–6; compare Sir. 48:9–10) and is linked especially to John the Baptist in the New Testament (for example, Mark 6:14–15; 8:27–28; 9:2–13). Elijah does return at the Mount of Transfiguration (Mark 9:2–9), providing continuity between his calling and that of Jesus. Comparable traditions developed around Enoch and Moses because of unusual departures from this life.

This ascent (introduced in a matter-of-fact way in v. 1) is less central to the narrative, however, than the transfer of authority from Elijah to Elisha and the continuity in Israel's prophetic leadership this represents. This will be shown further in the following narratives wherein Elisha's words and deeds parallel those of Elijah (for example, 4:18–37). The focus is on Elisha and establishing his faithfulness and authority for the narratives that follow; his ministry will span the reigns of four kings (over half a century, until his death in 13:14–21). This is not a "call narrative" (see 1 Kings 19:19–21) but a story of succession. With all the intertextual references (especially to Moses and Joshua, the only other comparable "prophetic" succession), it is a carefully crafted story and exhibits considerable knowledge of the tradition. Its context sets it off from "ordinary time" by regnal summaries of kings of the house of Omri and Ahab, whose dynasty Elisha is instrumental in ending (1:17–18; 3:1–3). The succession occurs in the course of a journey through various places; though not precisely plotted, the journey seems to trace Israel's trek under Joshua backward, climaxing in a crossing of the Jordan to the east and then, crossing back, retracing that journey (see Joshua 3–8).

The three stages of the journey (vv. 1–6) are reported in almost identical terms, probably to confirm Elisha's loyalty and the inexorability of its destination. Elijah tells Elisha to stay put, for he is being sent by God to another place and he will be resolute in pursuing it (this is *not* a test for Elisha, but the provision of a way for him to follow freely); Elisha swears an oath by Yahweh that he will not leave him; they move on to the next place; a company of prophets come out and inform Elisha that God is taking Elijah away from him "today" (the time is not in doubt); Elisha tells them to be silent for he knows what's happening (and their interpretation of events would be premature). This pattern is broken as they move from Jericho to the Jordan; a group of prophets accompany them and become witnesses of what is about to happen.

The succession of Elisha is accomplished by an unusual, even bizarre series of events, set apart from ordinary view. Verses 8–14 are framed by the use of the mantle in the same way, signifying that the transfer has taken place. Elijah uses the mantle (a symbol of authority, 1 Kings 19:19) to part the Jordan river and they cross over on dry ground; the language used recalls Israel's crossing of the Red Sea (Exodus 14; see 1 Kings 19 especially for other links to Moses). The rolled-up mantle would take the shape of Moses' rod. The crossing back over the Jordan (v. 14) recalls the entrance into the land under Joshua (Joshua 4). The links to Moses suggest the theme of deliverance (out of Egypt; Ahab becomes a new pharaoh) and the links to Joshua suggest new life in the land (a prominent theme in the Elisha stories). The symbolic value of a comparable succession is central here, not the "miraculous" character of what occurs. As it was with Moses and Joshua, so it is with Elijah and Elisha (the names Joshua and Elisha have a similar meaning: "the Lord saves"; "God saves").

In response to Elijah's open-ended offer, Elisha requests that he inherit "a double share" of Elijah's spirit (cf. Joshua in Deut. 34:9; Solomon's response to a comparable offer in 1 Kings 3:9–14). This language stems from laws of inheritance, wherein the firstborn alone among the children received a "double portion" of the inheritance (Deut. 21:17). This is not a request for twice as much spirit as Elijah has, but for twice the portion received by the other prophets (vv. 7, 15). The "spirit" is a theological *and* anthropological reference, linking God's spirit and the human spirit, issuing in authority, wisdom, and power. Elijah agrees, providing Elisha observes his departure ("seeing" is crucial to understanding). Interrupting their interaction (and having been removed from the others), a chariot with horses enveloped in fire separates them, and a whirlwind (not the chariots!) transports him to heaven. The images of fire and wind are emblematic for the presence of God and the chariot and horses for the character of the prophetic task.

Elisha's response is manifold, and each element of it is filled with not always clear symbolic value (vv. 12–14): He refers to Elijah as father (a traditional address for a master by a disciple) and shouts a phrase, the meaning of which is disputed. "The chariots of Israel and its horsemen" may refer either to the heavenly armies accompanying Elijah or, more likely, to a judgment (echoing God's use of these symbols) that Elijah's words and deeds, mediating God's power, have been like that of an army against spiritual enemies and so will Elisha's (see 13:14; 6:15–17; 7:6). Elisha tears his clothes, a sign of grief or unworthiness; the two pieces of cloth symbolize their separation. Elisha now stands alone. He takes up Elijah's mantle, goes back to the Jordan, and duplicates (except for the question to God, which sustains the continuity with Elijah) Elijah's parting of the Jordan. Elisha thereby demonstrates both to himself and to the witnessing prophets that Elijah's mantle has indeed passed to him.

The company of prophets formally state the point of the chapter (v. 15). They recognize that Elisha has properly succeeded Elijah; yet they linger over Elijah, hesitant to move on. They offer to initiate a search, recognizing that the spirit may have picked him up and taken him anywhere (see 1 Kings 18:10–12; Elijah is often searched for and not found). Elisha knows otherwise, yet lets them find out for themselves, and chides them in the end for not trusting his word (v. 18). Elisha is now the one in charge.

Two brief story fragments conclude this succession, both of which witness that the authority and power of Elijah has indeed been transferred to Elisha. They testify that the work of this prophet can be both positive and life-giving as well as negative and judgment-announcing. In the first (vv. 19–22), he sweetens the water of Jericho so that it is life-giving rather than death-dealing. While this action recalls that of Moses in the wilderness, Elisha uses the healing property of salt rather than a certain kind of wood (Exod. 15:22–25; cf. Fretheim, *Exodus*, 176–78, for ways in which God uses what is already available in the creation to bring life). The action is accompanied by a word of God (word plus visible means!). The permanency of the effect is especially noted, unlike the often ephemeral results of "miracle workers."

The second story (vv. 23–25) seems designed to make a point by push-ing the edges of reason and good sense. The concern is not to discuss the morality of the prophet's actions, but the nature of the prophetic task. Eli-jah curses forty-two boys (10:14) "in the name of the Lord" for mocking him, apparently to keep him away from Bethel (because he might speak against the shrine there? See 1 Kings 12:28–33). The gruesome effect of the curse on the boys is a mauling by bears; mocking issues in mauling (again, animals serve to mediate divine action; for a positive use, see 1 Kings 17:2–7). This illustrates in a forceful, if bizarre way that the prophet can be a dangerous figure, who may speak words of judgment that will be ef-fective. Even children may get caught up in the judgment (witness both Samaria and Jerusalem). This new prophetic leader will not be mocked; his ministry may entail speaking harsh words, but he will not be put off by de-tractors. In journeying to Mount Carmel and Samaria, Elisha visits famil-iar Elijah sites, returning finally to the burning center of both of their ministries.

On Symbolic Narrative

The modern reader should not interpret these texts in a narrowly histori-cal way, as if they were fundamentally concerned to reconstruct the his-tory of Israel. They do tell a story about the past and they frame that telling with a chronological schematic. But to consider them straightforward his-torical accounts is as reductionistic as to dismiss their historical grounding altogether or diminish them to fantasy, fairy tale, or morality play (for a consideration of the issues faced by the historiographer, see Fretheim, *Deuteronomic History*, 27–35). The various form-critical distinctions (ad-mirably laid out by Long in *1 Kings* and *2 Kings*) are helpful in sorting through the variety of types of literature that these chapters present. They cannot be flattened out into a single genre (though generally they are nar-rative), and the decisions made about genre will affect how one evaluates the degree to which they are grounded in actual occurrences.

One helpful way in which to think about many of these texts is in terms of symbolic narrative. By using this designation, I move in two primary directions. First, the characters are presented as "types." For example, while Ahaziah plays a minor historical role in chapter 1, he also portrays a typical apostate, embodies the sickness of Israel, and typifies the struggle between the adherents of the Lord and Baal for the soul of God's elect. He is portrayed in larger-than-life terms. Something simi-lar could be said about Elijah and Elisha. They emerge at a time when the future of Yahwism in Israel is deeply threatened. That the word of God was able to be heard and accomplished through them in such a time could, finally, be described only in less than ordinary terms. That Elijah was taken by God by means other than death expresses not only divine approval of his extraordinary ministry and the power of Israel's God to overcome death but the continuity in the ministries of these two prophets. In some inexplicable way, Elijah lives on in the ministry of Elisha; Elisha is Elijah one more time, larger than life (on miracle, see at 2 Kings 4:1–44).

Second, significant levels of intertextuality are present in the narrative, that is, direct and indirect allusions to other texts and traditions. By such linkages, the reader is invited to move imaginatively into other worlds that the tradition presents and connect them with the text at hand. Such intertextual work by the narrator implies a significant level of interpretation regarding the meaning of the matter under discussion. This means that the reader should not interpret in an overly literal way the wondrous events that are narrated, usually mediated by the word or deed of these prophets (the ascent itself is an exception, though still mediated; on the use of means, see at 1 Kings 17:1–24). The wonders enhance the authority of the prophetic word and are emblematic of God's commitments to the ministry of these prophets and of God's own remarkable actions in and through them.

A mysterious, elusive quality pervades the entire narrative and sets it off from "ordinary time" (between royal summaries) and "ordinary space" (in vv. 8–14). The narrator chooses not to "explain" what occurs, or spell out the details, or even connect God closely with the wondrous events (only in v. 1 does the *narrator* explicitly make God the subject of what occurs). Virtually every word and action is given symbolic value. The import of these twists and turns can only be discerned by considerable intertextual work (for example, connections with Moses and Joshua), and even then full interpretations do not become available. It is important to note that the narrator does not linger on the "miraculous" but presents each occasion in almost matter-of-fact terms. "The wonders themselves seem only little more than ordinary in this understated world" (Long, *2 Kings*, 34). The narrator does not pause to savor the marvel of it all nor express awe or wonder at what happens (even in v. 12). The reader is thereby pushed away from focusing on the spectacular in itself and asked to discern the theological and religious import of what is being stated. The center of that concern could be summarized in this way: In the face of numerous and powerful adversaries, God has not left himself without a mediator of the word of God and a faithful witness to God's purposes in Israel and the world. This, finally, is the real "miracle."

WAR AND WRATH IN MOAB
2 Kings 3:1–27

The chapter begins with a summary of the rule of King Jehoram (Joram) of Israel (849–842 B.C.). He is the second son of Ahab to reign in Israel (Amaziah having died childless); his reign was "evil," and though he introduced some reforms, he is adjudged by Elisha to stand in the tradition of his parents (v. 13). His reign provides the backdrop for the ministry of Elisha in chapters 3–9, at the end of which his violent death at the hands of Jehu brings the Omri dynasty to a close (finally fulfilling 1 Kings 21:29). The Moabite Stone of King Mesha, which speaks of Israel's expulsion from Moab, provides background for this rebellion.

This first major story about Elisha (vv. 4–27) is integrated with a battle story in which three kings attempt to put down the rebellion in Moab. It continues the king-prophet confrontation characteristic of the ministry of Elijah and others. Elisha here stands in the tradition of the unnamed prophet in 1 Kings 20:13–30, and he will be so involved again in 6:8–23 (cf. 6:24–7:20). The narrative resembles 1 Kings 22 in several respects, particularly the involvement of Jehoshaphat, the prophet, and the "king of Israel," again seldom named.

Jehoram goes to war against King Mesha of Moab (see 1:1), not least because he helped keep the coffers well supplied. He invites the support of Judah under Jehoshaphat (as in 1 Kings 22:4). The Edomites, vassals of Judah (8:20), also are joined in putting down the rebellion. The strategy proposed is to attack Moab from the south and east, going through Edom. A lack of water threatens the success of the mission, and Jehoram voices suspicions as to why God—of whom he never inquired, but whose will he thinks he knows—has stopped support (vv. 10, 13). This prompts the more faithful Jehoshaphat (see 1 Kings 22:7) to ask for a word from a prophet of the Lord. Differences in the piety of northern and southern kings is evident. Informed about Elisha (described as a servant of Elijah), Jehoshaphat testifies that Elisha is the mediator of the word of the Lord, and they consult him (v. 12). This witness provides an important mark of continuity with Elijah early in Elisha's ministry (see the witness to Elijah in 1 Kings 17:24).

The prophet's initial response is brusquely dismissive because Jehoram is linked to Ahab and Jezebel, and he ought to seek out their prophets (see 1 Kings 22:6). Elisha, ignoring Jehoram's claims that they have been victimized by *Yahweh* (not the god of Ahab's prophets), agrees because of the presence of Jehoshaphat, a Davidic king. His request for a musician stands in a prophetic tradition (see 1 Sam. 10:5–6) that links music with divine inspiration or power (literally, "the hand of the Lord"; see 1 Kings 18:46). The result is an oracle from the Lord, who promises that the wadi (normally dry in the summer) will have pools of water—from a source other than rain—to assuage their thirst (cf. Isa. 41:18). Moreover, moving beyond the word from God (which stops with v. 17), Elisha promises that God will accomplish a more difficult deed (some things are harder for God than others!) and bring victory over Moab. Elisha commands them to conquer every major city and ruin the environment of Moab (v. 19).

It is striking that Elisha's personal addition to the oracle from God stands in opposition to the guidelines for war in Deuteronomy 20:19–20, as well as against the divine command that Israel not harass or make war with Moab (Deut. 2:9; cf. Judg. 11:24). How could environmental devastation solve the commercial reason for the war in the first place (v. 4)? Yet the armies carry it out to the letter (v. 25). The next day (at dawn? as an effect of the sacrifice? cf. 1 Kings 18:36) water begins to flow from Edom, and the *country* (not just wadi pools) is filled with it (the source in Edom is not stated; the wordplay prevails—Edom means "red" and is assonant with *dam*, blood). Yet its coming is not linked to the promise (thirst); rather, the divine gift serves a strategic purpose that occasions miscalculation by Moab (vv. 22–23). The provision of water *to drink* is thus made secondary in the overall story.

Meanwhile, the Moabites muster all able-bodied men to counter the armies of Israel. Misinterpreting the sun-spangled waters as blood from feuding Israelites (mistaking life for death), they attack, only to be repelled and to have their cities and environment destroyed. But then a baffling turn of events occurs, the effect of which is that Elisha's word about victory is not (finally) fulfilled. When the king of Moab (at Kir-hareseth, near the Dead Sea) fails to break the Israelite ranks, he sacrifices his firstborn son to his god, Chemosh (cf. 16:3; 21:6 for possible parallels in Israel). The effect is that "great wrath comes upon Israel" (v. 27). This reality (see below) wreaks havoc; the Israelite armies return to their homes short of final victory (see 1 Kings 22:36). Moab is lost to Israel and will pester it until its death is complete (13:20; cf. 24:2).

The ambiguous ending recalls the battle with Aram in 1 Kings 22:29–36 and makes the reader wonder whether the presence of Ahab's son has adversely affected this one, too. In addition, the reader is given to wonder about Elisha's expansion of the oracle he received (vv. 18–19). Does he overextend himself here?

Great Wrath Came upon Israel

The ending of this story is puzzling. Israel, for all of its devastation of people and environment in Moab, has been driven home without victory. This raises several questions and forces the reader to go back and see if some clues have been missed.

We focus on the word "wrath." Wrath commonly "goes forth" or "comes upon" people, the effect of which may include plague or death (see Num. 1:53; 16:46; 18:5; 31:16; Josh. 22:20). Unlike other words used for divine anger in Kings (see at 1 Kings 14:21–16:34), wrath is an impersonal reality here, not a legal penalty or a divine response in view of apostasy. Wrath is an effect intrinsically related to or growing out of a violation of the moral order of God's creation. Wrath is usually the wrath of the Lord, as God sees to the movement from deed to consequence. The lack of reference to God in this text, however, makes it virtually deistic in its force. Something has happened that triggers wrath.

Whose wrath is it? Some scholars suggest it is the wrath of Chemosh upon the sacrifice of a child; the effect is the deliverance of the Moabites from Israel. But it seems unlikely that the larger narrative, so opposed to gods other than Yahweh, would ascribe such power to Chemosh or grant such an effect to child sacrifice. Hence it is best to see the wrath as having an origin from Israel's God.

What effect does the wrath have? It disrupts the military situation to such an extent that the Israelites have to give up the fight short of final victory and return home (as in 1 Kings 22:36).

Why does the wrath "come upon" *Israel?* The reader could appeal to God's mysterious ways, or suggest that the text is purposely ambiguous. Perhaps so, but some clues must be explored. The text up to this point suggests that Israel is mediating the wrath of God against *Moab,* and the child sacrifice on the part of Moabites should only intensify that wrath. It could be that the wrath comes upon Moab as well, but only Israel is mentioned. The narrator's interest in its impact on Israel is evident. But what if the wrath is not directly (or only) related to the child sacrifice? Might it not include the degradation of the environment (vv. 19, 25), an implicit violation of the law in Deuteronomy 20:19–20 (cf. also the violation of Deut. 2:9)?

Even more, the clue might be found in the numerous parallels to

1 Kings 22, many of which have been noted above. The question of the will of God in this confrontation has been suspiciously raised by Jehoram twice (vv. 10, 13). This suspicion may be grounded in the deceptive promissory word of both Micaiah and Ahab's prophets (on divine deception, see at 1 Kings 22:1–53), which sends Israel's armies against Aram precisely in order that they might fail. Might the word of Elisha in verses 18–19 be a counterpart to that of Micaiah in 1 Kings 22:15, that is, a deceptive word delivered (unknowingly? see 2 Kings 4:27) to lead to Israel's failure? The almost complete fulfillment of Elisha's word—Moab was not finally "handed over" (v. 18)—would thus be a part of this larger divine design in view of Israel's apostasy (and certainly takes the edge off his reputation). Whatever positive developments may occur in Israel's life, the buildup of its apostasy issues finally in devastation. The negative effect on Israel here would anticipate this final wrath against Israel (2 Kings 17:7–18; see Deut. 29:28).

ELISHA'S WONDROUS DEEDS
2 Kings 4:1–44

4:1 **Now the wife of a member of the company of prophets cried to Elisha, "Your servant my husband is dead; and you know that your servant feared the LORD, but a creditor has come to take my two children as slaves." 2 Elisha said to her, "What shall I do for you? Tell me, what do you have in the house?" She answered, "Your servant has nothing in the house, except a jar of oil." 3 He said, "Go outside, borrow vessels from all your neighbors, empty vessels and not just a few. 4 Then go in, and shut the door behind you and your children, and start pouring into all these vessels; when each is full, set it aside." 5 So she left him and shut the door behind her and her children; they kept bringing vessels to her, and she kept pouring. 6 When the vessels were full, she said to her son, "Bring me another vessel." But he said to her, "There are no more." Then the oil stopped flowing. 7 She came and told the man of God, and he said, "Go sell the oil and pay your debts, and you and your children can live on the rest." 8 One day Elisha was passing through Shunem, where a wealthy woman lived, who urged him to have a meal. So whenever he passed that way, he would stop there for a meal. 9 She said to her husband, "Look, I am sure that this man who regularly passes our way is a holy man of God. 10 Let us make a small roof chamber with walls, and put there for him a bed, a table, a chair, and a lamp, so that he can stay there whenever he comes to us." 11 One day when he came there, he went up to the chamber and lay down there. 12 He said to his servant Gehazi, "Call the Shunammite woman." When he had called her, she stood before him. 13 He** said to him, "Say to her, Since you have taken all this trouble for us, what may be done for you? Would you have a word spoken on your behalf to the king or to the commander of the army?" She answered, "I live among my own people." ¹⁴ He said, "What then may be done for her?" Gehazi answered, "Well, she has no son, and her husband is old." ¹⁵ He said, "Call her." When he had called her, she stood at the door. ¹⁶ He said, "At this season, in due time, you shall embrace a son." She replied, "No, my lord, O man of God; do not deceive your servant." ¹⁷ The woman conceived and bore a son at that season, in due time, as Elisha had declared to her. ¹⁸ When the child was older, he went out one day to his father among the reapers. ¹⁹ He complained to his father, "Oh, my head, my head!" The father said to his servant, "Carry him to his mother." ²⁰ He carried him and brought him to his mother; the child sat on her lap until noon, and he died. ²¹ She went up and laid him on the bed of the man of God, closed the door on him, and left. ²² Then she called to her husband, and said, "Send me one of the servants and one of the donkeys, so that I may quickly go to the man of God and come back again." ²³ He said, "Why go to him today? It is neither new moon nor sabbath." She said, "It will be all right." ²⁴ Then she saddled the donkey and said to her servant, "Urge the animal on; do not hold back for me unless I tell you." ²⁵ So she set out, and came to the man of God at Mount Carmel. When the man of God saw her coming, he said to Gehazi his servant, "Look, there is the Shunammite woman; ²⁶ run at once to meet her, and say to her, Are you all right? Is your husband all right? Is the child all right?" She answered, "It is all right." ²⁷ When she came to the man of God at the mountain, she caught hold of his feet. Gehazi approached to push her away. But the man of God said, "Let her alone, for she is in bitter distress; the LORD has hidden it from me and has not told me." ²⁸ Then she said, "Did I ask my lord for a son? Did I not say, Do not mislead me?" ²⁹ He said to Gehazi, "Gird up your loins, and take my staff in your hand, and go. If you meet anyone, give no greeting, and if anyone greets you, do not answer; and lay my staff on the face of the child." ³⁰ Then the mother of the child said, "As the LORD lives, and as you yourself live, I will not leave without you." So he rose up and followed her. ³¹ Gehazi went on ahead and laid the staff on the face of the child, but there was no sound or sign of life. He came back to meet him and told him, "The child has not awakened." ³² When Elisha came into the house, he saw the child lying dead on his bed. ³³ So he went in and closed the door on the two of them, and prayed to the LORD. ³⁴ Then he got up on the bed and lay upon the child, putting his mouth upon his mouth, his eyes upon his eyes, and his hands upon his hands; and while he lay bent over him, the flesh of the child became warm. ³⁵ He got down, walked once to and fro in the room, then got up again and bent over him; the child sneezed seven times, and the child opened his eyes. ³⁶ Elisha summoned Gehazi and said, "Call the Shunammite woman." So he called her. When she came to him, he said, "Take your son." [37] She came and fell at his feet, bowing to the ground; then she took her son and left. [38] When Elisha returned to Gilgal, there was a famine in the land. As the company of prophets was sitting before him, he said to his servant, "Put the large pot on, and make some stew for the company of prophets." [39] One of them went out into the field to gather herbs; he found a wild vine and gathered from it a lapful of wild gourds, and came and cut them up into the pot of stew, not knowing what they were. [40] They served some for the men to eat. But while they were eating the stew, they cried out, "O man of God, there is death in the pot!" They could not eat it. [41] He said, "Then bring some flour." He threw it into the pot, and said, "Serve the people and let them eat." And there was nothing harmful in the pot. [42] A man came from Baal-shalishah, bringing food from the first fruits to the man of God: twenty loaves of barley and fresh ears of grain in his sack. Elisha said, "Give it to the people and let them eat." [43] But his servant said, "How can I set this before a hundred people?" So he repeated, "Give it to the people and let them eat, for thus says the LORD, 'They shall eat and have some left.'" [44] He set it before them, they ate, and had some left, according to the word of the LORD.

This chapter comprises four miracle stories that highlight the deeds of Elisha, but not for the sake of his own reputation. They have in common the gift of life and well-being for those who are poor or needy (or both). Resembling the deeds of Elijah (1 Kings 17:8–24), they bear witness to the continuity between the two mediators of God's life-giving word. Yet Elisha's wondrous works are more dramatic than Elijah's and less specifically linked to the word of God (God-references in v. 1 and v. 44 bracket the chapter). Elisha's word is more fully integrated into the word of God so that to hear the one is to hear the other (God's word and the prophet's merge at 1 Kings 21:20–23; 2 Kings 3:16–19). The word of the prophet remains central throughout; without the word there is no deed. From this point on, Elisha will appear as the leader of a company of prophets, which magnifies the idea that God has not left himself without a witness in this apostate world.

4:1–7. The widow's oil. Standing in continuity with Elijah (1 Kings 17:8–16), Elisha by his word expands the food supplies for a needy widow of a prophet who cannot pay her debts. Her children are about to be given as a payoff to a creditor, a practice current in Israel (see Deut. 15:12). The widow states her lamentable situation to the prophet, carefully notes that her husband was faithful to the Lord, with a request for help implied. Elisha has no apparent access to the creditor involved and takes a direct route to meet the need.

Elisha is a model of approach to needy people (less so in the next story):

he responds openly to her, carefully draws her out and allows her to express her need, starts with what she has and can contribute, specifies a procedure to be followed, and gives minimal instructions for following through. She is to borrow (more than a few) vessels from the neighbors and, behind closed doors (this is not a public event), begin pouring from her jar of oil into each until they are full. She does as he says. The oil is not unlimited and stops "on its own" when the supply of vessels is exhausted. But it is sufficient to free her from debt and allow her family to remain intact. Economic realities do affect "family values." Her positive response to the prophet's instruction will be important; how she makes use of the gift matters.

4:8–37. The Shunammite woman and her son. Again, continuity with Elijah is evident (1 Kings 17:17–24). This finely wrought story centers on the birth (vv. 8–17), death, and resuscitation (vv. 18–37) of the son of a prominent woman from Shunem in the Jezreel valley. The unnamed woman's portrayal reveals a strong and independent person, respectful of Elisha but capable of direct and assertive action when called for (we encounter her again in 8:1–6).

The woman is host to Elisha whenever he passes through her town; she even has a special room built and furnished for him. In gratitude, Elisha asks what he can do for her (cf. v. 2). When a "reference letter" to the authorities is deemed not necessary because her physical needs are met by family, a second request through his servant Gehazi reveals that she and her husband are childless. Without consulting her (which she later sharply recalls for him, v. 28) or God, he announces that she will in due time "embrace a son" (see v. 20 for the irony; vv. 36–37 for the return). Her objection (typical for such stories, Gen. 18:12) is left open-ended (v. 16), but this makes the prophet morally accountable (see v. 28), and the narrator reports that a child is born "in due time" (=the next year), as Elisha had announced.

The child becomes sick or sustains a head injury and dies in his mother's embrace. Having placed him on Elisha's bed, and leaving her husband uninformed, she insists on hurrying to see Elisha at Mount Carmel, though no religious occasion prompts the visit. When Elisha sees her coming, he inquires through Gehazi of the health of each family member. She brushes Gehazi aside and over his objections persists in seeing a now responsive Elisha in person. To his complaint that God has not kept him informed is added her assertive complaint that she has been deceived after all (vv. 27–28). Elisha perceives the problem but insensitively asks his servant to go directly to the child and lay his staff on his face (cf. Moses' use of the staff in Exodus 7–17). But the mother insists that Elisha go as well (v. 30; ironically using Elisha's own oath to Elijah to jar him loose, 2:2–6); he goes silently. When Gehazi hurries ahead and lays the staff on the child, the child remains dead (showing the insight in the mother's tenacity). Elisha determinedly takes over and (away from public view) prays to God and places his own body over that of the boy in two stages, as the boy first warms and then sneezes (seven times, see 5:10, 14). On this combination of prayer and ritual, see at 1 Kings 17:17–24. Elisha finally speaks directly to her, gives the son back to his mother, who falls speechless before him in gratitude, takes her son, and leaves.

The absence of a verbal witness (contrast 1 Kings 17:24) suggests that the reputation of the prophet is not as central to this text as sometimes claimed. In fact, the various comings and goings associated with the son's revival suggest a witness to limitations regarding prophetic power (see Long, *2 Kings*, 61–62). The prophet himself admits that God has not kept him informed (v. 27), and the woman assertively bypasses the servant and challenges the man of God to become directly involved; her instincts are proven correct when Gehazi is not able to revive the child in spite of a prophetic word directed to the situation.

4:38–41. In this brief story, set at a time of famine (cf. 2:19–22), the prophet purifies a pot of stew that inadvertently had become spoiled through the addition of unidentified gourds. Hearing the cry of those eating due to the bitter taste ("death," even if not literally meant, is important for the point), Elisha uses flour (a symbol of life) as a means of purification, not magic; it apparently neutralizes the bitterness (poisons?) in the stew and the people are able to eat. They have no response to what the prophet has done.

4:42–44. In this story fragment, the prophet commands a person to feed one hundred people with his small offering of bread and grain. The man may be a member of the prophetic guild responsible for caring for their master. When Elisha's servant suggests that he has an insufficient supply, Elisha brings another perspective to bear on the situation. He presents a word from the Lord, namely, that it is sufficient and there will even be some left over. The man did as commanded and the word of the Lord spoken by the prophet was fulfilled. The people have no response to what the prophet has done. Gospel readers will recognize several points of similarity with Jesus' feeding miracles (e.g., Mark 6:30–44; 8:1–10).

Miracles of Life in the Midst of Death

These stories narrow the readers' focus from larger societal issues down to the needs of specific individuals in everyday life. These stories speak most fundamentally about a will for life that continues amid all that makes for wrath and death. The larger political and religious issues being faced by Israel are ignored. The needs of individuals—both rich and poor—are not lost within "society." Royal persons and policies are hardly in view (v. 13); they do not finally define reality. Apostasy and its effects have not taken over God's world. Needs are being met; life is being given and restored; God the Creator is still at work for good.

The needs met are not narrowly religious or spiritual—true also of the miracles of Jesus, which these stories anticipate and help interpret. They are concerned with quite mundane matters that have to do with enough food, safe food, freedom from debt that can break up families, sickness, and death. They recognize that suffering is real, that pain is an everyday experience for wealthy and poor, even for the faithful (v. 1). The people of God are not exempted from the pains and sorrows of life. As Psalm 23 puts it, "Thou preparest a table before me *in the presence of* my enemies." This is not escapist literature, designed to take one out of the world; rather, it puts life back into place according to God's creational design, and throws these people back into their everyday world.

Remarkably, these miracles are not presented in terms of divine intervention (God language is rare), or a violation of the natural order of things, or a disruption of God's creation. Indeed, these matter-of-fact stories witness that God's good creation is *properly* at work in the midst of those who would disrupt it. They are remarkably unconcerned to explain how these miracles take place (on symbolic narrative, see at 2:1–25). Such stories do not necessarily stand over against modern views of reality. Modern physics (quantum mechanics; chaos theory) has helped us see that this world is not a closed system of cause and effect; there is a loose, if complex, causal weave or "play" within God's design that makes novelty, freshness, surprise, and serendipity possible (see Job 38–41). Even more, such a world makes it possible for God to be at work *within* the interplay of natural law and the loose weave. God's creation is not fixed and static, but full of surprises and new possibilities. Historians still have their work to do in sorting out issues of probability as to whether these particular miracles occurred, but they cannot with integrity begin by saying they *could* not happen.

One key to understanding is that the Creator has placed within this world human beings with compassion and remarkable gifts who can bring life and well-being to those in need. Each of these stories involves human activity; a prophet enters into the life of another and seeks to ameliorate his or her life situation. Moreover, the prophet uses a variety of creational resources. His work is not a creation out of nothing, but the expansion and development of already existing gifts of God's creation (means are stated in each case; on means, see at 1 Kings 17:1–24). The contemporary links entail discerning the gifts the Creator has given that can enable such life-giving surprises in our own time—for example, medical research and the skills of surgeons and counselors. While the texts are not interested in promoting methods by which miracles might be brought about, they invite the reader to imagine creational resources not yet tapped.

The witness of these texts, finally, is that God's will for life working through human beings and other created realities is living and real even in the worst of times. They make clear that there are possibilities for life and healing in God's world that go beyond our present calculations and understandings, and they give us hope that God's working in this world through people like ourselves may indeed make miracles happen.

THE HEALING AND CONFESSION OF NAAMAN
2 Kings 5:1–27

5:1 Naaman, commander of the army of the king of Aram, was a great man and in high favor with his master, because by him the LORD had given victory to Aram. The man, though a mighty warrior, suffered from leprosy. [2] Now the Arameans on one of their raids had taken a young girl captive from the land of Israel, and she served Naaman's wife. [3] She said to her mistress, "If only my lord were with the prophet who is in Samaria! He would cure him of his leprosy." [4] So Naaman went in and told his lord just what the girl from the land of Israel had said. [5] And the king of Aram said, "Go then, and I will send along a letter to the king of Israel." He went, taking with him ten talents of silver, six thousand shekels of gold, and ten sets of garments. [6] He brought the letter to the king of Israel, which read, "When this letter reaches you, know that I have sent to you my servant Naaman, that you may cure him of his leprosy." [7] When the king of Israel read the letter, he tore his clothes and said, "Am I God, to give death or life, that this man sends word to me to cure a man of his leprosy? Just look and see how he is trying to pick a quarrel with me." [8] But when Elisha the man of God heard that the king of Israel had torn his clothes, he sent a message to the king, "Why have you torn your clothes? Let him come to me, that he may learn that there is a prophet in Israel." [9] So Naaman came with his horses and chariots, and halted at the entrance of Elisha's house. [10] Elisha sent a messenger to him, saying, "Go, wash in the Jordan seven times, and your flesh shall be restored and you shall be clean." [11] But Naaman became angry and went away, saying, "I thought that for me he would surely come out, and stand and call on the name of the LORD his God, and would wave his hand over the spot, and cure the leprosy! [12] Are not Abana and Pharpar, the rivers of Damascus, better than all the waters of Israel? Could I not wash in them, and be clean?" He turned and went away in a rage. [13] But his servants approached and said to him, "Father, if the prophet had commanded you to do something difficult, would you not have done it? How much more, when all he said to you was, 'Wash, and be clean'?" [14] So he went down and immersed himself seven times in the Jordan, according to the word of the man of God; his flesh was restored like the flesh of a young boy, and he was clean. [15] Then he returned to the man of God, he and all his company; he came and stood before him and said, "Now I know that there is no God in all the earth except in Israel; please accept a present from your servant." [16] But he said, "As the LORD lives, whom I serve, I will accept nothing!" He urged him to accept, but he refused. [17] Then Naaman said, "If not, please let two mule-loads of earth be given to your servant; for your servant will no longer offer burnt offering or sacrifice to any god except the LORD. [18] But may the LORD pardon your servant on one count: when my master goes into the house of Rimmon to worship there, leaning on my arm, and I bow down in the house of Rimmon, when I do bow down in the house of Rimmon, may the LORD pardon your servant on this one count." [19] He said to him, "Go in peace." But when Naaman had gone from him a short distance, [20] Gehazi, the servant of Elisha the man of God, thought, "My master has let that Aramean Naaman off too lightly by not accepting from him what he offered. As the LORD lives, I will run after him and get something out of him." [21] So Gehazi went after Naaman. When Naaman saw someone running after him, he jumped down from the chariot to meet him and said, "Is everything all right?" [22] He replied, "Yes, but my master has sent me to say, 'Two members of a company of prophets have just come to me from the hill country of Ephraim; please give them a talent of silver and two changes of clothing.'" [23] Naaman said, "Please accept two talents." He urged him, and tied up two talents of silver in two bags, with two changes of clothing, and gave them to two of his servants, who carried them in front of Gehazi. [24] When he came to the citadel, he took the bags from them, and stored them inside; he dismissed the men, and they left. [25] He went in and stood before his master; and Elisha said to him, "Where have you been, Gehazi?" He answered, "Your servant has not gone anywhere at all." [26] But he said to him, "Did I not go with you in spirit when someone left his chariot to meet you? Is this a time to accept money and to accept clothing, olive orchards and vineyards, sheep and oxen, and male and female slaves? [27] Therefore the leprosy of Naaman shall cling to you, and to your descendants forever." So he left his presence leprous, as white as snow.

At one level this narrative is a miracle story; a leper is healed. At another level it lifts up the ministry of the prophet Elisha, though his role remains secondary. At still another level, and perhaps most centrally, the story tells of a foreigner's witness to the one true God (see at 1 Kings 8:1–66; 17:17–24). In the larger context, this stands in contrast to the apostate Israelites and their kings. Finally, the story contrasts Elisha and Gehazi among Israel's prophets regarding ways in which a prophet mediates the work and word of God. The story begins and ends with a person who has leprosy; Naaman the outsider is delivered *from* it; Gehazi the insider is delivered *to* it. The story is marked by an unusual number of characters (ten) and a complex plot (see Cohn, 1983; R. D. Moore, *God Saves*).

The story begins by reporting that Naaman, a prominent Syrian official (cf. 4:8), has experienced communal salvation (the history is uncertain) from the Lord but is in need of individual salvation (leprosy, a skin disease). His newly acquired Israelite slave-girl has the right counsel: Naaman must go to the prophet (whose God is the source of the communal salvation). The kings of Aram and Israel come on the scene and mismanage the matter, almost comically. The King of Aram misdirects the message (and doesn't tell the full truth) by sending Naaman laden with an immense gift to the king of Israel (Jehoram), thinking that he could find a cure (v. 6). Jehoram interprets the matter mostly in political terms and expresses despair (tearing his clothes); the King of Aram knows he cannot cure leprosy and when that becomes clear he will have an excuse to invade Israel again. Yet his "Am I God . . . " does recognize royal limitations (cf. 6:27; the reader should not uncritically accept the king's theology, for example, his assertion that God does not work through means).

The story continues only because Elisha hears about the situation. He sends a message to Jehoram and asks that Naaman be sent to him, so "that he may learn that there is a prophet in Israel" (v. 8), an agenda more extended than Naaman's; it shortly becomes clear that Elisha refers to the prophet as bearer of the word of *God*. Irony continues as Naaman appears at the front door of Elisha's modest house with all his horses, chariots, and money (vv. 5, 9). And Elisha sends a servant to meet him! In fact, Elisha does not put in an appearance until the healing is complete. The word he speaks stands front and center.

That word consists of both command and promise. Naaman is to go and wash in the Jordan seven times and he will be healed. A few similarities with levitical rites of purification are evident (Lev. 14:1–9; seven is a number common to rituals). Naaman's angry reply threatens to block progress. He recognizes the source of healing (the Lord!) but claims the rivers of Damascus would have done even better and saved him the trip! He is also angry because Elisha did not show up in person, engage in a familiar ritual, and cure him on the spot! Elisha does have a ritual, but obedience to the command is integral to its efficacy. Naaman's servants (again, little people) insightfully observe a case of misplaced pride; the great cannot be bothered with the simple. Verse 14 clarifies that the Jordan does not have magical properties; it is water together with obedience "to the word of the man of God," which includes the promise, that leads to cure. Elisha lets the word stand in the center and uses means that are available in that culture (see at 1 Kings 17:1–24). Naaman is healed and restored with the flesh of a "young boy."

Naaman comes to Elisha and stands before him for the first time (see v. 3), emphasizing his servant status. In this climactic moment, Naaman bears witness to his healing (cf. Exod. 18:11); his is a word about God, not the prophet (moving beyond, but not denying Elisha in v. 8). God's healing action has created his faith. There is no God in all the world except in Israel (cf. the questions of 1:3, 6, 16). What are the effects of this confession for Naaman? He moves from an arrogant stance to a subservient one (using "servant" five times). He promises that he will worship no other god than the Lord, a First Commandment concern so important for the narrator. Naaman, a foreigner, witnesses to the Lord in a way not typical of Israelites (but of David and Solomon, 2 Sam. 7:22; 1 Kings 8:23 and 41–43; see at 1 Kings 8:1–66). Naaman offers his gift to Elisha, whose refusal takes the form of an oath (see 2 Kings 2:2–6).

Verses 17–18 develop as they do because of Elisha's refusal. No credit is to redound to him for the healing. To accept Naaman's gifts might have obscured the gracious gift of God (see below). In response, Naaman requests something from Elisha—two loads of Israelite earth (compare his prior disdain of the Jordan). This is not because he thinks that the Lord is present only on Israelite soil. He wants to build an altar with it, providing a tangible and material tie to the community of faith Elisha represents. Being sensitive to a potential issue, Naaman asks that he be pardoned when he finds it necessary to accompany his king into the temple of Rimmon (a Syrian form of Baal). This is not a lapse into syncretism, but a recognition that the life of faith must be lived out in ambiguous situations and away from the community of faith. His insight into the nature of God's grace is evident here, and Elisha simply gives him his blessing. He discerns that Naaman would not "go limping with two different opinions" (1 Kings 18:21); in another time and place he might have made Elijah's speech about divided loyalties.

The final section presents a contrast to Elisha's refusal of gifts from Naaman in the person of Gehazi (see also at 2 Kings 4:8–37; 8:1–6). He thinks that Naaman (that Aramean!) has gotten off too lightly—received grace too freely!—and, deceitfully, gets him to hand over (gladly!) a part of his treasure (two talents of silver is the amount Omri paid for the hill of Samaria!; 1 Kings 16:24). Naaman's servants haul the loot home for Gehazi; he hides it well and goes to stand next to Elisha, who traps his deception with a simple question. Elisha sees through the lie (God-given insight into his servant, not extrasensory perception; note the absence of specifics), lists what Gehazi could have purchased with the money, and announces that Naaman's leprosy will also become his (and his family's). It does.

Salvation and the Universal Grace of God

The universality of divine activity is present in a variety of ways in this chapter, not least through several ironic contrasts.

1. "The Lord had given victory to *Aram*" (v. 1)—over an enemy named Israel (v. 2)! The word "victory" is derived from the Hebrew root *yasha'*, to save. Salvation here is victory in national conflict, understood in a comprehensive sense as the experience of life and well-being by a *community*. The point is not the defeat of Israel (there is no interest in the reason), but God's salvation experienced by Aram, a non-elect people.

2. The leader of the victorious Arameans experiences *individual* salvation through the witness of one who has been defeated and captured, an Israelite slave-girl (vv. 2–4). Salvation is here defined in the sense of both healing and conversion, which leads to a change in perspective and in conduct. Both Aram and Naaman experience salvation through *Israel's* defeat and the witness of one from the defeated side. God is portrayed as salvifically active through both a non-elect leader of Israel's enemy and an Israelite slave-girl.

3. Naaman is strong but weak with leprosy; he cannot heal himself. The weak "young girl" has access to strength that enables Naaman to become a "young boy" (v. 14) and a "servant" (vv. 15–18). This should not take away from the salvation wrought for Naaman's people through his strength (v. 1, "by him"). God mediates salvation through both the strong and the weak, through both outsider and insider.

4. Here we see the contrast between Naaman and another insider, Gehazi. The narrative begins with salvation coming to Aram at Israel's expense; it ends when Elisha disallows that an Israelite should benefit at Aram's expense. The Aramean becomes a servant of the God of Israel, but

does not become a "servant" of Gehazi's opportunistic methods. The Arameans are the servants of God, not of Israel.

Naaman's confession is remarkably sophisticated in its understanding of God in both particular and universal terms ("in Israel"; "all the earth"). Both of these dimensions are crucial for a proper understanding of the nature of the faith of Israel. Neither Naaman's confession nor his request regarding soil localizes Yahweh in Israel. The confession excludes all gods that other lands may have to offer (the universal dimension), but the confession is linked to a particular community, namely, Israel (in contrast to Ahaziah's efforts to go outside of Israel in 2 Kings 1:2); Naaman's request for soil recognizes the continuing import of links to the particular community that is inextricably associated with the confession and guards its integrity.

Gehazi's judgment is connected to the point of integrity. The issue at stake for Elisha is more than the deception or the greed. The phrase, "is this a time?" (v. 26), suggests that the issue is the possible effect Gehazi's behavior may have on Naaman. Gehazi represents his request as Elisha's (v. 22) and that would neutralize Elisha's earlier refusal (v. 16). Naaman might conclude that his healing had been bought and the grace of God would thereby be eclipsed. Note how the gifts are made prominent in being carried before Gehazi (v. 23). There may be "a time" to speak in terms of gifts to be offered, but right now the grace of God needs to fill Naaman's vision and the freedom of the life of faith needs to be reinforced. Gehazi's sin is, finally, a *theological* sin, for it endangers the very nature of faith and obscures the gracious work of God. The effect of the judgment is that Gehazi is returned to the pre-healing situation of Naaman, and he now stands in need of a Naaman-like journey (on miracle, see at 2 Kings 4:1–44). The insider has experienced God's judgment; the outsider has received salvation. The outsider has become an insider and the insider an outsider. The boundary lines of the community of faith are less clear than the insiders often suggest.

ELISHA AND THE ARAMEANS
2 Kings 6:1–7:20

The opening story in a semiprivate setting prefaces two stories about public conflicts with the Arameans. The story of the ax head may be designed to prepare the reader for the powers Elisha exhibits in that larger arena. When placed beside Elisha's accomplishments in the story that follows, manipulating ax heads seems not only trivial but downright elementary.

The story of the ax head also looks back to an Aramean coming to faith through a healing at the Jordan; this is another miracle at the same river.

An Ax Head Brought to the Surface
(2 Kings 6:1–7)

This brief story finds Elisha again among his followers; in this circle he demonstrates his prophetic powers. They have outgrown their gathering place, where some prophets may stay on a (semi-) permanent basis and be instructed by the master. Parallels have been drawn with monasteries (though prophets could be married, 4:1). In an expedition to cut logs for the building, Elisha agrees to accompany them. When a borrowed ax head (or other iron implement) falls into the Jordan, Elisha comes to the rescue (iron was rare and valuable), though he has to ask where it fell! He cuts a stick, throws it in the water, and the ax head comes to the surface. The stick is an important means, and may function in terms of imitative magic; the iron floats like the stick. The newness of the stick may be thought important (see 2:20; 1 Kings 11:29). No wonder or awe is expressed; it is just an ordinary event in the life of this prophet, who solves problems so that people can get on with their work.

To make iron float to the surface is not your usual daily event. The common options for interpretation have been three (or some combination thereof): to interpret literally, to dismiss as impossible, or to understand as symbolic narrative (see discussion at 2 Kings 2:1–25). The story typifies those remarkable kinds of activity in which God and prophets are engaged, say, enabling life in the midst of death-dealing battles, or healing Aramean leaders and bringing them to faith. Miracles are concentrated at two points in the Old Testament—the exodus complex of events and Elijah/Elisha stories—both crucial turning points in the history of the people of God. (On miracles, see the discussion at 2 Kings 4:1–44.)

The Prophet Blindsides the Arameans
(2 Kings 6:8–23)

In 5:1 God had given Aram victory over Israel (with no evident prophetic activity). Here God gives Israel victory over Aram; the difference between defeat and victory is the word and work of the prophet. Royal power, within Israel or without, is dependent upon Elisha's use of power. This story anticipates the ultimate defeat of Israel at the hands of outsiders because it rejected the word of the prophets (17:13–14). The prophets' engagement in ongoing conflict between Israel and Aram has varied since God announced Elijah's role in 1 Kings 19:15–17. Prophets spoke both negative and positive words in 1 Kings 20 and 22 and the results were somewhat mixed; Elisha takes a pro-Israel stance in the next story (6:24–7:20), as he does here.

Aram's army movements are regularly anticipated by the king of Israel with the "military intelligence" of Elisha—due to God-given insight, not extrasensory perception. The King of Aram suspects treason among his troops, but is informed about Elisha, who is said (hyperbolically) to overhear the king's pillow-talk! When told that Elisha was in Dothan (near Samaria), he sends "a great army" (!) by night to capture this one man and neutralize him. Elisha's servant is fearful when he sees them, but Elisha tells him not to fear (see Exod. 14:13), for they are surrounded by God's army—embodied in Elisha (see 2:11). When Elisha prays that the servant might be reassured with a vision of this army (as he himself was, 2:12), the Lord opens his eyes to see the true nature of the situation, that reality has a depth unavailable to ordinary sight.

When the Arameans move to capture Elisha, he prays that God will dazzle them (in contrast to the opening of eyes in v. 17; cf. Gen. 19:11); God responds to the prayer in just those terms. The effect: an Israelite who moves from ordinary seeing to true sight into the nature of the situation and an Aramean army that moves from sight to blindness. Elisha dupes the soldiers into thinking that the object of their search is in another city and leads them to Samaria. The capturers have become the captured. In a remarkably ironic pied-piper scene, the prophet leads a great, but dazzled (not physically blinded) foreign army on horses and chariots up a winding country road to the center of Israelite power. Elisha here assumes the role of the commander of Aram's army that Naaman played in 5:1, and it leads also to a saving event.

Elisha prays again for sight, this time for the Aramean army, and their eyes are opened to see where they are: delivered into the hands of the Israelite king. Jehoram, acknowledging Elisha's authority ("father"), excitedly asks whether he shouldn't kill them. What an opportunity! He may recall that the prophet condemned his father Ahab when he refused to have Ben-hadad killed (1 Kings 20:35–43). Elisha forbids it, for the king has not done the capturing (it is not a holy war situation), and commands that they be fed and allowed to return home instead. Elisha here assumes the role of leadership of the Israelite army. With both armies under his control (!), Elisha holds back on the power options available to him. Jehoram obeys him; the army of Aram returns to its king, and its raids stop (at least for a time).

The Prophets, Power, and Foreign Affairs

As in 2 Kings 3, and like the prophets of 1 Kings 20 and 22, Elisha again becomes involved in international politics (see the divine charter in 1 Kings

19:15–17). What Elisha says and does has considerable impact upon foreign affairs and military engagements. The king of Israel is dependent upon his insight; the king of Aram is undermined by his intelligence gathering. Both parties to the conflict receive a new vision into both the power and the kindness of (the man of) God, who had struck them blind, restored their sight, and fed them rather than killed them. Both Israelites and Arameans have been given new powers to see—new insight into the nature of reality, appropriate ways to exercise power under prophetic leadership, and the concern of Israel's God to bring peace rather than war.

The key for Elisha is his penetrating insight—his vision to interpret events in terms of the will of God. It is not that Elisha just sees what God is going to do anyway, however, with only an appearance of efficacy; his insight in itself is important in shaping what happens, in redefining the situation. Without his engagement on behalf of the will and word of God, we do not know what God would have gotten done. Elisha's use of prayer as a vehicle for divine action, even twice addressing God with a "please" (vv. 17–18), is seen to be important. His prayer is efficacious—a means in and through which God gets things done in the world. Thereby *God* has access to power and resources that would not otherwise be available (see at 1 Kings 8:1–66; 2 Kings 20:1–8).

Several questions present themselves. Are the affairs of the kings futile in the face of Elisha's words and deeds? Is this a "no contest" from the word "Go"? Is it true that what the prophet decides to do gets done, irrespective of the nature of the opposition? It seems wise for the interpreter not to generalize from this specific situation. The specific wise and unwise actions of the two kings are important with respect to how the situation develops. There are moments in the life of a people when the insights and prayers of key individuals are decisive in human affairs, even miraculously so. Such a salutary effect may not always come to be, but one prays as if it would make all the difference in the world.

The Arameans Foiled Again
(2 Kings 6:24–7:20)

This extensive story about Aram's siege of Samaria clearly moves into another time from verse 23; relationships with other texts regarding Aram are uncertain, as is the historical setting. The Ben-hadad here is likely different from others encountered. The role of Elisha is more subdued than in the prior text, but the power of his word remains central; through it God works a saving deed. In the larger context, this story functions to lift up that word and the supporting roles of "little people" in shaping Israel's future (see at 5:1–27). The continuing ineffectiveness of the king, though qualified here, reinforces a negative evaluation, yet once again issues of apostasy are left aside.

Aram's siege of Samaria is described in graphic terms. The famine that grips the city is so severe that prices skyrocket, even for such unappetizing food as a donkey's head or dove's dung (*kab*=about a quart). What is more, cannibalism has occurred (see Deut. 28:53–57; Lam. 2:20; 4:10). This is vividly portrayed in the poignant plaint of a mother who has just eaten her own child! Truly remarkable in this mother's story is the matter-of-fact way in which she describes her pact with another woman to eat their children in turn. Even more, her concern addressed to the king is one of justice—the other woman didn't follow through on the agreement—rather than guilt or shame (see Lasine, 1991).

When the king first hears the cry for help (literally, Save me! Hebrew: *yashaʿ*) he throws up his hands, claiming that he (the king!) has no resources to put an end to the famine. In exclaiming, "let the Lord help" (*yashaʿ*) he ironically points to the source from which help will come. Yet the king hears her plea for justice and tears his clothes in distress (see 5:7), publicly displaying his impotence (v. 30). This act reveals that he is wearing sackcloth; given that it is inadvertently revealed, Jehoram's remorse is probably sincere (see 1 Kings 20:31). The king, believing the famine to be God's doing (v. 33), lays the blame on God's man Elisha and threatens him with decapitation. After all, if Elisha could multiply food for the many (see 4:42–44), he could, if he would, put an end to the famine. This implicit indictment of Elisha's passivity responds to the woman's cry for justice. In response, the king lays a siege for Elisha within the larger siege of the city.

Elisha, again given insight into the situation (v. 32; see 5:26; 6:8–10), alerts his "students" to bar the door to the king's messenger; he wants to speak directly with the king, who will not be far behind. When the king claims that the dire situation is from God and he is without hope, Elisha replies with a surprising, concrete promise from the Lord, using classic prophetic speech. From within a situation of entrapment, he speaks a word of freedom: The very next day prices for food in the marketplace will return to their normal levels. This prophetic word suggests that Elisha disagrees with the royal assessment that the siege was the Lord's doing; on the contrary, God's activity in this situation saves. The king's confidant (the king has no reaction) expresses doubts that this would be possible—even for God. This is a realistic move, for major rains (windows in the sky) could not make the earth produce food that quickly! But such an evaluation of the situation is unimaginative. Elisha meets the skepticism with a word of judgment: He will come to know that the food is there but die before eating it (7:17–20).

Meanwhile, four starving lepers (see 5:1, 27) ironically come to the rescue; once again, through minor, bumbling figures God works salvation. Their role is both imaginative and verbal. In dire straits they desert to the Arameans, reasoning that it is worth the chance because death will come whatever else they do. They discover that the Aramean camp is deserted (though the army escapes, as in 6:23). The narrator pauses to tell the reader why: God has tricked them, creating the noise of an advancing army (see 2:11–12; 6:17); thinking that the lepers are Hittites and Egyptians (the Hebrew word for lepers is similar to the word for Egypt), they flee for their lives (abandoning even their horses!). What now will the lepers do in response to this "good news"? The lepers make merry with what the army has left behind, even hiding valuables for later use. With ethical sensitivities suddenly sharpened (out of fear), they recognize that this is indeed "good news" (with only potential theological content) that must be shared with the king. Having delivered the good news, the lepers drop out of the story. When the "proclamation" reaches the king, he suspects an Aramean trick to get him to let down his defenses. But he accepts a servant's common sense suggestion to check it out with horses which would be lost anyway.

When the messengers return with a confirmation of the good news of the Aramean retreat, their camp is cleaned out, and the supplies are so great that food is sold for exactly the price the prophet had foretold (7:1). In the melee, the king's captain is trampled to death before he can eat of the bounty, also just as the prophet had announced. Verses 18–20 recapitulate the word of the prophet—to make sure the point is not missed amid all the good news about Samaria. Yet without the words and actions of key figures along the way (for example, the lepers), the word would not have had the chance to be fulfilled. This turns out to be another war that God does not have to fight alone.

Sieges, Famines, and Hope in God

In the face of communal disaster (Israel's situation in both religious and political terms), with horrendous consequences, the text suggests several responses:

1. Cope with the disaster in whatever way one can; extreme situations may call for extreme measures (the women). One may wonder about the

way in which the mothers seek to resolve their dilemma, but those who have not faced such hunger should be very hesitant to pass judgment. Though they may wait too long to cry for help, at the least their cry does finally start them and their community on the road to deliverance.

2. Blame God, lose hope, and kill the prophet (the king). When the king comes to Elisha (v. 33), he shifts from blaming the prophet (v. 31) to blaming God and losing hope. God is the cause of the problem, so why hope that God will bring relief? This seems not to be an unfaithful question (only the captain is judged); the king could even be said to mediate the resolution by bringing the issue before the prophet. But if God is viewed as the problem behind every community disaster (an image of a scary God is often encouraged by the religious establishment to keep people in line), it is understandable how one could strike out against such a God or his chosen representative. Blaming of God and loss of hope, even a loss of faith, often go together. Elisha's response addresses the king's concern directly, in both theological and economic terms. Contrary to the king's theological view, God is *not* to be blamed for the famine and its effects (only the Arameans are cited, 6:24). Rather, God will act quickly to resolve the problem, namely, food for all at reasonable prices. Indeed, God may have been dependent on the emergence of the right configuration of circumstances in order to make this move. There may be other times when God is involved in community disaster (and commonly so in Kings), and prophetic discernment will be needed to sort out the issues at stake, but one dare not generalize regarding the nature of the divine involvement.

3. Doubt that God can ameliorate the situation (the captain). His doubt seems not to be a problem in itself, but because it is rooted in a lack of imagination regarding God's possibilities. He can only imagine that choice meal and barley would come from field growth (7:2), and that takes time. He cannot imagine another source (such as what turns out to be the source of food). Elisha's judgment comes not because he limits God's power in some abstract way, but because he has narrowed the divine possibilities—God's possible ways of working in the world—to his own limited vision.

4. Act imaginatively and with some abandon regarding one's own life, and spread the "good news" that miraculously becomes available, even if one is not fully cognizant of the theological issues involved (the lepers). Elisha's word about the future does not make its way in total independence of how people speak and act. What people do counts; what even minor characters do can make a difference with respect to the shaping of the future. These somewhat comical outcasts stumble upon a treasure and bumble in their ethical considerations of what to do about their newfound

bounty, but they do get some things straight. They refuse simply to lie down and die in the face of disaster, but use their imaginations in thinking through life-giving possibilities. They recognize "good news" when they see it and refuse to keep it to themselves. Though they don't see the full theological potential in that news, they pass it along and let others carry it further.

5. Trust that God has Israel's best interests at heart and will bring salvation (the prophet). In the face of threats and entrapment and his own seeming passivity, Elisha sees that, even in the midst of the worst that life can throw Israel's way, God's purposes and possibilities cannot be delimited by the shape of the disaster. He trusts that God has the best for the people's life and well-being in view and, discerning that the time is right, speaks a word that gives hope that God's saving purposes are at work. This basic perspective is also available even in those situations where community disaster is related to God's judgment, though issues of discernment will need attention.

ELISHA FOLLOWS THROUGH
2 Kings 8:1–15

This segment comprises two brief stories that follow through on threads provided by earlier narratives. The first gives further favorable witness to the ministry of Elisha—even by the king and Gehazi! The second brings closure to God's word to Elijah in 1 Kings 19:15 about anointing Hazael. The long-awaited fulfillment of that prophecy takes place.

The Shunammite Woman, Once Again
(2 Kings 8:1–6)

8:1 Now Elisha had said to the woman whose son he had restored to life, "Get up and go with your household, and settle wherever you can; for the LORD has called for a famine, and it will come on the land for seven years." ² So the woman got up and did according to the word of the man of God; she went with her household and settled in the land of the Philistines seven years. ³ At the end of the seven years, when the woman returned from the land of the Philistines, she set out to appeal to the king for her house and her land. ⁴ Now the king was talking with Gehazi the servant of the man of God, saying, "Tell me all the great things that Elisha has done." ⁵ While he was telling the king how Elisha had restored a dead person to life, the woman whose son he had restored to life appealed to the king for her house and her land. Gehazi said, "My lord king, here is the woman, and here is her son whom Elisha restored to life." ⁶ When the king questioned the woman, she told him. So the king appointed an official for her, saying, "Restore all that was hers, together with all the revenue of the fields from the day that she left the land until now."

This story is a sequel to the narrative about the Shunammite woman in 4:8–37; it testifies to Elisha's past action in her life (note the repetition in v. 5) and how that affects her present situation. Though Elisha is not present, he lives on! The internal witness to Elisha in the story supports the larger narrative witness. Implicitly, the reader is to respond as do the king and Gehazi (still leprous, 5:27?).

Seven years earlier, it is recalled, Elisha had warned the woman about a coming seven-year famine (different from the one in the city in 6:25) as a judgment from God (for unspecified reasons). She had responded by settling in the land of the Philistines (along the coast). When she now returns, she sets out to appeal to the king for the return of her property, lost for an unknown reason (did it become crown property?). She happens upon the king speaking with Gehazi, the servant of Elisha, about "all the great things that Elisha has done," especially the resuscitation of her son. This is sufficient reason for the king to order that her property be restored to her and that she be given the revenue earned from the fields while she was gone (probably not much during the famine!). The king resolves the issue of the negative effect of Elisha's advice, but it is the witness to Elisha's miraculous deed that prompts the king to make the move he does.

The Accession of Hazael
(2 Kings 8:7–15)

8:7 Elisha went to Damascus while King Ben-hadad of Aram was ill. When it was told him, "The man of God has come here," ⁸ the king said to Hazael, "Take a present with you and go to meet the man of God. Inquire of the LORD through him, whether I shall recover from this illness." ⁹ So Hazael went to meet him, taking a present with him, all kinds of goods of Damascus, forty camel loads. When he entered and stood before him, he said, "Your son King Ben-hadad of Aram has sent me to you, saying, 'Shall I recover from this illness?'" ¹⁰ Elisha said to him, "Go, say to him, 'You shall certainly recover'; but the LORD has shown me that he shall certainly die." ¹¹ He fixed his gaze and stared at him, until he was ashamed. Then the man of God wept. ¹² Hazael asked, "Why does my lord weep?" He answered, "Because I know the evil that you will do to the people of Israel; you will set their fortresses on fire, you will kill their young men with the sword, dash in pieces their little ones, and rip up their pregnant women." [13] Hazael said, "What is your servant, who is a mere dog, that he should do this great thing?" Elisha answered, "The LORD has shown me that you are to be king over Aram." [14] Then he left Elisha, and went to his master Ben-hadad, who said to him, "What did Elisha say to you?" And he answered, "He told me that you would certainly recover." [15] But the next day he took the bed-cover and dipped it in water and spread it over the king's face, until he died. And Hazael succeeded him.

This story is a sequel to 1 Kings 19:15–18, where Elijah was commanded to anoint Hazael king of Aram. It falls to Elisha to move on that front and he visits Damascus, the capital of Aram; the occasion is the illness of King Ben-hadad. Elisha is welcome in this setting (after Naaman's healing? but cf. 6:8–23), and Ben-hadad sends an officer named Hazael to inquire regarding the prognosis of his illness (see 1:2–8). Hazael brings a huge present, perhaps in hope that the prophet's healing powers can be extended to the king, who is called Elisha's "son" (deference to a prophet from Israel!).

Elisha commands Hazael to tell the king that he will recover but then reports (to Hazael only) a contrary word from the Lord that Ben-hadad will actually die (cf. Micaiah in 1 Kings 22:15, 17). The second word makes the first word a deception (on the use of deception, see at 22:1–40). What purpose these contrary words serve is not entirely clear; it may alert Hazael (and the reader) that Elisha has given a signal for Hazael to accede to the throne by deposing him quickly (on the ruthlessness of succession, see 1 Kings 2:1–9). Hazael stares at him (perhaps disbelievingly) until he (apparently Hazael) lowers his eyes and then Elisha breaks down. He explains his behavior as due to knowledge of Israel's future devastation (="evil") at the hands of Hazael (in inexact fulfillment of 1 Kings 19:17); the actual destruction will be described as less extreme (10:32–33; 13:3–7; compare Hos. 13:16; Amos 1:13). When Hazael self-effacingly ("dog") questions him, Elisha gets to his main point with clarity: Hazael will become king of Aram. Hazael returns to Ben-hadad and reports only part of what Elisha had said: a word of recovery. But the next day—picking up on Elisha's clues—he returns to suffocate him, making it look like it happened naturally (apparently), and Hazael becomes king. He will be heavily involved in Israel's history until his death (reported in 13:24).

Prophecy and International Affairs

This text is further testimony to the religious factor at work in national and international affairs (see the discussion at 6:1–23). The prophet involves himself in political life beyond the specifically religious sphere. Even more, the prophet engages in specific actions with respect to the internal political affairs of countries other than Israel. The theological grounding for such prophetic activity is the belief that God is the Creator who is caught up in the life of the world and its peoples beyond the boundaries of Israel and pursues the divine will in every time and place. The prophet not only claims *that* God is so involved (an important first step) but also seeks to delineate *how* God is so engaged and to act in ways congruent with that. The prophet's powers of discernment are key. He interprets what is happening on the world scene in terms of the will of God, and then has the energy, courage, and sheer audacity *both* to speak and to act in such a way as to bring that will to effect (remembering that the will of God is not irresistible). In the person and work of the prophet more resources can be accessed for interpreting the world's affairs than what political and military leaders conventionally consider to be available.

Though prophets often spoke oracles regarding other nations (e.g., Amos 1:3–2:3), only Elisha becomes personally involved in social and political affairs outside of Israel (see also Jonah). This international involvement does enhance Elisha's reputation, but the fundamental point has to do with God's recurring activity among such peoples, for purposes of both judgment and salvation. In this text, Hazael is raised up to be an instrument of divine judgment against the Northern Kingdom. This is likely viewed as anticipatory of a much more devastating foreign visit by the Assyrians (chap. 17). God's involvement among non-Israelite peoples for purposes of salvation has already been clearly presented regarding Aram (see 5:1; see the discussion at 1 Kings 8:1–66; 11:14–25). This perspective is congruent with that of Amos, a northern prophet (see Amos 9:7).

THE ZEAL OF JEHU
2 Kings 8:16–10:36

The story of King Jehu of Israel (842–815 B.C.) is marked by his purging of the house of Ahab and the associated worship of Baal. The narrative details various actions taken by Jehu in explicit (if less than exact) fulfillment of Elijah's prophecy regarding the house of Ahab (1 Kings 21:21–24) and God's explicit word about Jehu to Elijah (1 Kings 19:17). Jehu uses violence in pursuit of two objectives—political change and religious reform. His brilliantly conceived, if ruthless and uncompassionate, purge is assessed by the narrator in ambiguous terms (see below).

Two Kings of Judah
(2 Kings 8:16–27)

The narrator shifts to report on kings of Judah, for the first time since 1 Kings 22:41–50. Both Jehoram and Ahaziah, linked to the house of Ahab by marriage, are negatively evaluated. This report connects the apostasy of the North to developing unfaithfulness in Judah, anticipating the fall of both. The family of Ahab has now deeply infected both kingdoms (see 11:18; 21:3), and Jehu's purge catches up the South as well. Looking back, one can understand why the narrator gave so much space to Ahab. At the same time, God is caught up in these events, and the divine authorization of Jehu's coup stands at the beginning of all the violence that follows.

Jehoram (or Joram) is king of Judah (849–843 B.C.), while his namesake is king of Israel. He was as apostate as Ahab, whose daughter Athaliah became his wife. Athaliah stands in the tradition of her mother Jezebel and later becomes the apostate queen of Judah (see 11:1–16). In spite of Jehoram's evil reign, the narrator reports that God would not destroy Judah because of the covenant promise (2 Sam. 7:14–16; cf. 1 Kings 11:36; 15:4–5) that David would always have a lamp (=a dynasty) on the throne. How this promise works out is a question that hangs over the subsequent narrative. The only other events reported are Jehoram's unsuccessful attempt to put down an Edomite rebellion (and Libnah, near Philistia); the empire is slowly being trimmed back.

Ahaziah (843–842 B.C.) followed in the ways of his parents. The brief notice of his reign is "interrupted" by the story of Jehu's anointing and coup in the North. The death of Ahaziah is part of this coup, and its report (9:27–29) is only a transition within the larger unit focusing on Jehu. A conflict between the Arameans (under Hazael) and Israel/Judah over Ramoth-gilead (Ramah) is again reported (see 1 Kings 22:1–40). King Joram of Israel was wounded in the conflict, an event which sets up the coup by Jehu that follows.

Anointing Jehu King over Israel
(2 Kings 8:28–9:13)

8:28 **He went with Joram son of Ahab to wage war against King Hazael of Aram at Ramoth-gilead, where the Arameans wounded Joram.** [29] **King Joram returned to be healed in Jezreel of the wounds that the Arameans had inflicted on him at Ramah, when he fought against King Hazael of Aram. King Ahaziah son of Jehoram of Judah went down to see Joram son of Ahab in Jezreel, because he was wounded.**

9:1 **Then the prophet Elisha called a member of the company of prophets and said to him, "Gird up your loins; take this flask of oil in your hand, and go to Ramoth-gilead.** 2 **When you arrive, look there for Jehu son of Jehoshaphat, son of Nimshi; go in and get him to leave his companions, and take him into an inner chamber.** 3 **Then take the flask of oil, pour it on his head, and say, 'Thus says the LORD: I anoint you king over Israel.' Then open the door and flee; do not linger."** 4 **So the young man, the young prophet, went to Ramoth-gilead.** 5 **He arrived while the commanders of the army were in council, and he announced, "I have a message for you, commander." "For which one of us?" asked Jehu. "For you, commander."** 6 **So Jehu got up and went inside; the young man poured the oil on his head, saying to him, "Thus says the LORD the God of Israel: I anoint you king over the people of the LORD, over Israel.** 7 **You shall strike down the house of your master Ahab, so that I may avenge on Jezebel the blood of my servants the prophets, and the blood of all the servants of the LORD.** 8 **For the whole house of Ahab shall perish; I will cut off from Ahab every male, bond or free, in Israel.** 9 **I will make the house of Ahab like the house of Jeroboam son of Nebat, and like the house of Baasha son of Ahijah.** 10 **The dogs shall eat Jezebel in the territory of Jezreel, and no one shall bury her." Then he opened the door and fled.** 11 **When Jehu came back to his master's officers, they said to him, "Is everything all right? Why did that madman come to you?" He answered them, "You know the sort and how they babble."** 12 **They said, "Liar! Come on, tell us!" So he said, "This is just what he said to me: 'Thus says the LORD, I anoint you king over Israel.'"** 13 **Then hurriedly they all took their cloaks and spread them for him on the bare steps; and they blew the trumpet, and proclaimed, "Jehu is king."**

During the war with Aram, with the king wounded and removed from the situation, Elisha gives detailed instructions to a member of his guild: take a flask of oil, go to Ramoth-gilead, and secretly (this was treason) anoint one of the army commanders, Jehu, to be king of Israel. Jehu's coup is thus given explicit divine authorization. This anointing fulfills one more command of God to Elijah (1 Kings 19:16; on prophetic anointing of kings, see 1 Sam. 16:3; 1 Kings 1:34). This is the last reported action of Elisha until the time of his death (13:14–21).

The "young prophet" finds Jehu (who is appropriately modest, v. 5) and anoints him, setting him apart for his role with divine blessing. Then he expands upon Elisha's word. While expansiveness is not uncommon among prophets (note the divine first person), that he does not follow Elisha's precise directives should give the reader pause. Jehu is to purge the house of Ahab because of the killing of prophets and other servants (1 Kings 18:4; 19:10). Verses 8–10 essentially repeat the prophecy of Elijah (1 Kings 21:21–24; for the harsh language, see at 1 Kings 14:10–11). Elisha (and other prophets) play no role in the ensuing events; Jehu and his activities fill the scene, but Elisha's actions have set everything in motion. When Jehu reports the anointing and gives the essence of the oracle (vv. 3, 6, 12) to his fellow commanders (at their insistence), they respond by acclaiming him king of Israel in a "rump" coronation.

Jehu Kills Joram and Ahaziah
(2 Kings 9:14–29)

9:14 Thus Jehu son of Jehoshaphat son of Nimshi conspired against Joram. Joram with all Israel had been on guard at Ramoth-gilead against King Hazael of Aram; [15] but King Joram had returned to be healed in Jezreel of the wounds that the Arameans had inflicted on him, when he fought against King Hazael of Aram. So Jehu said, "If this is your wish, then let no one slip out of the city to go and tell the news in Jezreel." [16] Then Jehu mounted his chariot and went to Jezreel, where Joram was lying ill. King Ahaziah of Judah had come down to visit Joram. [17] In Jezreel, the sentinel standing on the tower spied the company of Jehu arriving, and said, "I see a company." Joram said, "Take a horseman; send him to meet them, and let him say, 'Is it peace?'" [18] So the horseman went to meet him; he said, "Thus says the king, 'Is it peace?'" Jehu responded, "What have you to do with peace? Fall in behind me." The sentinel reported, saying, "The messenger reached them, but he is not coming back." [19] Then he sent out a second horseman, who came to them and said, "Thus says the king, 'Is it peace?'" Jehu answered, "What have you to do with peace? Fall in behind me." [20] Again the sentinel reported, "He reached them, but he is not coming back. It looks like the driving of Jehu son of Nimshi; for he drives like a maniac." [21] Joram said, "Get ready." And they got his chariot ready. Then King Joram of Israel and King Ahaziah of Judah set out, each in his chariot, and went to meet Jehu; they met him at the property of Naboth the Jezreelite. [22] When Joram saw Jehu, he said, "Is it peace, Jehu?" He answered, "What peace can there be, so long as the many whoredoms and sorceries of your mother Jezebel continue?" [23] Then Joram reined about and fled, saying to Ahaziah, "Treason, Ahaziah!" [24] Jehu drew his bow with all his strength, and shot Joram between the shoulders, so that the arrow pierced his heart; and he sank in his chariot. [25] Jehu said to his aide Bidkar, "Lift him out, and throw him on the plot of ground belonging to Naboth the Jezreelite; for remember, when you and I rode side by side behind his father Ahab how the LORD uttered this oracle against him: [26] 'For the blood of Naboth and for the blood of his children that I saw yesterday, says the LORD, I swear I will repay you on this very plot of ground.' Now therefore lift him out and throw him on the plot of ground, in accordance with the word of the LORD." [27] When King Ahaziah of Judah saw this, he fled in the direction of Beth-haggan. Jehu pursued him, saying, "Shoot him also!" And they shot him in the chariot at the ascent to Gur, which is by Ibleam. Then he fled to Megiddo, and died there. [28] His officers carried him in a chariot to Jerusalem, and buried him in his tomb with his ancestors in the city of David. [29] In the eleventh year of Joram son of Ahab, Ahaziah began to reign over Judah.

Advising his supporters to keep his anointing secret (in effect, a test of allegiance), Jehu takes the conspiratorial steps necessary to "activate" his kingship. He travels to Jezreel, where King Joram is recovering from wounds and King Ahaziah of Judah is visiting (9:14–16 repeat the information of 8:28–29). Alerted to Jehu's coming by a sentinel, Joram sends out two reconnaissance men in succession to determine whether the news from the front is good (Hebrew: *shalom*, a key word here, means harmony and well-being in both political and religious senses). In each case, the men do not return to Joram but fall in behind Jehu—join his cause—in response to Jehu's rhetorical question that implies a judgment: neither Jehoram *nor* his supporters are promoters of genuine *shalom* in this kingdom, only Jehu is (vv. 18–19). The sentinel reports the situation to Joram and identifies the person as Jehu—one of Joram's commanders known for driving like a maniac (from the same root as "madman" in v. 11; an image for his zeal)!

Joram and Ahaziah then set out to meet Jehu personally and, meeting at the property of Naboth (see 1 Kings 21:19), again Joram inquires about *shalom* (the third and climactic time). Jehu's rhetorical question states—in prophetic terms—that there can be no *shalom* as long as his mother Jezebel's apostasy continues (v. 22). The language of prostitution commonly refers to religious infidelity, the worship of gods other than the Lord (Hosea 1–3; see Deut. 31:16; Exod. 34:16). Realizing that Jehu is treasonous, Joram seeks to flee but is killed by Jehu in the cause of *shalom* (concluding his reign, begun at 3:1). Jehu commands—twice—that his body be thrown onto Naboth's land, framing the word of fulfillment of Elijah's prophecy (vv. 25–26; here noted explicitly as a word from God; see at 1 Kings 21:21–22). This fulfillment is inexact, representing a conflation of oracles against Ahab and against his house (1 Kings 21:19, 21–22). Both Ahab's apostasy and injustice thus shape Jehu's actions, and both are seen in terms of the prophetic word taking shape in the judgment against his house. Jehu also commands that Ahaziah of Judah be killed, probably because he was a grandson of Ahab and followed in his steps (8:27), but no prophetic fulfillment is linked to his murder.

The Death of Jezebel
(2 Kings 9:30–37)

> 9:30 When Jehu came to Jezreel, Jezebel heard of it; she painted her eyes, and adorned her head, and looked out of the window. [31] As Jehu entered the gate, she said, "Is it peace, Zimri, murderer of your master?" [32] He looked up to the window and said, "Who is on my side? Who?" Two or three eunuchs looked out at him. [33] He said, "Throw her down." So they threw her down; some of her blood spattered on the wall and on the horses, which trampled on her. [34] Then he went in and ate and drank; he said, "See to that cursed woman and bury her; for she is a king's daughter." [35] But when they went to bury her, they found no more of her than the skull and the feet and the palms of her hands. [36] When they came back and told him, he said, "This is the word of the LORD, which he spoke by his servant Elijah the Tishbite, 'In the territory of Jezreel the dogs shall eat the flesh of Jezebel; [37] the corpse of Jezebel shall be like dung on the field in the territory of Jezreel, so that no one can say, This is Jezebel.'"

Jehu proceeds to the royal palace in Jezreel where Jezebel (Joram's mother) resides; she has played a key role in this narrative since 1 Kings 16:31. She makes herself up, not to seduce Jehu, but as if it were a royal audience. In this way she maintains a queenly role that ironically links her back to the "whoredoms" of 9:22. She sarcastically asks whether he comes in *shalom*, calling him Zimri (who had assassinated all of Baasha's family, 1 Kings 16:8–14, but only reigned for seven days). When Jehu asks whether anyone is on his side, only some eunuchs respond and they obey his command to throw Jezebel out a window; the narrator reports the results in gruesome terms (compare the death of Ahab in 1 Kings 22:38). When Jehu thought—after hours of eating and drinking!—to have the "cursed woman" buried because of her royal lineage, his servants report that not enough is left for burial—a disgrace in Israel. No one will be able to say: Jezebel is buried here. He interprets this as a fulfillment of the word of the Lord (vv. 36–37) by elaborating on the oracle given by Elijah in 1 Kings 21:23 (cf. 2 Kings 9:10).

Jehu Destroys the House
of Ahab and Baal
(2 Kings 10:1–36)

Having begun by eliminating key individuals, Jehu turns to groups, the first being the descendants of Ahab in Samaria (seventy is a round number). To this end, he sends a letter from Jezreel to their guardians and other leaders still in place in Samaria, challenging them to pick a king from among Ahab's sons and defend him. They are afraid to do so, given Jehu's success to this point, and declare their homage to Jehu. Jehu tests their allegiance by asking them to take the "heads" of Ahab's sons *and* come to him by the next day. Interpreting "heads" literally (as Jehu intended, but the ambiguity left him an escape), they behead all of Ahab's sons, but only send the heads to Jehu, personally removed from the slaughter at Jezreel. He has the heads placed in heaps at the most public place in the city and the next day speaks to the people. In a clever move, he declares them innocent of any killings (or, fair-minded in assessing what has happened) and admits that he has killed Joram. And then he asks who killed the seventy. This removes him from direct responsibility and implies that others (leaders in Samaria that had not come to him as he asked) are involved in the elimination of Ahab's house. Jehu grounds these deaths (and others that may occur) in the prophetic word as the will and work of God (v. 10). In effect, their death is God's work! And the crowd serves as the silent jury. This gives him reason for further slaughter of Ahab's leaders in Jezreel as well (v. 11).

Next in line are relatives of King Ahaziah of Judah (vv. 12–14). Jehu meets them on a *shalom*-visit to Ahab's family; but there can be no *shalom* at this moment in Israel. Taking them alive (!), he slaughters them all. It is not certain why he does this—either because they are descendants of Ahab through Athaliah, or Jehu thinks they may have tried to retaliate for their relative's murder and he removes any danger to his power from the Southern Kingdom. This text also places the fate of Judah into the mind of the reader, anticipating later developments.

After this slaughter he meets up with Jehonadab son of Rechab (coming to see *him*, not Ahab's relatives) and makes common cause with him. Jehonadab is associated with a group of zealous Yahweh worshipers who support a radical separation from Canaanite culture (Rechabites; see Jeremiah 35). Jehu invites him to be a public witness (vv. 17, 23), to verify his own zeal for the Lord, a match that would lend support to his moves among other zealots. He proceeds to wipe out every trace of Ahab in the city of Samaria. The prophecy of Elijah (1 Kings 22:21–24) is fulfilled.

Having slaughtered all members of Ahab's family and their associates, he moves to "reform" Israel's worship and its leadership. This is the key objective behind all the prior moves. In a remarkably ambiguous statement, which the narrator names approvingly as "cunning" (v. 19), he claims he will offer Baal a much greater "service" (probably a pun on the word "destroy") than did Ahab. For purposes of entrapment he will outdo

Ahab's Baalism (Baal is mentioned eleven times in this segment!). An-
nouncing a "great sacrifice" (the word can also mean "slaughter") and
"solemn assembly" (in more than one sense) for Baal, he summons everyone associated with Baal worship (prophets, priests, worshipers)—at
penalty of death! Everyone obeys, the total number filling the temple of
Baal (one would have thought there were more Baal worshipers in Israel
by this time; perhaps only the enthusiasts are in view). Keeping the ruse
intact, Jehu has everyone dress in their proper vestments and offer their
sacrifices, making sure that no worshipers of Yahweh are among them
(Jehu presents himself as a Baal fundamentalist). He alerts his soldiers that
they are to kill everyone present (or forfeit their own life). After completing the "worshipful entrapment," Jehu orders his soldiers to kill everyone
present. They do so, throw their bodies out, destroy the pillars associated
with Baal, and demolish his temple (built by Ahab, 16:32)—making it a toi-
let (a sarcastic monument that remains in place at the time of writing).

The narrator sums up the reign of Jehu (10:28–36). He eliminated Baalism from the country, for which he is commended by God and given a dynasty to last for four generations (about 102 years; v. 30). Yet he did not
remove Jeroboam's calves, and hence his evaluation is, finally, mixed.
Tacked on is a report of the external threat to Israel in the person of Hazael of Aram. Even with Jehu on the throne, he succeeded—and God is explicitly involved—in "trimming" sections from Israel that lay to the east of
the Jordan (see the prophecy of Elisha to Hazael in 8:12).

Zeal for Yahweh and Violence

These two chapters contain much violent material; parents may wish to
prevent their children from reading them! To the modern reader (at least),
much of this activity smells like personal ambition and political oppor-
tunism. We question those who justify political moves by an appeal to religion and are deeply suspicious of zealous behaviors, especially when
associated with violence and brutality. Time and time again, God-inspired
revolutions are turned into bloodbaths, and the oppressed become the op-
pressors (see Exod. 22:21–27). Walter Brueggemann (2 Kings, 36) wisely
speaks of true faith living in the tension "between a careless toleration
which won't sort things out and a misguided zeal which too easily equates
God's way and ours."

Yet the narrator presents Jehu as Elijah in royal robes: zealous on behalf of the Lord (1 Kings 19:10, 14; 2 Kings 10:16), unyielding in oppos-
ing royal apostasy (see 2 Kings 9:22), and single-minded in eliminating

Baal adherents (see 1 Kings 18:40). Jehu and his killing role are explicitly rooted deep in the Elijah tradition (1 Kings 19:16–17). In a virtual refrain Jehu's actions are grounded in prior divine words. God himself authorizes the coup at the first and then at the end places his imprimatur on what Jehu has done (10:30). He has done "well," his actions are "right," he has executed "all that was in [God's] heart," and God bases a promise on that activity (see 15:12 for fulfillment). The links to the Rechabites also ground a positive assessment of his zeal. The recurrent theme of *shalom* (peace) seems positively linked to objectives pursued by Jehu; *shalom*—the "right" kind—is established through violence (see Olyan, 1984).

Yet the narrator does have some misgivings regarding Jehu's reign (cf. 1 Kings 1:1–2:46 regarding Solomon). Jehu did not follow through in ridding the country of apostasy, an assessment that brackets the positive evaluation (10:29, 31). One might say that his evaluation is less than fully positive because he did not go far enough! Yet the more general evaluation that "he was not careful to follow the law . . . with all his heart" (v. 31) suggests a more wide-ranging disobedience (see Deut. 17:18–19); the revolution did not go *deep* enough—into Jehu's own "heart." The "trimming" of Israel's lands by Hazael in 10:32–33 is also a negative judgment for the "sins of Jeroboam"; these actions of Hazael are envisioned by Elisha (8:12) and supported by God (10:32), and in this context they represent an Israel that is being squeezed from the outside. Finally, the violence of Jehu may be explicitly contrasted with the minimal violence perpetrated by Jehoiada on Joash's behalf in a comparable move to power in chapters 11–12.

This mixed evaluation means that *shalom*, in both its religious (Jeroboam's calves) and political (Hazael) senses, is not finally established in Israel by violence. Violence finally does not bring true peace. The *shalom* of Ahab, Jezebel, and Baal is no real peace and needs to be subverted and undone; but Jehu falls short of establishing a *shalom* that is genuine. Any biblical assessment of Jehu must take Hosea 1:4–5 into account. Critical of Jehu's violence, it shows that Israel was not of one mind regarding his brutality. This inner-biblical critique means that no unequivocal approval of Jehu's violence in the service of Yahweh is possible.

Another critical perspective may also be available. While God does initiate the coup of Jehu, and approves the results in a general way, God does not necessarily sanction the means by which Jehu works it out (though the narrator's citation at 10:17 does cover much violence). Two angles on this may be found in Jehu's own citation of the prophetic basis for his moves (9:25–26, 36–37; 10:10)—interestingly, no such basis is given for his actions in 10:18–27. First, these texts have to do with the basic objective and not necessarily the means to achieve them, though Jehu seems to cite them as if they did. Second, he adjusts or conflates these texts (so also does the young prophet in 9:6–10 in launching his coup), which personalizes his link to them (too conveniently?).

Jehu's violence must also be seen from another angle. The narrative will soon demonstrate, in the Assyrian and Babylonian destructions of Samaria and Jerusalem, that Israel is not done experiencing brutality and violence. Moreover, it will be made clear that, once again, God stands behind the violence. How does the violence of Jehu relate to that later violence? It could be viewed as a failed effort on the part of Jehu (and God!), which necessitates a more radical violence later. Even the brutal levels of Jehu's violence were not able to achieve *shalom* for Israel and overturn the buildup of chaotic forces, not least because of his own failures. All the violence of Jehu was not able to stop the decline and death of the North. It is as if God, in using Jehu as a means to turn that situation around, had limited choices available; the brutal instrument through which God chose to work proved inadequate to the task and bought only a little time (four generations). It would take a more violent overthrow of Israel by foreign armies, from the outside, in order to restore the *shalom* that had been violated. And even then such a peace is thrown onto an eschatological screen (Isa. 2:1–4).

In these considerations, the narrator must be commended for the realistic portrayal. Such brutal acts are the way it often is in a violent world, and the narrator does not back off from telling it like it is. At the same time, the narrator insists on integrating theological realities into this picture. God is at work in every such history, and the prophets interpret the significance of that divine work. They claim that God does not shy away from being involved in the political and military maneuverings of peoples and nations, no matter how messy they may be. God initiates new political arrangements, even if not democratically legitimated, though how they are carried out may not conform to God's will. No existing political establishment or societal order, however *shalom*-like it may appear to be, is sacrosanct.

So the testimony of the texts is that God does not cease to be at work simply because everything is so ungodlike. God will be at work in and through the human means available (see the discussion at 1 Kings 1–2), even though it may appear that God is absent. And God's purposes, because they extend over time and integrate highly disparate human motivations and actions, are not often fully discernible at any one moment or embodied in any one individual or movement. Generally speaking, one might understand the violence in terms of God mediating the moral order (on divine judgment, see at 1 Kings 11:1–43; 21:1–29; 2 Kings 17). Finally, the issue for God should not be simply stated in terms of apostasy; the idolatry of the house of Ahab is front and center, but injustice perpetrated against Naboth is also brought into play (9:21, 25–26). The understanding of infidelity to Yahweh is broad enough to include both of these dimensions, and the narrator integrates them as being finally of one piece and having disastrous effects for the life and well-being of the community.

5. The Endangered Promise
2 Kings 11:1–12:21

The narrative now turns to the effects of the turmoil in the North on life in the South (most of the rest of Kings is focused there). Jehu had murdered King Ahaziah (9:27–28) and many members of the royal household (10:12–14). The future of the Davidic throne was threatened, and this is intensified under Athaliah (for her own reasons). This is the story of a promise endangered. It is parallel in many ways to the final verses of 2 Kings, where once again the future of the Davidic dynasty hangs by the thread of one individual's life.

Parallels with the preceding story are instructive. Both are stories of reform. The actions of Jehoiada in overthrowing Athaliah parallel those of Jehu in ending Ahab's house in the North, except that the former is restoration (of the Davidic dynasty) while the latter is revolution (a new dynasty). Changes in the South are also accomplished with considerably less violence, undertaken with a Solomon-like wisdom rather than a cunning that issues in brutality. The God-directed role of the prophet Elisha with respect to Jehu parallels the priest Jehoiada's (not explicitly God-directed) role with respect to Joash's succession.

ATHALIAH AND JOASH
2 Kings 11:1–21

> 11:1 Now when Athaliah, Ahaziah's mother, saw that her son was dead, she set about to destroy all the royal family. ² But Jehosheba, King Joram's daughter, Ahaziah's sister, took Joash son of Ahaziah, and stole him away from among the king's children who were about to be killed; she put him and his nurse in a bedroom. Thus she hid him from Athaliah, so that he was not killed; ³ he remained with her six years, hidden in the house of the LORD, while Athaliah reigned over the land. ⁴ But in the seventh year Jehoiada sum-

moned the captains of the Carites and of the guards and had them come to him in the house of the LORD. He made a covenant with them and put them under oath in the house of the LORD; then he showed them the king's son. [5] He commanded them, "This is what you are to do: one-third of you, those who go off duty on the sabbath and guard the king's house [6] (another third being at the gate Sur and a third at the gate behind the guards), shall guard the palace; [7] and your two divisions that come on duty in force on the sabbath and guard the house of the LORD [8] shall surround the king, each with weapons in hand; and whoever approaches the ranks is to be killed. Be with the king in his comings and goings." [9] The captains did according to all that the priest Jehoiada commanded; each brought his men who were to go off duty on the sabbath, with those who were to come on duty on the sabbath, and came to the priest Jehoiada. [10] The priest delivered to the captains the spears and shields that had been King David's, which were in the house of the LORD; [11] the guards stood, every man with his weapons in his hand, from the south side of the house to the north side of the house, around the altar and the house, to guard the king on every side. [12] Then he brought out the king's son, put the crown on him, and gave him the covenant; they proclaimed him king, and anointed him; they clapped their hands and shouted, "Long live the king!" [13] When Athaliah heard the noise of the guard and of the people, she went into the house of the LORD to the people; [14] when she looked, there was the king standing by the pillar, according to custom, with the captains and the trumpeters beside the king, and all the people of the land rejoicing and blowing trumpets. Athaliah tore her clothes and cried, "Treason! Treason!" [15] Then the priest Jehoiada commanded the captains who were set over the army, "Bring her out between the ranks, and kill with the sword anyone who follows her." For the priest said, "Let her not be killed in the house of the LORD." [16] So they laid hands on her; she went through the horses' entrance to the king's house, and there she was put to death. [17] Jehoiada made a covenant between the LORD and the king and people, that they should be the LORD's people; also between the king and the people. [18] Then all the people of the land went to the house of Baal, and tore it down; his altars and his images they broke in pieces, and they killed Mattan, the priest of Baal, before the altars. The priest posted guards over the house of the LORD. [19] He took the captains, the Carites, the guards, and all the people of the land; then they brought the king down from the house of the LORD, marching through the gate of the guards to the king's house. He took his seat on the throne of the kings. [20] So all the people of the land rejoiced; and the city was quiet after Athaliah had been killed with the sword at the king's house. [21] Jehoash was seven years old when he began to reign.

After Ahaziah is murdered, his mother Athaliah (Ahab and Jezebel's daughter) seizes the throne (843–837 B.C.). Because her reign is considered perverse and illegitimate, the narrator omits the usual summary of rule. Athaliah sets about to destroy the remaining heirs of the Davidic line. Her reasons are not made clear (she is given voice only briefly, 11:14), but she likely sought to solidify the worship of Baal in the South in view of Jehu's purge in the North (11:18). In anticipation of her action, Jehosheba, a princess (sister of Ahaziah), quietly challenges the control of this "queen," takes the one remaining member of the Davidic line, her nephew Joash (or Jehoash) to "the house of the Lord," where he is unrecognized as such for six years (cf. 2 Chron. 22:10–12). The relation between temple ("the house of the Lord"; 22 times in chaps. 11–12) and palace ("the king's house") shapes the movement of the narrative. The true king is associated with God's presence throughout.

Jehosheba's husband, the priest Jehoiada (11:9), undertakes the religious instruction of Joash (12:2). These faithful persons are committed to the continuity of the Davidic line. While Jehoiada is the primary "mover and shaker," the concern of the narrative is the Davidic king (to whom the priest is subservient, 12:7). In the seventh year, Jehoiada gathers the palace guard (the Carites were an elite company) and, swearing them to secrecy (="covenant," 11:4), shows them that Joash is still alive. Apparently (the text is not clear) he commands that two-thirds of the palace guard be taken from normal duties and be used to protect the young king "in his comings and goings" at the temple (11:8). The remaining third are divided into three subgroups to assume normal tasks at the palace. All are secretly committed to Jehoiada, and Athaliah is now without evident military support. Compare the military guards surrounding the temple with the role of the Levites at the sacred space of the tabernacle in Numbers 1:53 (note that Levites replace the military in the Kings parallel in 2 Chron. 23:7).

Jehoiada secretly stations the protective force at strategic places around the sacred spaces of the temple. They carry weapons from David's time (a link to the dynastic issue involved); the risks are patent. Then he brings Joash out, places him by one of the two pillars in front of the temple (v. 14; 1 Kings 7:15–22), invests him with the symbols of royal office, and crowns him king (cf. Solomon in 1 Kings 1:39–40). The gathered group demonstrates much popular support, including the guard, trumpeters, "the people of the land" (an influential group of faithful leaders, 21:24; 23:30), and the people generally. All acclaim him king in a joyful spirit (cf. 2 Chron. 23:3). The "covenant" given him (11:12) is the "decree" of Psalm 2:7 (cf. 132:12), a document that specifies the fundamental character of the Davidic covenant, highlighting God's promises and royal responsibilities (2 Sam. 7:14–16).

When Athaliah comes to the temple to inquire about all the commotion, she attempts to arouse opposition by a cry of treason. Jehoiada commands that she be taken out of the temple and killed along with any who follow her. She journeys to her death alone—in the palace. Jehoiada then presides over a covenant ceremony, needed after such a disruptive time. In this ritual the relationship between God, the king, and the people is renewed, as is the relationship between king and people (see below). They proceed to destroy the temple of Baal and its religious trappings (apparently built and furnished by Athaliah). All groups involved take the seven-year-old Joash from temple to palace and he is seated as the Davidic heir, "on the throne of the kings" (cf. Solomon in 1 Kings 1:46). The summary statement in 11:20 describes the effect in a nutshell: The people rejoiced and "the city was quiet." The "peace" Jehu sought in the North here falls upon Jerusalem/Judah and its people.

THE REIGN OF JOASH
2 Kings 12:1–21

The reign of Joash (837–800 B.C.) is marked especially by a renovation of the temple (on the temple, see 1 Kings 6–7). This activity is virtually the only matter recalled from a nearly forty-year reign. His rule is evaluated in positive terms, though he does not centralize all worship in Jerusalem (12:3; 2 Chron. 24:15–22 speaks of his reign more critically). This renovation anticipates that of Josiah (2 Kings 22:3–7), for whom Joash is an exemplar. Josiah does destroy the high places but is finally not able to reverse all the effects of apostasy imported by the family of Ahab either.

The king commands the priests to collect donations for the repair (census taxes; voluntary offerings). The priests, however, keep the donations for their own use and so, without much ado, Joash makes a new arrangement. He involves more people in the disbursement to ensure ongoing provision for temple renovation. The priests are not to accept these donations for their own use, but they also no longer are responsible for the repairs (they do retain the donations from guilt and sin offerings, 12:16; see Lev. 4:1–6:7). Instead, the donations are to be placed by a priest in a chest provided by Jehoiada. When they had accumulated to a certain level, representatives of *both* the crown and the temple would count it and give it to foremen (commended for their honesty, 12:15), who in turn pay all the craftsmen. None could be used for the various vessels of the temple; it is all given to support the workers.

The story of Joash concludes on a sour note. Hazael of Aram threatens

Judah (see 10:32–33), but is bought off by Joash with gold given to the temple by his predecessors as an expression of their piety (12:17–18; cf. 18:15; 24:13). Joash's care of the temple is thereby qualified. His reign ends tragically when he is killed by servants, who are in turn killed by his son Amaziah (14:5; 2 Chron. 24:23–27 speaks of Joash's infidelity and ascribes his murder to retaliation for Joash's murder of Jehoiada's son).

A Promise Endangered and Renewed

The theme that comes to the fore in this story is the threat to the Davidic promise. The apostasies and injustices of Ahab and Jezebel have put the North on its sickbed, and it looks to be a sickness unto death. Now their influence has come to the South in the person of their daughter, Athaliah, and her fellow Baal adherents. Her impact on Judah's worship can be seen in 11:18; she built a temple for Baal, established a rival priesthood, and ran her own liturgical show. The cancer of Baalism has spread to the South and the malignancy is metastasizing quickly.

When these Baalistic apostasies are combined with the possible elimination of the Davidic dynasty, the threat to the South takes on a new urgency. If the line of David disappears from history, then what happens to the promise (2 Sam. 7:11–16)? What happens to the God who made the promise in the first place? God's promise is unconditional; if it fails, then does God fail? Athaliah not only undercuts the links to Moses in violating the First Commandment but threatens the links to David as well (and Abraham). If both David and Moses go, the major pillars of the Yahwistic tradition have been undermined, and Israel's future is deeply in doubt. The promise hangs on the preservation of a baby boy. The reader thinks of an earlier time, with a child named Moses, and a later time, and a threatened child with a name not unlike Joash—Jesus. Even more, this text anticipates the end of Kings (25:27–30), when the future of the Davidic dynasty is again endangered; it rests then on the shoulders of a king in prison and exile.

Two faithful, resolute, and wise Yahwists save the day, Jehosheba and Jehoiada. Because of them the Davidic promise has a future. They take this issue directly into their own hands by hiding Joash and instructing him, and *not a single word* is spoken about God inspiring them or acting through them (not unlike at 25:27–30). God it seems has simply *entrusted* this most significant work to faithful people and chosen to be dependent upon what they do. God continues to work in unobtrusive ways, to be sure, but God's decision to work through people means that what they do truly counts for something and, in this case, actually removes the danger to the Davidic dynasty and shapes the future of the promise.

From another angle, a priest is at the center of reforming activity, and a written covenant gives shape to renewed structures of life. Prophetic figures, so prominent heretofore, are not in view. Elisha doesn't pass from the scene until 13:14–21, but his sphere of activity is in the North. Yet God is not left without still other faithful people (cf. 1 Kings 19:18), and God is at work in and through more traditional structures than the prophetic word. In this case, the religious (priestly) *establishment* provides the wisdom and energy to rescue the endangered promise from the threats of the political regime. The impetus for reformation does not come from prophetic "outsiders," but from "insiders," whose work is often criticized by prophets. And when the priestly work is finished, the royal work continues.

Joash embodies the hope for a future beyond Athaliah, though she rules the country. The temple space—the house of Yahweh—remains linked to the presence of the Davidic heir through priestly intervention. In turn, that place of God's presence imbues the king with the divine blessing and legitimation within the larger social order. His assumption of the throne will extend the blessings and order of that space to the entire city (11:20). Here the presence of God mediated in and through the temple (and its personnel and rituals) is added to the prior witness and energy of the prophetic word and also brings life and well-being to the community.

Restoration of Davidic dynasty leads to covenant renewal at every level. The covenant with David shapes the entire story; indeed, its future is at stake (see 2 Sam. 17:11–16). The covenant in 11:12 centers in God's promise to the king and the basic obligations assumed by both God and king (see Pss. 2:7; 89:3–4; 132:12) and hence probably is assumed in 11:17. By its very nature this promissory covenant with David catches up the people within it and shapes their future, as is so clearly evident in this chapter. This is an old promise, to be sure, but it is new by virtue of the threat being removed. In 11:17, the king is an essential element in both parts, relating to God and people and then just to people. First, this covenant (more fully spelled out in 23:1–3; cf. Exod. 24:3–8) has reference to the Mosaic covenant so central to Deuteronomy (see 27:9–10; 31:9–13). The focus is covenant renewal, "by which they would be the LORD's people" (NAB). The people are reconstituted as the people of God and renew the responsibilities of covenant partner. Second, the covenant between king and people spells out relationships between them and the mutual obligations necessary for the sake of stability and peace (not specified, but no doubt related to texts such as Deut. 17:14–20; compare 2 Sam. 5:3). The cleansed temple and restored Davidic dynasty is consonant with a renewed covenant. They complement each other in mediating the work of God anew in this time of endangered promises. (See Dutcher-Walls, 1996.)

6. Kings Come and Go
2 Kings 13:1–16:20

This section includes brief treatments of a succession of kings in both Israel and Judah, covering less than a century (about 815–732 B.C.). That prophets are rarely active creates an eerie silence regarding the nature of God's involvement; Elisha dies in 13:20, and Jonah makes a brief appearance at 14:25. Two kings have long and successful reigns (Jeroboam II and Azariah/Uzziah), but the narrator expresses little interest in them. Their reigns are woven into an overall roller coaster pattern of occasional success and precipitous decline. In Israel King Jehu's dynasty continues for four generations: Jehoahaz, J(eh)oash, Jeroboam II, and Zechariah. Thereafter, Israel falls under increasing pressure from the Assyrians; this leads to rapid dynastic changes and its end becomes increasingly clear. In the South, less decline is evident, but its kings are unremarkable. Several textual difficulties affect order and chronology, but no scholarly surmise has proved convincing.

THE RENEWED FORTUNES OF ISRAEL
2 Kings 13:1–14:29

In these chapters, Israel achieves remarkable success under divine care and deliverance, even though its rulers are evil. On the other hand, Judah's fortunes do not match its good kings (see comment below).

13:1–9. Jehoahaz of Israel (815–802 B.C.) receives the usual appraisal from the narrator, with some qualifications. Because he did what was evil, God was provoked to anger (on anger, see at 1 Kings 14:21–16:34) and gave Israel into the hand of the Arameans "repeatedly." Conflict with the Arameans has been a periodic reality for Israel since Ahab (1 Kings 20; 22; 2 Kings 6–10).

Jehoahaz, in an unusual response for a king of Israel (cf. Ahab, 1 Kings

21:27–29), entreats the Lord (repeatedly?) for relief from Aramean oppression. In response, God gives the people of Israel "a savior" to deliver them (v. 5). This sin-judgment-entreaty-savior pattern is familiar from Judges 2:11–23, though here the identity of the "savior" is not given (Elisha, 13:14? Jeroboam II is the savior in 14:27; perhaps both if the cycle is ongoing, "repeatedly," v. 3). This pattern is summarized in somewhat different terms at 13:22–23 and, under Jeroboam II, at 14:26–27 (see discussion below). Israel did not depart from its apostasies (v. 6; on the Asherah, see 1 Kings 14:15), and so Aramean oppressions are renewed, including the devastation of Israel's army (v. 7). The cycle of verses 3–5 presumably begins again (see vv. 22–23).

13:10–25. The reign of J(eh)oash of Israel (802–786 B.C.) is initially treated in a regnal summary (vv. 10–13). Yet additional stories about his reign continue (vv. 14–25; 14:8–14), after which the end of his summary (13:12–13) is repeated in 14:15–16. The reason for this repetition is uncertain.

The first of these stories speaks of the death of Elisha (vv. 14–21). Jehoash pays a visit to Elisha, now dying after a ministry of about fifty years (beginning in 1 Kings 19:19–21). Joash laments Elisha's departing, using language that Elisha himself used at the departure of Elijah (see at 2:12)— "father" here indicates respect. Jehoash thereby may recognize that Elisha's ministry has been more valuable to Israel than its military might. The mourning of the king at Elisha's passing may signal the end of an era; Elisha leaves no disciples. The die is cast for the future of Israel, and the most appropriate response is one of mourning.

Elisha performs two symbolic acts (see 1 Kings 11:29–39) that initiate historical events. Elisha involves the king in both acts, and the king's response also shapes the character of events. The first (vv. 15–17) directs him (assisted by Elisha) to shoot "the Lord's arrow" to the east (Aram lay to the east of Israel). When Joash follows commands precisely, Elisha's interpretation is that Israel will defeat Aram at Aphek (near the Sea of Galilee), indeed, *the king* "will make an end of them." In a second action (vv. 18–19), in what amounts to a test, Elisha commands Jehoash to strike the ground with *God's* arrows (a gesture of confidence in their efficacy); he does so three times. Elisha upbraids him because he did not strike the ground more often, interpreting this to mean that Jehoash's confidence in God is less than it ought be. Hence, Israel will not make an end to Aram (thus qualifying the first act; Jeroboam II does succeed later, 14:25–28), but will only be victorious three times (see v. 25). Note that the action of the king (and not just the prophetic word) shapes the nature of Israel's history. Jehoash had a chance to succeed fully; he failed, and in effect determined his own future. It is likely that this failure has such effects, not simply because of this one test, but because the test reveals the shape of a life.

Even in death Elisha's life-giving powers are evident. During the burial of an unnamed man, those burying him are hurried by some marauding Moabites and dispose of his body in Elisha's grave (perhaps in a cave). Their action mediates what follows! When the body touches Elisha's "bones" (=body) the man comes to life (see 4:32–37). The Hebrew verb "throw" (v. 21) is the same as "banish" in verse 23 (and 17:20), suggesting that Israel's banishment will not be the end of its life. The verse thus gives hope that Israel will continue to live beyond its exile, in "their homes as formerly" (13:5). Hence, this is less legend than symbolic narrative giving a hopeful testimony regarding Israel's future life (see below; on symbolic narrative, see at 2 Kings 2:1–25).

The chapter concludes with a summary of the previously noted pattern under Jehoahaz (vv. 22–23) and of the three victories by Jehoash over the Arameans (vv. 24–25), consonant with Elisha's word (v. 19). Yet the victories (under both kings, presumably) are not simply fulfillment of prophecy, whether Elisha's word or the word of God to Jehu at 10:30. Verse 23 gives an explicit divine motivation for Israel's deliverance. In a statement unique in Kings, God's grace and compassion issuing in deliverance is grounded in the ancestral covenant (see Genesis 15; 17; Deut. 4:31; 9:27; 1 Kings 18:36). Because of this promise, God "would not destroy them" nor "banish them from his presence." The concluding "until now" (v. 23), the narrator's own time, is linked only with the banishment. The phrase reflects the fall of Israel in 721 B.C., when Israel was banished (17:20, 23). Yet even in the narrator's own time, Israel would not be "destroyed" or "blotted out" (14:27). Israel still has a future in God's eyes (see above on vv. 20–21). It is remarkable that this ancestral promise is cited in connection with the Northern Kingdom (for the first and only time in Kings); only the Davidic form of the promise is associated with the Southern Kingdom (2 Kings 8:19).

14:1–22. The narrator turns to the South and the reign of Amaziah (800–783 B.C.; the twenty-nine years [v. 2] probably include years of co-regency with his son Azariah/Uzziah). His reign receives a basically positive assessment. His first reported act is the killing of the servants who murdered his father (12:19–21); their children are not killed, however, in obedience to the law in Deuteronomy 24:16, which limits punishment to those actually committing the crime (see Jer. 31:29–30; Ezek. 18:2–4). The explicit notice given to the law is unusual (see 10:31; Deut. 17:18–19).

Ironically, the family members he left alive because of the law are likely those who kill him (v. 19). He is also successful in battles against the Edomites (at a place somewhere near the Dead Sea).

His relationship with Israel (under Jehoash) is, however, more problematic; Israel is much the stronger here. For some time, Judah has been under the control of Israel (cf. 1 Kings 22:4), and Amaziah proposes a "face-off" (v. 8). Jehoash interprets these words as hostile, sending Amaziah a word in the form of a fable (cf. Judg. 9:7–15). In effect: Amaziah is not as strong as his victories over Edom suggest, and he should stay home and be content with what he has. Amaziah is the thornbush (a useless shrub); Jehoash is the strong and majestic cedar, as well as the wild animal that tramples the thornbush in response. Jehoash is remarkably wise in his assessment of Amaziah, who rejects the message and loses face. Jehoash defeats him at Beth-shemesh (in Judah near Jerusalem), capturing him, breaking down about 600 feet of the walls of Jerusalem, and raiding the temple treasuries (all at the cost of a little bravado!). This is an anticipation of the eventual fall of Jerusalem to the Babylonians (see 24:10–16). The hostages (v. 14) may be in exchange for the freedom of Amaziah, who remains on the throne. Yet in the face of an internal rebellion (for unknown reasons) he flees to Lachish (southwest of Jerusalem), is captured, and killed (2 Chron. 25:27 interprets this as a consequence of his apostasy). The rebels make his young son, Azariah/Uzziah, king in his stead.

14:23–29. Turning to the North, the reign of Jeroboam II (786–746 B.C.) is given little narrative time, though his reign was marked by peace and prosperity unparalleled among Israel's kings. His "evil" evaluation is typical for northern kings, but the only description of his reign is positive: his expansion of Israel's territory encompasses the northern half of Solomon's empire (hence Judah in v. 28?), from Lebo-hamath (see 1 Kings 8:65) to the Sea of the Arabah (=Dead Sea). Lebo-hamath, Damascus, and Hamath are in Aram, indicating that Jeroboam broke its hold on Israel. This territorial expansion is linked to a fulfillment of a prophecy by Jonah. Jonah's prophecy has not been preserved; he is otherwise known only from the book of Jonah. Some have suggested that Jonah was a "prophet" like the prophets of Ahab (1 Kings 22:6–8), but the narrator gives his word a positive interpretation (14:26–27). This prophecy is a divine response to Israel's distress; Jeroboam is understood to be Israel's savior, though his evaluation is negative. God's saving work is not unmediated; God "saved them" *by the hand of* ("evil") Jeroboam. What Jeroboam did meant the *help* and *salvation* of Israel! The statement that God "had not said that he would blot out the name of Israel" is remarkable. This statement recalls, if negatively, the promises of 13:23; 8:19 (for Judah); 1 Samuel 12:22; and Judges 2:1 that God would never destroy or cast off his people.

Two other prophetic books are dated to his reign (Amos 1:1; 7:9–11; Hosea 1:1); these prophets are sharply negative about Jeroboam explicitly (Amos) and about developments in Israel during his reign, highlighting both issues of justice (Amos) and apostasy (Hosea). One wonders why the narrator ignores them (though not Isaiah, see chaps. 18–20).

THE DECLINE OF ISRAEL
2 Kings 15:1–38

While dynastic stability marks the South (the reigns of two of its kings frame this chapter), the North slides precipitously downward through several dynasties toward its end.

15:1–7. Returning to Judah, the reign of Azariah/Uzziah (783–742 B.C.) is lengthy (the chronology is unclear), but the narrator has little interest in it. His name is probably most familiar from the call of Isaiah (6:1), "in the year that King Uzziah died." He receives the same evaluation as his father and grandfather (Joash). The only matter that interests the narrator is his leprosy and the resultant co-regency with his son, Jotham. 2 Chronicles 26 gives more detail about his reign. Whereas 2 Kings 15:5 only implies a reason for God's striking Uzziah with leprosy (v. 4), Chronicles interprets it as punishment for intruding upon the priestly domain.

15:8–31. Turning to Israel, the narrator treats five kings in quick succession (Zechariah [746–745 B.C.]; Shallum [745 B.C.]; Menahem [745–737 B.C.]; Pekahiah [737–736 B.C.]; Pekah [736–732 B.C.]). They are all evaluated in negative terms (this note is missing for Shallum); tumbling so quickly on one another, these evaluations become a refrain of decline and death. Their reigns are marked by frequent dynastic change (Zechariah is the last of Jehu's dynasty, 15:12), assassination (15:10, 14, 25, 30), barbarism (15:16; cf. Amos 1:13), and heavy taxation (15:20). This dismal record occurs in tandem with the rise of the Assyrians, who increasingly intrude upon Israel's affairs under King Pul (the Tiglath-Pileser III, 745–727 B.C., of v. 29); under Menahem they exact tribute (15:19–20) and under Pekah they capture numerous cities in the north and east (15:29; the chronology for these events is uncertain). Pekah is succeeded by Hoshea, Israel's last king before the Assyrian onslaught (see Isa. 10:5–10).

15:32–38. Turning to Judah, the narrator briefly treats the reign of Jotham (742–735 B.C.), evaluated like his predecessors. His reign is marked by the increasing pressure from Assyrian expansion; God's involvement is specifically linked to the policies of the kings of Aram and Israel as they seek to have Judah join them in an anti-Assyrian coalition; this becomes a concern in chapter 16. During his reign, the ministry of Micah begins (Micah 1:1).

Royal Deeds and Divine Action and Evaluation

God's compassion and saving acts are cited more often in these chapters (13:5, 23; 14:25–27) than God's anger (13:3; compare the predominance of anger in 1 Kings 14:21–16:34). These promissory texts (focused on the North) could be linked to God's promise to Jehu of a four-generation dynasty (10:30). Yet the Jehu link is never explicit (as it will be at 15:12), and dynastic stability is never offered as a reason for God's gracious action. Other reasons are given—the prophecies of Elisha (13:14–19) and Jonah (14:25), and the prayers of Jehoahaz (13:4). God's action is also grounded in the ancestral promises (13:23; see above discussion) and motivated by human suffering and the divine "seeing" of oppression and distress (14:26; probably social and economic). These motivations and the language of salvation and compassion recall the programmatic formulations in Exodus 2:23–25; 3:7–10 (compare Deut. 26:7–9) and also certain rhythms in the book of Judges (2:11–22).

Moreover, though God's motivations and actions are central in these few verses, God does not act alone. God raises up human "saviors" (13:5) and "saves by the hand of" persons such as Jeroboam II. What these human agents do truly counts. That Kings picks up these themes from earlier traditions witnesses to a basic continuity in the life of the people of God. The theme of divine deliverance disappears in 2 Kings 15–17, however; the accumulated effects of evil have their way with Israel. God remains gracious and compassionate, but judgment is the only way into the future.

The variation in the summaries of reigns and related comments about specific kings shows that there is a less rigid analysis and a more subtle theology at work in these texts than might at first appear. Despite the appearance of reducing these kings to a formula, oppression is not always connected to sin nor prosperity to faithfulness to God. To say that kings do right but do not succeed, or are evil and do succeed, indicates no little subtlety in assessing the overall character of the reign. For example, God acts on behalf of *faithless* Israel in chapters 13–14. Jeroboam II is "evil," but recovers Solomon's empire. Jehoahaz is "evil" but his prayers are answered (13:4–5) and Jehoash receives a (qualified) word from Elisha about deliverance from the Arameans (13:14–19). God's compassion and promises continue to shape Israel's life in the midst of its evil ways. The story is somewhat different in Judah at this time, for Azariah/Uzziah is judged by God for his sins (15:5)—though he reigns for fifty-two years! Moreover, Amaziah is a good king who scrupulously obeys the law (14:6), but he is bested in battle by an evil king of Israel and is assassinated.

These promissory and "inconsistent" texts are often considered intrusive, unusual, surprising, or uncharacteristically positive. Yet, in such theological comment the narrator qualifies his own somewhat mechanical royal summaries. The summaries give the basic direction of a reign and its more long-range impact, but the narrator has no precise retributive sense of the relationship between good and bad kings and what happens to them individually (cf. also the earlier list in 1 Kings 14:21–16:34; for example, Zimri, 16:15–20, rules only seven days but is sharply condemned). Both divine and human activity upset any individualistic and mechanistic understandings of these summaries. God is at work, pursuing the divine designs, making people accountable, pursuing well-being for all, but no dogma of retribution is evident.

One claim of these summaries seems incontestable. Because God is at work in all aspects of life—social, economic, political, and military—issues of moral accountability will regularly surface. Leaders will be held accountable by God, often through other human beings, for all aspects of their work within the community. To pass such theological judgments is to be true to the way in which God evaluates life in our world. God will not be evicted from the public arena, for God's purposes for life are at stake in those precincts far removed from churchly buildings and confessions.

THE REIGN OF AHAZ
2 Kings 16:1–20

Ahaz (735–715 B.C.) received a negative evaluation like the kings of Israel, uncommon for Judean kings (see also the negative account in 2 Chronicles 28). With him the downward spiral of Judah is intensified, yet not irrevocably so. The reasons stated are his apostate and "abominable" worship practices (vv. 3–4; note the comparable language for Manasseh at 21:2–6). This included making "his son pass through fire" (as did Manasseh, 21:6). Child sacrifice by fire was associated with the indigenous religions of

Canaan, especially the cult of Molech, and was prohibited in the law (Deut. 18:10; 12:31). Moreover, he actually worshiped at the high places, the first king since Solomon to do so.

Ahaz may also be condemned for his political actions. He sought to protect Judah from the invasion of Aram and Israel by appealing for help from the Assyrians and buying their protection (from the temple treasury). The Assyrians gladly respond by taking Damascus, the capital of Aram, and killing its king (about 732 B.C.). By this appeal (note the subservient language) Ahaz makes Judah in effect a vassal state of Assyria (he also lost territory to Edom, v. 6). On this issue Ahaz is addressed by the prophet Isaiah, who warns against foreign alliances and urges trust in God alone (Isa. 7:1–8:10); the book of Kings ignores this tradition. Because pressures from Aram and Israel are sent by God (15:37), whether to appeal to Assyria for help becomes a kind of test for Ahaz.

The brevity of the political report contrasts with the detail regarding an altar. When in Damascus, Ahaz is attracted by a "great altar" (v. 15) and sends word to the priest Uriah (a supporter of Isaiah, 8:2) to build one just like it. It is completed posthaste and displaces the existing bronze altar (v. 14; too small according to 1 Kings 8:64). When Ahaz returns, he himself offers various traditional sacrifices upon it (Solomon and Jeroboam I also functioned as priests, 1 Kings 8:63; 12:32) and commands Uriah to use this altar for all future sacrifices (v. 15). Ahaz also made other (not always clear) changes in the temple furnishings, perhaps in the interests of appeasing the king of Assyria (v. 18b). This worship and temple redesign are apparently not considered apostate as such (see also Ahaz's own use of the bronze altar for prayer, v. 15), but the links to the Assyrians are considered ominous and will adversely affect the South in short order.

7. The Destruction and Exile of Israel
2 Kings 17:1–41

This chapter provides a key theological interpretation of the fall of the Northern Kingdom. The northern prophets, Amos and Hosea, provide further reflection on the reasons for this fall. This chapter begins with the reign of the last of Israel's kings (Hoshea) and the fall of Samaria (vv. 1–6), moves to theological analysis (vv. 7–23), and concludes with an interpretation of the situation in Samaria after Israel's dispersion (vv. 24–41).

THE FALL OF SAMARIA
2 Kings 17:1–6

> 17:1 In the twelfth year of King Ahaz of Judah, Hoshea son of Elah began to reign in Samaria over Israel; he reigned nine years. ² He did what was evil in the sight of the LORD, yet not like the kings of Israel who were before him. ³ King Shalmaneser of Assyria came up against him; Hoshea became his vassal, and paid him tribute. ⁴ But the king of Assyria found treachery in Hoshea; for he had sent messengers to King So of Egypt, and offered no tribute to the king of Assyria, as he had done year by year; therefore the king of Assyria confined him and imprisoned him. ⁵ Then the king of Assyria invaded all the land and came to Samaria; for three years he besieged it. ⁶ In the ninth year of Hoshea the king of Assyria captured Samaria; he carried the Israelites away to Assyria. He placed them in Halah, on the Habor, the river of Gozan, and in the cities of the Medes.

King Hoshea (732–724 B.C.) presides over this disastrous time for Israel. Surprisingly, his reign is evaluated less negatively than that of most northern kings, for unclear reasons. In the face of Assyrian threats under Shalmaneser (727–722 B.C.), Hoshea first offers tribute, then refuses and appeals to Egypt for help (King So is not otherwise known). In response, Assyria imprisons him. Verses 5–6 are not a report of a second Assyrian invasion, but a summary of the fall, including the two-to-three year siege and the capture of Samaria in 722/721 B.C. (under the Assyrian king Sargon II). Pursuant to Assyrian policies during this time, many Israelites are dispersed to various parts of the Assyrian empire, including the cities of the Medes, to the east of Assyria. (See 18:9–12 for a further use of this text in view of Hezekiah's reign.)

THEOLOGICAL INTERPRETATION OF THE FALL
2 Kings 17:7–23

17:7 This occurred because the people of Israel had sinned against the LORD their God, who had brought them up out of the land of Egypt from under the hand of Pharaoh king of Egypt. They had worshiped other gods 8 and walked in the customs of the nations whom the LORD drove out before the people of Israel, and in the customs that the kings of Israel had introduced. 9 The people of Israel secretly did things that were not right against the LORD their God. They built for themselves high places at all their towns, from watchtower to fortified city; 10 they set up for themselves pillars and sacred poles on every high hill and under every green tree; 11 there they made offerings on all the high places, as the nations did whom the LORD carried away before them. They did wicked things, provoking the LORD to anger; 12 they served idols, of which the LORD had said to them, "You shall not do this." 13 Yet the LORD warned Israel and Judah by every prophet and every seer, saying, "Turn from your evil ways and keep my commandments and my statutes, in accordance with all the law that I commanded your ancestors and that I sent to you by my servants the prophets." 14 They would not listen but were stubborn, as their ancestors had been, who did not believe in the LORD their God. 15 They despised his statutes, and his covenant that he made with their ancestors, and the warnings that he gave them. They went after false idols and became false; they followed the nations that were around them, concerning whom the LORD had commanded them that they should not do as they did. 16 They rejected all the commandments of the LORD their God and made for themselves cast images of two calves; they made a sacred pole, worshiped all the host of heaven, and served Baal. 17 They made their sons and their daughters pass through fire; they used divination and augury; and they sold themselves to do evil in the sight of the LORD, provoking him to anger. 18 Therefore the LORD was very angry with Israel and removed them out of his sight; none was left but the tribe of Judah alone. 19 Judah also did not keep the commandments of the LORD their God but walked in the customs that Israel had introduced. 20 The LORD rejected all the descendants of Israel; he punished them and gave them into the hand of plunderers, until he had banished them from his presence. [21] **When he had torn Israel from the house of David, they made Jeroboam son of Nebat king. Jeroboam drove Israel from following the LORD and made them commit great sin.** [22] **The people of Israel continued in all the sins that Jeroboam committed; they did not depart from them** [23] **until the LORD removed Israel out of his sight, as he had foretold through all his servants the prophets. So Israel was exiled from their own land to Assyria until this day.**

This Deuteronomic theological analysis suspends the narrative flow in order to reflect on the meaning of the fall of Samaria to Assyrian armies. This event has been anticipated in earlier narratives, and here the use of repeated words and phrases pounds the point home. On the one hand, the text explains why Israel was destroyed and exiled. In doing so, it does not focus on the kings (as the narrative to this point has), though kings frame the account (vv. 8, 21–22). Rather, the narrator centers on the sins of the people of Israel as a whole, with every sin interpreted as a general or specific violation of the First Commandment.

On the other hand, the text also claims that Judah did no better; comparable religious developments have taken place in Judah as well and hence it can anticipate a comparable end (vv. 13, 18–20). The narrator's own time ("to this day") is evident at verses 23, 34, 41, demonstrating a concern to make a theological and religious point to readers. These are matters that deserve their careful attention, lest they succumb in comparable ways!

The narrator begins by alerting the reader that what follows is an explanation: "This occurred because" the people had sinned against the Lord. The Lord is specifically identified in terms of the exodus, as the one who "brought them up out of the land of Egypt." This is ironic, for God has now brought them up out of a land again, this time the land of Canaan. The God who drove others from the land of Canaan because of their wickedness (Deut. 9:5) has now driven Israel out for the same reason; they have followed in the ways of these peoples. Notable is the fact that Israel's sin is initially focused on God's gracious action and not on the giving of the law. Israel's is a rebellion against grace before it is a disobedience of the law (this is also identified as the problem for Judah; see the discussion at 2 Kings 21:1–26). The sin of the people is specifically identified in terms of the First Commandment of the Decalogue—worshiping gods other than Yahweh and walking in their ways—an issue central to the entire Deuteronomic corpus (see Introduction). This activity was often "secretly" pursued (v. 9). That is, though their syncretistic worship places and practices were public, they carried on with a Yahwistic veneer. In fact, however, they were idolatrous and unfaithful to Yahweh. This theme of the First Commandment functions like a refrain in these verses. All their sins are grounded in this fundamental infidelity.

God had graciously sent prophets to Israel to call them to repentance and new life (vv. 13–14, 23), but they were stubborn (like their ancestors, see Ps. 81:11–12; Exodus 32) and wouldn't listen. The narrative has not reported any prophets who called them to repent, but Amos and Hosea may be in mind. The people even "sold themselves to do evil" (v. 17); that is, they followed that which is false (or empty) and themselves "became false" (v. 15). Israel has become false like the very Baals they follow. The explanation climaxes in a double statement of God's anger (vv. 17–18; on anger, see at 1 Kings 14:21–16:34) which has issued in the destruction and exile. The "therefore" of verse 18 makes the link between sin and judgment clear; this is no arbitrary divine move.

The divine judgment is stated in various ways. God "removed them out of his sight" begins a litany of judgment (vv. 18, 21); and then, apparently including Judah in "*all* the descendants of Israel [Jacob]," God rejected, punished (or humbled), banished and exiled, and gave them over to the enemy (v. 20; see 24:2). Israel has been "torn" from the house of David (v. 21; see 1 Kings 11:31). Verses 21–23 recapitulate the basic points. The Israelites remain exiled to the time of the narrator (v. 23). We know that they became so thoroughly integrated into these foreign populations that they ceased to exist as a people (hence "the ten lost tribes"); yet many fled to the south and were preserved within that grouping of the people of God (see also 2 Chron. 30:6–11).

Judah alone is left, but Judah too has walked in comparably unfaithful ways (v. 19). At the time, Judah probably thought it had escaped. But verses 21–22 imply that Judah has a comparable future if it persists in these ways, though this is finally written from the perspective of the exile and anticipates what will in fact occur.

RESETTLEMENT IN SAMARIA
2 Kings 17:24–41

This section explains why it is that the people in Samaria at the narrator's time have syncretistic forms of worship (the later Samaritans are not yet in view, though they descend from this mixed group). At the same time, it demonstrates the continuing ill effects of Israel's sin upon subsequent history. The way it looks now (at the time of the readers) is like it used to be. The Israelites remaining in the land are still syncretists, and that syncretism has been explicitly taught by an Israelite priest to the people who were settled in Canaan by Assyria (v. 28). This perpetuation of idolatry in the North—not finally resolved by the Assyrian invasion—will be addressed by Josiah (see 23:15–20).

Assyria not only exiled Israelites into the far reaches of its empire, it also brought peoples from various parts of its empire and settled them in Samaria. These settlers initially experience hardships (killed by lions; see 1 Kings 13:24), and the narrator faults their failure to worship Yahweh. The non-worship of Yahweh on the part of *every* people will have ill effects, but this people's presence in the land of Canaan seems to make them especially vulnerable; somehow even the land itself is polluted. The king of Assyria is given an interpretation of these hardships, namely, their failure to "know the law of the god of the land." The king (remarkably!) responds by sending an Israelite priest to Bethel to teach them the law and the "proper" way to worship Yahweh. The results are ironic: He succeeds in teaching them the same syncretism that Israel practiced before they were exiled. The Israelites have perpetuated themselves.

On the one hand, the settlers continue to worship their own gods, make images of them, pursue traditional practices, and appoint their own priests (as they had in their homelands, v. 33, and as was true also in Israel before the fall). On the other hand, in a syncretistic move familiar to Israel (see 1 Kings 18:21), they also worship the Lord. This syncretism continues up to the narrator's own time (v. 34a, 41). In between these "to this day" references, the narrator denies this syncretistic possibility (vv. 34b–41): "they do not worship the Lord." That is, they do not "properly" or "actually" worship Yahweh, though from all appearances this seems to be the case; the inherited tradition cited in verses 35–39 shows that it is improper. Not that these settlers should know this to be case (though see v. 28), but this is the basis upon which one shows that this worship is apostate. Insofar as the inhabitants included remaining Israelites, they would know it applied to them.

The Story of God and Divine Judgment

Another perspective from which to view the text is in terms of God's own history with this people. The sin of Israel has an effect on God that is cumulative. God's history with this people begins with the exodus (v. 7) and includes the giving of the law (v. 12) and the land settlement (v. 8). Israel's is a rebellion against God's *gracious* actions. This story begins and continues over time with God's graciousness manifest again and again; the longer the relationship has been in place, and the greater the intimacy between them, the more the people's infidelity is sharpened *for God*. The patience of God over this long stretch of apostasy is again and again evident, but that is not without cost to God. Hosea 11:1–9, set close to this time in Israel's history, witnesses to the inner turmoil suffered by God over the children's rejection. Given the unfaithfulness, God warns the people again and again through the prophets (v. 13), and the hope is always that it might lead the prodigals to come back home. When the anger of the Lord comes into view (vv. 17–18), it is followed by exile (vv. 18, 20, 23) but not final destruction (2 Kings 13:23; 14:27; Hosea 11:9).

This is a story of Israel; it is also a story of God and how God has related to this people in a variety of ways in view of their life together. God does not remove God's self from this journey, with all of its twists and turns; this journey is a genuine one for God, and that means that it has ill effects upon the divine life. Because God goes on this journey with Israel to the very end, even the disaster is not meaningless but is given theological significance within God's overarching purposes. Given the "ten lost tribes," one might raise the question as to whether this major part of the body of Israel (some of whom certainly remained faithful through it all) was cut off forever from God's promises. But a northern remnant persists through the disaster (see 1 Kings 19:18). At the least, the people who fled to the south were caught up in shaping a future for Israel. It is even likely that some of these faithful ones were involved in the production of the Deuteronomic tradition. The promise to Abraham, tucked into a corner of this tradition (2 Kings 13:23; cf. Deut. 4:31) is a continuing witness to a God who will be faithful through the worst possible judgments.

The journey of Israel is most fundamentally one of infidelity; the issue for Israel is at its deepest level an issue of faith and not of law ("they did not believe," v. 14). The people have rebelled against the gracious action of God on their behalf (see also at 2 Kings 21:1–26) and have violated the marriage relationship (seen in terms of the First [and the Second] Commandment). This is not basically a matter of disobedience of laws, but of unfaithfulness within relationship. Virtually every sin that is detailed in this chapter is focused on the First Commandment. This failure has in turn led to the violation of *all* of the commandments. Disobedience of law is not the primal sin; disobedience is symptomatic of, and grows out of, a more fundamental problem—mistrust and infidelity.

Judgment is understood fundamentally in terms of the moral order. Their evil (Hebrew: *ra*ʿ) led to God's disaster (*ra*ʿ). Just as the people had rejected Yahweh, so Yahweh rejected them; just as they had not departed from their sins, God caused them to depart from the land. Just as they had banished Yahweh from their life, so God banished them from their inheritance (on judgment, see further at 1 Kings 11:1–43; 21:1–29; 2 Kings 3:1–27).

8. Judah: Reform and Fall
2 Kings 18:1–25:30

The final section of the book of Kings consists of somewhat contrary elements. On the one hand, two of the most thoroughgoing reforms in the history of Israel are undertaken by Hezekiah (18:1–20:21) and Josiah (22:1–23:30). Yet their reforming activities are not sufficient to overcome the buildup of the effects of sin and evil over Israel's long history, especially during the reigns of Manasseh and Amon (21:1–26). And so, on the other hand, the final chapters witness to the rapid decline of Judah and the destruction of temple, city, and country at the hands of the Babylonian armies (24:1–25:26). Yet there is a glimmer of hope that shines through the gloom in the final verses (25:27–30).

THE REIGN OF HEZEKIAH
2 Kings 18:1–20:21

This lengthy treatment of Hezekiah (715–687 B.C.) is dominated by Assyria's invasion of Judah under Sennacherib in 701 B.C. Parallels, with additional material, are found in Isaiah 36–39 and 2 Chronicles 29–32 (Assyrian records are also available). In the Kings context, Hezekiah appears as a contrast to the wicked kings of the previous chapters. He is a new David, one for whom God and people had long been waiting. He may have been the incentive for the messianic oracles of Isaiah (see 9:1–6; 11:1–9). Yet finally his reign does not cut off a negative future for Judah.

Evaluation of Hezekiah
(2 Kings 18:1–12)

18:1 **In the third year of King Hoshea son of Elah of Israel, Hezekiah son of King Ahaz of Judah began to reign.** 2 **He was twenty-five years old when he**

196

began to reign; he reigned twenty-nine years in Jerusalem. His mother's name was Abi daughter of Zechariah. ³ He did what was right in the sight of the LORD just as his ancestor David had done. ⁴ He removed the high places, broke down the pillars, and cut down the sacred pole. He broke in pieces the bronze serpent that Moses had made, for until those days the people of Israel had made offerings to it; it was called Nehushtan. ⁵ He trusted in the LORD the God of Israel; so that there was no one like him among all the kings of Judah after him, or among those who were before him. ⁶ For he held fast to the LORD; he did not depart from following him but kept the commandments that the LORD commanded Moses. ⁷ The LORD was with him; wherever he went, he prospered. He rebelled against the king of Assyria and would not serve him. ⁸ He attacked the Philistines as far as Gaza and its territory, from watchtower to fortified city.

Hezekiah is the most positively evaluated king, even more than David and Josiah. He "trusts in" and "holds fast to" the Lord (vv. 5–6), obeys the commandments, and institutes numerous religious reforms. The theme of "trust" will echo throughout the following narrative. He centralizes all worship in Jerusalem by removing the high places (for the first time) and destroys other sacred objects of idolatrous import. This includes the "bronze serpent" (Nehushtan is a wordplay on the phrase) that Moses had made in the wilderness (Num. 21:4–9) but which had apparently been drawn into apostate worship practice at some point. From God's side, God is "with him" and wherever he goes, he prospers (v. 7). He rebels against the Assyrians and recaptures territory from the days of the Solomonic empire (Gaza is near the southwest boundary). Verses 9–12 are borrowed from 17:5–8 and adapted to say, in effect, that Hezekiah is different from Israel's kings. Yet, will his trust make a difference in this profound threat to Judah?

Hezekiah and Sennacherib
(18:13–19:37)

18:13 In the fourteenth year of King Hezekiah, King Sennacherib of Assyria came up against all the fortified cities of Judah and captured them. ¹⁴ King Hezekiah of Judah sent to the king of Assyria at Lachish, saying, "I have done wrong; withdraw from me; whatever you impose on me I will bear." The king of Assyria demanded of King Hezekiah of Judah three hundred talents of silver and thirty talents of gold. ¹⁵ Hezekiah gave him all the silver that was found in the house of the LORD and in the treasuries of the king's house. ¹⁶ At that time Hezekiah stripped the gold from the doors of the temple of the LORD, and from the doorposts that King Hezekiah of Judah had overlaid and gave it to the king of Assyria. [17] The king of Assyria sent the Tartan, the Rab-saris, and the Rabshakeh with a great army from Lachish to King Hezekiah at Jerusalem. They went up and came to Jerusalem. When they arrived, they came and stood by the conduit of the upper pool, which is on the highway to the Fuller's Field. [18] When they called for the king, there came out to them Eliakim son of Hilkiah, who was in charge of the palace, and Shebnah the secretary, and Joah son of Asaph, the recorder. [19] The Rabshakeh said to them, "Say to Hezekiah: Thus says the great king, the king of Assyria: On what do you base this confidence of yours? [20] Do you think that mere words are strategy and power for war? On whom do you now rely, that you have rebelled against me? [21] See, you are relying now on Egypt, that broken reed of a staff, which will pierce the hand of anyone who leans on it. Such is Pharaoh king of Egypt to all who rely on him. [22] But if you say to me, 'We rely on the LORD our God,' is it not he whose high places and altars Hezekiah has removed, saying to Judah and to Jerusalem, 'You shall worship before this altar in Jerusalem'? [23] Come now, make a wager with my master the king of Assyria: I will give you two thousand horses, if you are able on your part to set riders on them. [24] How then can you repulse a single captain among the least of my master's servants, when you rely on Egypt for chariots and for horsemen? [25] Moreover, is it without the LORD that I have come up against this place to destroy it? The LORD said to me, Go up against this land, and destroy it." [26] Then Eliakim son of Hilkiah, and Shebnah, and Joah said to the Rabshakeh, "Please speak to your servants in the Aramaic language, for we understand it; do not speak to us in the language of Judah within the hearing of the people who are on the wall." [27] But the Rabshakeh said to them, "Has my master sent me to speak these words to your master and to you, and not to the people sitting on the wall, who are doomed with you to eat their own dung and to drink their own urine?" [28] Then the Rabshakeh stood and called out in a loud voice in the language of Judah, "Hear the word of the great king, the king of Assyria! [29] Thus says the king: 'Do not let Hezekiah deceive you, for he will not be able to deliver you out of my hand. [30] Do not let Hezekiah make you rely on the LORD by saying, The LORD will surely deliver us, and this city will not be given into the hand of the king of Assyria.' [31] Do not listen to Hezekiah; for thus says the king of Assyria: 'Make your peace with me and come out to me; then every one of you will eat from your own vine and your own fig tree, and drink water from your own cis-tern, [32] until I come and take you away to a land like your own land, a land of grain and wine, a land of bread and vineyards, a land of olive oil and honey, that you may live and not die. Do not listen to Hezekiah when he mis-leads you by saying, The LORD will deliver us. [33] Has any of the gods of the nations ever delivered its land out of the hand of the king of Assyria? [34] Where are the gods of Hamath and Arpad? Where are the gods of Sephar-vaim, Hena, and Ivvah? Have they delivered Samaria out of my hand? [35] Who among all the gods of the countries have delivered their countries out of my hand, that the LORD should deliver Jerusalem out of my hand?'" ³⁶ But the people were silent and answered him not a word, for the king's command was, "Do not answer him." ³⁷ Then Eliakim son of Hilkiah, who was in charge of the palace, and Shebna the secretary, and Joah son of Asaph, the recorder, came to Hezekiah with their clothes torn and told him the words of the Rabshakeh.

19:1 When King Hezekiah heard it, he tore his clothes, covered himself with sackcloth, and went into the house of the LORD. ² And he sent Eliakim, who was in charge of the palace, and Shebna the secretary, and the senior priests, covered with sackcloth, to the prophet Isaiah son of Amoz. ³ They said to him, "Thus says Hezekiah, This day is a day of distress, of rebuke, and of disgrace; children have come to the birth, and there is no strength to bring them forth. ⁴ It may be that the LORD your God heard all the words of the Rabshakeh, whom his master the king of Assyria has sent to mock the living God, and will rebuke the words that the LORD your God has heard; therefore lift up your prayer for the remnant that is left." ⁵ When the servants of King Hezekiah came to Isaiah, ⁶ Isaiah said to them, "Say to your master, 'Thus says the LORD: Do not be afraid because of the words that you have heard, with which the servants of the king of Assyria have reviled me. ⁷ I myself will put a spirit in him, so that he shall hear a rumor and return to his own land; I will cause him to fall by the sword in his own land.'" ⁸ The Rabshakeh returned, and found the king of Assyria fighting against Libnah; for he had heard that the king had left Lachish. ⁹ When the king heard concerning King Tirhakah of Ethiopia, "See, he has set out to fight against you," he sent messengers again to Hezekiah, saying, ¹⁰ "Thus shall you speak to King Hezekiah of Judah: Do not let your God on whom you rely deceive you by promising that Jerusalem will not be given into the hand of the king of Assyria. ¹¹ See, you have heard what the kings of Assyria have done to all lands, destroying them utterly. Shall you be delivered? ¹² Have the gods of the nations delivered them, the nations that my predecessors destroyed, Gozan, Haran, Rezeph, and the people of Eden who were in Telassar? ¹³ Where is the king of Hamath, the king of Arpad, the king of the city of Sepharvaim, the king of Hena, or the king of Ivvah?" ¹⁴ Hezekiah received the letter from the hand of the messengers and read it; then Hezekiah went up to the house of the LORD and spread it before the LORD. ¹⁵ And Hezekiah prayed before the LORD, and said: "O LORD the God of Israel, who are enthroned above the cherubim, you are God, you alone, of all the kingdoms of the earth; you have made heaven and earth. ¹⁶ Incline your ear, O LORD, and hear; open your eyes, O LORD, and see; hear the words of Sennacherib, which he has sent to mock the living God. ¹⁷ Truly, O LORD, the kings of Assyria have laid waste the nations and their lands, ¹⁸ and have hurled their gods into the fire, though they were no gods but the work of human hands—wood and stone—and so they were destroyed. [19] So now, O LORD our God, save us, I pray you, from his hand, so that all the kingdoms of the earth may know that you, O LORD, are God alone." [20] Then Isaiah son of Amoz sent to Hezekiah, saying, "Thus says the LORD, the God of Israel: I have heard your prayer to me about King Sennacherib of Assyria. [21] This is the word that the LORD has spoken concerning him:

> She despises you, she scorns you—
> virgin daughter Zion;
> she tosses her head—behind your back,
> daughter Jerusalem.

[22] Whom have you mocked and reviled?
> Against whom have you raised your voice
> and haughtily lifted your eyes?
> Against the Holy One of Israel!

[23] By your messengers you have mocked the LORD,
> and you have said, 'With my many chariots
> I have gone up the heights of the mountains,
> to the far recesses of Lebanon;
> I felled its tallest cedars,
> its choicest cypresses;
> I entered its farthest retreat,
> its densest forest.

[24] I dug wells
> and drank foreign waters,
> I dried up with the sole of my foot
> all the streams of Egypt.'

[25] Have you not heard
> that I determined it long ago?
> I planned from days of old
> what now I bring to pass,
> that you should make fortified cities
> crash into heaps of ruins,

[26] while their inhabitants, shorn of strength,
> are dismayed and confounded;
> they have become like plants of the field
> and like tender grass,
> like grass on the housetops,
> blighted before it is grown.

[27] "But I know your rising and your sitting,
> your going out and coming in,
> and your raging against me.

[28] Because you have raged against me
> and your arrogance has come to my ears,

I will put my hook in your nose
    and my bit in your mouth;
I will turn you back on the way
    by which you came.

29 "And this shall be the sign for you: This year you shall eat what grows of itself, and in the second year what springs from that; then in the third year sow, reap, plant vineyards, and eat their fruit. 30 The surviving remnant of the house of Judah shall again take root downward, and bear fruit upward; 31 for from Jerusalem a remnant shall go out, and from Mount Zion a band of survivors. The zeal of the LORD of hosts will do this. 32 "Therefore thus says the LORD concerning the king of Assyria: He shall not come into this city, shoot an arrow there, come before it with a shield, or cast up a siege ramp against it. 33 By the way that he came, by the same he shall return; he shall not come into this city, says the LORD. 34 For I will defend this city to save it, for my own sake and for the sake of my servant David." 35 That very night the angel of the LORD set out and struck down one hundred eighty-five thousand in the camp of the Assyrians; when morning dawned, they were all dead bodies. 36 Then King Sennacherib of Assyria left, went home, and lived at Nineveh. 37 As he was worshiping in the house of his god Nisroch, his sons Adrammelech and Sharezer killed him with the sword, and they escaped into the land of Ararat. His son Esar-haddon succeeded him.

The heart of this section consists of two similar verbal duels regarding the Assyria-Judah conflict. Sennacherib's envoys confront Hezekiah's in 18:17–35 and 19:8–13 (their argument moves from God's will to God's power to God's integrity); Hezekiah responds with appeal and prayer to God (19:1–4, 14–19; his prayers do have efficacy); Isaiah announces God's word of salvation (19:6–7, 20–34). The focus is verbal confrontation rather than military. The issue becomes: Whose *word* will prevail (cf. 18:19 with 19:6, 20)? Sennacherib's arrogant taunts or God's response through the prophet Isaiah? And will Hezekiah's trust make a difference in this face-off? (see Fewell, 1986).

Assyria's attack is prompted by Hezekiah's rebellion (v. 7) and initially is successful in capturing cities and pressing Hezekiah's back to the wall. Not a promising beginning for one who trusts Yahweh! Hezekiah calls for a truce, admits his wrongdoing, and offers to pay tribute. In response Sennacherib demands an amazingly large amount (some 25,000 pounds of gold and silver!) and Hezekiah strips temple and palace to provide it. But this move fails (it is omitted in Isaiah and 2 Chronicles).

18:17–19:7. First confrontation. Deciding that tribute is not enough, Sennacherib sends his "big guns," Tartan (=second in rank), Rabsaris (commander-in-chief), and Rabshakeh (=chief butler, in charge of the king's affairs) to confront Hezekiah. Perhaps he can gain what he wants through verbal bombast and save his armies. Hezekiah sends three of his key officials—three against three—and meets the Assyrians at a place central to Jerusalem's water supply.

The Rabshakeh's message (in typical royal style in that world) raises the key issue in these texts: Whom do you trust (see vv. 5–6)? He upbraids Hezekiah (plausibly) for appealing to weak Egypt for help (v. 21), for relying upon a god whose very institutions he had destroyed in centralizing worship (v. 22; he assumes they were legitimate), and for thinking he is strong enough to rebel (vv. 23–24). Hezekiah is so weak that he would not even be able to provide riders if he were given 2,000 horses! Then, with a flourish he claims the blessing of *Yahweh* to destroy Jerusalem (v. 25). This is an extension of the *truth* regarding the destruction of the Northern Kingdom (see 19:25–26). But will it be true for the South? How can Hezekiah trust in the Lord, given such firepower and a God whose *will* stands against him?

Hezekiah's officials feel the force of the speech and ask them to speak in the official Aramaic so that the soldiers on guard would not understand. But the Rabshakeh boasts that they should hear it because they are the ones who will suffer (stating this in gross terms, v. 27). Hoping to divide the enemy, he makes an appeal to the soldiers with a loud and boastful speech, questioning their trust in Hezekiah and Hezekiah's trust in the Lord. If they want good food, water, and land (gifts that Yahweh had given in Deut. 8:7–9!), both now (v. 31) and after they are exiled (v. 32), the people should trust in the king of Assyria. Their God will not be able to deliver them any more than any other god has, including Israel's (vv. 28–35). This is a real slap, claiming that the Lord's *power* is no greater than that of other gods (which are nothing). The soldiers respond with studied silence, however, and Hezekiah's officials despair in their report back to the king, as he does when he hears it (19:1).

Hezekiah has officials and priests consult Isaiah and request his prayers for the city's salvation. They inform Isaiah of the great hardships and taunts ("rebuke and disgrace") the city is enduring and the mocking God is having to suffer; the proverb about children indicates that the moment of truth has arrived for Jerusalem but it does not have the strength to succeed (19:3). Isaiah responds with an oracle of salvation (vv. 6–7): God has heard the taunts and will deliver the city by putting a spirit in Sennacherib (a confused mind) so that he is deceived by a rumor (on deception, see at 1 Kings 22:1–40) and in fear will return to his own land and be killed. This rumor is reported in verse 9, but his return to his own land is delayed.

19:8–37. Second confrontation. The Rabshakeh returns to Sennacherib, now fighting on another front (Libnah was near Lachish), but still a threat. A further stage in the negotiations now ensues, though some scholars think this text recounts a second campaign of Sennacherib from a later time. The king reports an advance by Tirhakah (actually of Egypt, north of Ethiopia); this is the rumor of verse 7, but it hardens Sennacherib's approach. He sends his officials back to Hezekiah with a message that advances the speech of 18:19–35. He claims that Hezekiah's God lacks *integrity* and is deceiving him with promises (v. 10)! This must be so because his God cannot deliver against Sennacherib's might—listing a few more cities (including Israel's) as notches on his "gun barrel."

Hezekiah's response is not military or political in nature, but prayer to God (vv. 15–19). In the face of the charge of divine deception, he addresses God as trustworthy Lord of all creation, not one god among many, and hence powerfully active among all nations. Lamenting the mocking of "the living God" and the destruction of other nations (put in terms of their gods, who would be nothing to defeat compared to Yahweh), he appeals to God to save his people from Assyria "so that all the kingdoms of the earth" may know that Yahweh is God alone (cf. 1 Kings 18:37). Notable here is Hezekiah's move beyond Judah's own salvation to a concern for the knowledge of God among all the nations of the earth. The Rabshakeh has raised issues that will affect God's honor and reputation; God must address this for the sake of the divine future in the eyes of the world.

God responds to Hezekiah through the prophet Isaiah with a definitive "*word*" about Sennacherib in poetic form (vv. 21–34; its content is similar to Isa. 10:12–19; 14:24–27). One characteristic of poetry is the repetition of similar ideas in successive lines (for example, virgin daughter Zion; daughter Jerusalem in v. 21).

God speaks as if Sennacherib were directly addressed; this is an issue between the two of them. In effect, God returns Sennacherib's taunt back upon him and draws out the judgmental implications of his arrogance and blasphemy. The people of Jerusalem despise him, with a scornful toss of their hair behind his back (v. 21). But it is not a young woman whom he has mocked in his pride, but God, the Holy One of Israel (v. 22). God quotes his arrogant boasts of military might against several nations, exaggerating for effect and using metaphors from the natural world (as if *he* were the Creator); he has climbed the highest mountain, felled the tallest trees, and dried up the Nile, exodus-like, with a foot gesture (vv. 23–24). Does he not know that the Lord has long planned to use Assyria as the agent of divine judgment, destroying cities and confounding their inhabitants like blighted grass (vv. 25–26; see Isa. 10:5–11)? Ironically, this is not a show of Sennacherib's power, but of God's use of him. Because of his boasting, however, God, who knows him well, will turn him home as if he were a harnessed animal (copying Assyrian army practices; vv. 27–28). The upshot of this for Hezekiah is that the Assyrian threat will be removed (the essence of which is repeated in vv. 32–34).

God then addresses Hezekiah directly (vv. 29–34), giving him a *future* sign that this will happen, that is, authenticating that the prophecy is from God and will come to pass (see 20:8). The ravaged land will not recover quickly. The people will only be able to eat what grows naturally for two years; in the third year agriculture will return to normal. This cycle is a sign that the land will be repopulated from the remnant of people now left in Jerusalem (an encouraging word for exilic readers). Sennacherib will not come into Jerusalem, but will return home. God will defend Jerusalem, not only for the sake of David, but for God's own sake. That is, the deliverance of Jerusalem is a matter in which God has something at stake: God is committed because of the promise made to David, and his reputation in the world, given Sennacherib's taunts, is at risk (see 20:6; 19:19; cf. Isaiah 30–33). The trust of Hezekiah in Yahweh proves to be decisive after all.

Verses 35–37 describe the Assyrian retreat in fulfillment of Isaiah's prophecies. The means used by the angel of the Lord to decimate the Assyrian armies is not specified (cf. Exod. 12:29). And Sennacherib is killed in the very "presence" of his own god!

The Illness of Hezekiah
(2 Kings 20:1–11)

20:1 **In those days Hezekiah became sick and was at the point of death. The prophet Isaiah son of Amoz came to him, and said to him, "Thus says the LORD: Set your house in order, for you shall die; you shall not recover."** 2 **Then Hezekiah turned his face to the wall and prayed to the LORD:** 3 **"Remember now, O LORD, I implore you, how I have walked before you in faithfulness with a whole heart, and have done what is good in your sight." Hezekiah wept bitterly.** 4 **Before Isaiah had gone out of the middle court, the word of the LORD came to him:** 5 **"Turn back, and say to Hezekiah prince of my people, Thus says the LORD, the God of your ancestor David: I have heard your prayer, I have seen your tears; indeed, I will heal you; on the third day you shall go up to the house of the LORD.** 6 **I will add fifteen years to your life. I will deliver you and this city out of the hand of the king of Assyria; I will defend this city for my own sake and for my servant David's sake."** 7 **Then Isaiah said, "Bring a lump of figs. Let them take it and apply it to the** boil, so that he may recover." ⁸ Hezekiah said to Isaiah, "What shall be the sign that the LORD will heal me, and that I shall go up to the house of the LORD on the third day?" ⁹ Isaiah said, "This is the sign to you from the LORD, that the LORD will do the thing that he has promised: the shadow has now advanced ten intervals; shall it retreat ten intervals?" ¹⁰ Hezekiah answered, "It is normal for the shadow to lengthen ten intervals; rather let the shadow retreat ten intervals." ¹¹ The prophet Isaiah cried to the LORD; and he brought the shadow back the ten intervals, by which the sun had declined on the dial of Ahaz.

The chronology of this story of Hezekiah's illness is disputed (for a longer account see Isa. 38:1–22). Verse 6 suggests that it happened before or during the events of chapters 18–19; its present placement presents a flashback regarding that word of victory and takes it a step further. Hezekiah's nearness to death and his healing are a parallel to what happens to the city of Jerusalem (v. 6). But it also implies that, just as Hezekiah has only fifteen years to live, Judah too has a limited time left.

Isaiah comes to Hezekiah with a word from God that he will not recover. Hezekiah does not simply accept this word, but prays for recovery and voices a deep lament, properly recalling his faithfulness (see 18:5–6; Ps. 17:3–5). Note that there is no repentance; he does not understand his illness to be due to sin. In response to prayer, God changes his mind (see below) and tells Isaiah to return to Hezekiah with a new word. He shall recover after all (by the third day), fifteen years will be added to his life, and (repeating 19:34) the city will be delivered from the Assyrians—again for *God's* sake as well as David's. Isaiah is not, however, simply content with the word from God; he requests that medical means (figs were thought to have healing properties) be used in the healing process as well. The use of both prayer and medicine is a remarkable combination.

The sign (see 19:29; 1 Kings 13:3) that Hezekiah requests is given in terms of a delay in the movement of time (see Josh. 10:12–13). If God can delay time, the time of his death can be delayed. Upon Isaiah's suggestion, Hezekiah requests a reversal of the shadow. The sundial (or steps) was marked by intervals (the amount of time covered by an interval is not stated) that tracked the shadow of the sun (which had nearly set, just as Hezekiah had neared death); it reverses ten intervals. As had been the case in the previous story (19:14–19), prayer is the means for the divine delay of the sunset as it was for Hezekiah's own death. God here works through human prayer in both healing and temporal delay to accomplish the divine purposes (on miracle, see 2 Kings 4:1–44).

Hezekiah and the Babylonians
(2 Kings 20:12–21)

The chronology of this encounter between Hezekiah and envoys from the Babylonian king Merodach-baladan is difficult to resolve; he was king prior to the Assyrian invasion in 701 B.C. It thus represents a flashback, designed to show that the pressures against Jerusalem are ongoing and to anticipate further troubles. Sennacherib's defeat will not make Jerusalem eternally invincible. This textual order reflects the order of the threats; first the Assyrians, then the Babylonians.

The purpose of the Babylonian visit is uncertain. Hezekiah's tour of his treasuries (note the emphasis; see 18:14–16) suggests that the Babylonian envoys are enlisting Hezekiah's help against the Assyrians; his showing them his resources implies that he has agreed to do so. Isaiah (who stands against all foreign alliances) confronts him and asks about the visitors and what they had seen. Without indicting Hezekiah, Isaiah links his commitment of Israel's treasures to Babylon to an announcement of the judgment of exile a century later, when they will be forcibly taken to "the far country" (v. 14) along with many people (see 24:10–17). The Babylonians will take what they had been shown. These will include sons of Hezekiah, who will be eunuchs (servants stripped of power) in the Babylonian king's palace.

Hezekiah's reply seems inane, but he will take whatever "goodness" (!) God has to offer. The summary of Hezekiah's rule includes a reference to his building of the Siloam tunnel through solid rock (1,749 feet long) to bring water from the Gihon spring into the city. The tunnel can still be traversed today.

Trust and Prayer
in the Face of Disaster

At one basic level, this narrative is about trust: Whom will you trust? The beginning of the story lays out the thesis (18:5–7): Hezekiah trusted in God and God was with him. The narrative moves through a variety of complications that seem to call that trust and that God into question. That trust is questioned by clever and powerful enemies, whose strength seems invincible. Is the trust a misplaced trust? All the external signs suggest that it is. In the end, the trust proves not to be misplaced at all.

Yet trust will not necessarily issue in a blessing-filled future for God's people. This point is intimated by anticipations of exile for Judah

(20:16–18; cf. 17:19–20). These texts do not imply that good kings (or others) can do nothing to stave off that future. Rather, they show forth the remarkable insight that only hindsight can give. From the perspective of exile, there were signs of this negative future deep within Israel's life long before it happened. This, of course, does not mean that no other future *was* possible *at that time;* only that, looking back, one could see signs of what in fact came to be. One should be careful in drawing "lessons" from such hindsight, say, that God is in total control of history or that trust like Hezekiah's will surely bring deliverance from foreign powers in any time or place. The point seems rather to be: In spite of trusting persons like Hezekiah, or even God's will, a good future may not be possible. Exile may not be able to be staved off by even a faithful king. If a Hezekiah can be followed by a Manasseh, then no amount of trust can secure the future.

At another level, the question becomes: Whose word will you trust? The Rabshakeh puts the question early on: Is Hezekiah basing his trust on "mere words" (18:19–20)? If so, then let the battle be one of words: "Thus says the great king, the king of Assyria." Whose word can stand against his? The strategy pursued by the Rabshakeh is powerful rhetoric. He suggests a variety of theses that Hezekiah might put forward and offers his countertheses at each point. He strikes out against the God of Hezekiah at three seemingly vulnerable points: God's will, God's power, and God's integrity. Against this formidable rhetoric, however, comes "Thus says the LORD" (19:6, 20, 32). This word proves to be a more powerful rhetorical strategy in which the bombast and arrogance of the king is subverted and turned back against him so that he suffers the effects of his own words. When this happens, God's will, power, and integrity are shown to be intact and decisively at work in this situation.

Alongside the prophetic word, the prayers of Hezekiah (19:14–19; 20:2–3) are a crucial factor in the mediation of divine will and power to counteract the will and power of Sennacherib. In 19:14–19, his prayers (his *words*) intrude into this battle of words with an efficacy of their own. In fact, when Hezekiah does *not* pray (9:1–4) the word spoken by Isaiah is only partly effective (the rumor does not do what he says it will, 19:7) and the battle of words continues. When Hezekiah does pray, the salvation oracle of God comes in triplicate (!), and the rhetoric is especially forceful. Hezekiah's prayer is not some innocuous sandwich between the Rabshakeh's words and God's; they are crucial to the energy of the overall rhetoric in leading to the decisive end of Sennacherib (see the prayers in 13:4–5).

In 20:2–3, Hezekiah's prayer is even able to reverse the prophetic word of *God*! Isaiah's initial word from God to Hezekiah was unconditional; he would not recover—no ifs, ands, or buts. The prayer has such an effect on God, however, that God commands Isaiah to return and speak a contrary word: Hezekiah *will* recover. Once again, the power of prayer, indeed the power of prayer to effect changes in God's word, is demonstrated. In this relationship, God is not the only one who has something important to say. Hezekiah's prayers bring his will, energy, and insight into the equation, and they become ingredients with which God works to shape the future, even a future God had not initially declared. This understanding is congruent with other prayers (compare Josiah, 22:18–20; Ahab, 1 Kings 21:27–29; Moses, Exod. 32:11–14, on which see Fretheim, *Exodus*, 285–87; Balentine, 1993, 61–64, 91–97). Given the power of this prayer to reverse a prophetic word, one wonders why Hezekiah did not pray to reverse the word of Isaiah in 20:17–18. Verse 19 suggests that this was because it would not affect him personally.

TWO EVIL KINGS OF JUDAH
2 Kings 21:1–26

21:1 **Manasseh was twelve years old when he began to reign; he reigned fifty-five years in Jerusalem. His mother's name was Hephzibah.** [2] **He did what was evil in the sight of the LORD, following the abominable practices of the nations that the LORD drove out before the people of Israel.** [3] **For he rebuilt the high places that his father Hezekiah had destroyed; he erected altars for Baal, made a sacred pole, as King Ahab of Israel had done, worshiped all the host of heaven, and served them.** [4] **He built altars in the house of the LORD, of which the LORD had said, "In Jerusalem I will put my name."** [5] **He built altars for all the host of heaven in the two courts of the house of the LORD.** [6] **He made his son pass through fire; he practiced soothsaying and augury, and dealt with mediums and with wizards. He did much evil in the sight of the LORD, provoking him to anger.** [7] **The carved image of Asherah that he had made he set in the house of which the LORD said to David and to his son Solomon, "In this house, and in Jerusalem, which I have chosen out of all the tribes of Israel, I will put my name forever;** [8] **I will not cause the feet of Israel to wander any more out of the land that I gave to their ancestors, if only they will be careful to do according to all that I have commanded them, and according to all the law that my servant Moses commanded them."** [9] **But they did not listen; Manasseh misled them to do more evil than the nations had done that the LORD destroyed before the people of Israel.** [10] **The LORD said by his servants the prophets,** [11] **"Because King Manasseh of Judah has commit-**

ted these abominations, has done things more wicked than all that the Amorites did, who were before him, and has caused Judah also to sin with his idols; [12] therefore thus says the LORD, the God of Israel, I am bringing upon Jerusalem and Judah such evil that the ears of everyone who hears of it will tingle. [13] I will stretch over Jerusalem the measuring line for Samaria, and the plummet for the house of Ahab; I will wipe Jerusalem as one wipes a dish, wiping it and turning it upside down. [14] I will cast off the remnant of my heritage, and give them into the hand of their enemies; they shall become a prey and a spoil to all their enemies, [15] because they have done what is evil in my sight and have provoked me to anger, since the day their ancestors came out of Egypt, even to this day." [16] Moreover Manasseh shed very much innocent blood, until he had filled Jerusalem from one end to another, besides the sin that he caused Judah to sin so that they did what was evil in the sight of the LORD. [17] Now the rest of the acts of Manasseh, all that he did, and the sin that he committed, are they not written in the Book of the Annals of the Kings of Judah? [18] Manasseh slept with his ancestors, and was buried in the garden of his house, in the garden of Uzza. His son Amon succeeded him.

The reign of Manasseh (687–642 B.C.) is evaluated as the most evil in Israel's history. More than any other person, he led Judah to destruction and exile. And as if to counter retributionary schemes, he reigns longer than any other king! The account in 2 Chronicles 33:10–20 is somewhat more positive in its portrayal of Manasseh, including references to his repentance and divine restoration. Perhaps Kings paints a bleaker picture to set him off from Hezekiah and Josiah. The goodness of those two kings could not overcome the evil of Manasseh.

The list of the evils of Manasseh constitutes a veritable litany of apostasies (vv. 1–9). They focus on the violation of the First Commandment—infidelity. Manasseh reverts to the practices of the Canaanites, as had Israel (17:7–8), and then proceeds to outdo them! He overturns the reforms of Hezekiah and reverts to the practices of Ahaz. His apostate policies are linked to the worst of the northern kings, Ahab (1 Kings 16:31–33); he does for Judah what Ahab did for Israel. His introduction of idolatries into the inner precincts of the temple and its worship is noted as especially heinous (the Asherah was probably a consort for Yahweh). Such an infidelity is like moving a mistress into the house to live with one's wife. To all of this Josiah will respond (23:4–12, 24), but the end is in sight (23:26–27; 24:3; Jer. 15:4). Adding it all up (v. 9), the narrator claims that the evil has now built up to a greater extent in Israel than it had among Canaan's pre-Israelite inhabitants (see Deut. 9:5).

The prophetic word (vv. 10–15) gathers up the key points of indictment and announces judgment. As with verses 7–8, no prior word is being quoted here and no prophets are known from Manasseh's reign; it is as if this word captures the essence of what every prophet said. Because Manasseh has caused the evil to accumulate beyond that of the Amorites (=Canaanites, v. 9) and has led the people to sin, God has been provoked to anger (vv. 6, 15). God will bring judgment upon Jerusalem and Judah, using the same standards (measuring line and plummet) as were used for the Northern Kingdom. Note that God will bring "evil" (Hebrew: *ra*ʿ) in response to Judah's *ra*ʿ; God's judgment does not introduce anything new into the situation. The images used for judgment are piled up like the judgment itself. It will be so severe that the ears of those who hear of it will tingle (or quiver; see Jer. 19:3); it will be like wiping a dish clean and turning it upside down; the remnant (that is, Judah) will be cast off; they will be given into the hands of their enemies as prey and spoil. Note that none of these images specify annihilation. Interestingly, the final clause in verse 15 takes some of the blame for what happens off of Manasseh; his acts are only the culmination of a long history of evil from the time of the exodus (Exodus 32 may be especially in mind).

Verse 16 adds, as if to make sure the reader doesn't escape the point, that the sins of Manasseh and the people were not simply sins of idolatry, but also sins of injustice. Jerusalem was filled with the dead bodies of the innocent (royal opponents?).

Manasseh's son Amon (642–640 B.C.) simply continued down the road his father had traveled (vv. 20–22). Amon was assassinated by his servants, who were in turn assassinated by "the people of the land" (a group of leaders faithful to Yahweh, 11:14), who put his son Josiah on the throne.

Infidelity, Grace, and Promise

In assessing the idolatrous situation under Manasseh, the narrator recalls words of the Lord regarding the temple (vv. 4, 7–8). These words are remarkable in that they lift up what God has done *for* his people (see also 2 Kings 17:7–8 for a comparable word about the North). Along with verses 2 and 15 and their reference to exodus and conquest, the text stresses that Israel has been unfaithful in the face of God's ongoing gracious action on their behalf. Hence, the disobedience of the law is, at its deepest level, a rebellion against *grace* (within which one ought also to include the gift of the law). In the bright light of God's love and mercy, Israel's sins become all the more apparent and profound. The issue between God and Israel, at its heart, is infidelity to a relationship.

Verses 7–8 surprise for what they do and do not say. These words are not quotations from any prior text (as also with vv. 11–15). This is remarkable given that tendency in Kings to this point; one text that might have been used is 1 Kings 9:3–9. If this text does lie in the background, it is striking that the verses about the conditioning of the land settlement (9:6–7) are picked up, but those conditioning the Davidic house and the temple are not (9:4–5, 8). In 21:7, God has chosen the temple as the place in which to put his name *forever*; this promise is not conditioned here (23:27 moves to "rejection," though no suggestion is made that this is a permanent state of affairs). Neither the Davidic promise nor Israel's identity as the people of God is called into question. Expulsion from the land apparently did not entail the rejection of either. Given the moral order and God's tending to that order, the Israelites must suffer judgment; but, from all that is said (even in vv. 10–15), they remain God's people and the Davidic promise is still in place. The testimony to God's grace and mercy, evident all along Israel's journey, continues.

THE REIGN OF JOSIAH
2 Kings 22:1–23:30

Josiah (640–609 B.C.) is one of the great kings of the line of David. His light is especially clear and bright because he follows the worst of the southern kings, Manasseh; yet even he was not able to overcome the negative impact of that reign (23:26; 24:3). The summary of his rule (22:1–2) is briefer and less laudatory than that of Hezekiah (18:1–7); still, only he is said to fulfill the expectation of obedience in Deuteronomy 17:20 (see also 23:25). These positive evaluations bracket the entire story (22:2; 23:25). If Hezekiah was a new David, Josiah was a new Moses. The positive evaluation is centered in both his personal piety and the depth and breadth of his public reform, explicitly anticipated already in 1 Kings 13:2. That his public reform is focused on making the temple the center of Israel's life is especially exemplary.

Considerable scholarly effort has been focused on these chapters, and this in two major respects. First, a long-standing theory has discerned links between these chapters—particularly the nature of the reform in 23:4–24—and the book of Deuteronomy, with implications for the composition of the Pentateuch. An early form of Deuteronomy (chaps. 12–28?) is usually identified with "the book of the law" found in the temple (22:8; only Deuteronomy is called "the book of the law" in the Pentateuch, for example, 28:61).

The question of the book's origins remains contested. Second, research more recently has focused on the formation of the Deuteronomistic History (Joshua, Judges, Samuel, Kings). On the basis of distinctive vocabulary, theological perspective, and literary style, it is common to discern (at least) two redactions of this material, one from the time of Josiah and one from the exile. But whatever the redactional history, it is important to read the text as it presently stands.

The Book of the Law
(2 Kings 22:1–20)

22:1 Josiah was eight years old when he began to reign; he reigned thirty-one years in Jerusalem. His mother's name was Jedidah daughter of Adaiah of Bozkath. [2] He did what was right in the sight of the LORD, and walked in all the way of his father David; he did not turn aside to the right or to the left. [3] In the eighteenth year of King Josiah, the king sent Shaphan son of Azaliah, son of Meshullam, the secretary, to the house of the LORD, saying, [4] "Go up to the high priest Hilkiah, and have him count the entire sum of the money that has been brought into the house of the LORD, which the keepers of the threshold have collected from the people; [5] let it be given into the hand of the workers who have the oversight of the house of the LORD; let them give it to the workers who are at the house of the LORD, repairing the house, [6] that is, to the carpenters, to the builders, to the masons; and let them use it to buy timber and quarried stone to repair the house. [7] But no accounting shall be asked from them for the money that is delivered into their hand, for they deal honestly." [8] The high priest Hilkiah said to Shaphan the secretary, "I have found the book of the law in the house of the LORD." When Hilkiah gave the book to Shaphan, he read it. [9] Then Shaphan the secretary came to the king, and reported to the king, "Your servants have emptied out the money that was found in the house, and have delivered it into the hand of the workers who have oversight of the house of the LORD." [10] Shaphan the secretary informed the king, "The priest Hilkiah has given me a book." Shaphan then read it aloud to the king. [11] When the king heard the words of the book of the law, he tore his clothes. [12] Then the king commanded the priest Hilkiah, Ahikam son of Shaphan, Achbor son of Micaiah, Shaphan the secretary, and the king's servant Asaiah, saying, [13] "Go, inquire of the LORD for me, for the people, and for all Judah, concerning the words of this book that has been found; for great is the wrath of the LORD that is kindled against us, because our ancestors did not obey the words of this book, to do according to all that is written concerning us." [14] So the priest Hilkiah, Ahikam, Achbor, Shaphan, and Asaiah went to the prophetess Huldah the wife of Shallum son of Tikvah, son of Harhas, keeper of the wardrobe; she resided in Jerusalem in the Second Quarter, where they consulted her. [15] She declared to them, "Thus says the LORD, the God of Israel: Tell the man who sent you to me, [16] Thus says the LORD, I will indeed bring disaster on this place and on its inhabitants—all the words of the book that the king of Judah has read. [17] Because they have abandoned me and have made offerings to other gods, so that they have provoked me to anger with all the work of their hands, therefore my wrath will be kindled against this place, and it will not be quenched. [18] But as to the king of Judah, who sent you to inquire of the LORD, thus shall you say to him, Thus says the LORD, the God of Israel: Regarding the words that you have heard, [19] because your heart was penitent, and you humbled yourself before the LORD, when you heard how I spoke against this place, and against its inhabitants, that they should become a desolation and a curse, and because you have torn your clothes and wept before me, I also have heard you, says the LORD. [20] Therefore, I will gather you to your ancestors, and you shall be gathered to your grave in peace; your eyes shall not see all the disaster that I will bring on this place." They took the message back to the king.

The narrative begins in 622 B.C., with some form of temple activity already underway (22:3–7); earlier stages of reform are described in 2 Chronicles 34:1–7, but are of no apparent interest to this narrator. Key figures in this reform are Shaphan, the secretary to the king (see Jer. 26:24), and Hilkiah the high priest. Josiah commands Shaphan to go to Hilkiah and make appropriate financial arrangements with those working on temple renovations. These arrangements correspond to those put in place by Joash (also a young king) and the priest Jehoiada some two hundred years earlier (see 2 Kings 12:4–16). The honesty of the officials involved is stressed (v. 7).

Hilkiah tells Shaphan that a "book of the law" has been "found" in the temple (v. 8). The origins of this book (probably a scroll of papyrus or animal skin) are uncertain. Earlier references to such a book occur, though after Joshua (1:8; 8:31, 34; 23:6; 24:26) only 2 Kings 14:6 explicitly refers to "the book of the law" (and adds "of Moses"). Kings has a few prior references to the law/commandments or the law of Moses (1 Kings 2:3; 2 Kings 10:31; 17:13, 34, 37; 18:6). Many scholars suggest that an older book, of uncertain age, had been sequestered in the temple during the evil reign of Manasseh. But it is not entirely clear what "found" means; persons like Hilkiah may have been privy to its existence (and even edited it?). Perhaps the book (in some form) was used to shape the reform of Hezekiah as well (see 18:1–7).

Having read the book (it is read four times in these verses! 22:8, 10, 14 [implicit]; 23:2), Shaphan reports back to Josiah that the financial arrangements have been made (v. 9) and that "a book" has been found. When Josiah hears its contents, he is filled with fear and remorse and commands that an interpretation of its import be sought. He is especially concerned that, in view of Israel's disobedience (literally, not hearing) of the law, God's wrath has been provoked against them (anticipating Huldah's words). (His comprehensive "our ancestors," may refer to the kings or recognize the human condition.) The book is taken to the prophetess, Huldah, an otherwise unknown but apparently prominent figure (one wonders why Jeremiah was not consulted).

Huldah's assessment of the book is given in the form of a prophetic oracle, to be delivered to Josiah (22:15–20). Her interpretation—the first unequivocal announcement of the South's destruction—constitutes a parallel to that of the narrator regarding the sin and judgment of the North in 17:7–20. Josiah's initial assessment of the book is correct (v. 13); the divine anger has been provoked (on anger, see at 1 Kings 14:21–16:34) and God is about to bring judgment upon the people because of their failure to attend to its words. The focus of the failure is the First Commandment: Israel has deserted Yahweh and worshiped other gods (v. 17). God's personalizing of the word (unlike the third person in 2 Kings 17:7–17) is striking: "they have abandoned *me* . . . provoked *me* to anger . . . *my* wrath." God's anger is such that this disaster will certainly be forthcoming. Yet because Josiah has been penitent, the judgment will not fall during his lifetime. Note the mutuality; because Josiah has heard the words, God hears Josiah (vv. 18–19). The word that Josiah would die in peace is likely a reference to his death (see Gen. 15:15), not to his burial or to a peaceful time before community disaster. This word is not literally fulfilled, given his violent death (23:29–20). This is another example of inexact prophecy in Kings.

The Reform of Josiah
(2 Kings 23:1–30)

> 23:1 **Then the king directed that all the elders of Judah and Jerusalem should be gathered to him. 2 The king went up to the house of the LORD, and with him went all the people of Judah, all the inhabitants of Jerusalem, the priests, the prophets, and all the people, both small and great; he read in their hearing all the words of the book of the covenant that had been found in the house of the LORD. 3 The king stood by the pillar and made a covenant before the LORD, to follow the LORD, keeping his commandments, his decrees, and his statutes, with all his heart and all his soul, to perform the words of this covenant that were written in this book. All the people joined in the covenant. 4 The king commanded the high priest Hilkiah, the priests of the**

second order, and the guardians of the threshold, to bring out of the temple of the LORD all the vessels made for Baal, for Asherah, and for all the host of heaven; he burned them outside Jerusalem in the fields of the Kidron, and carried their ashes to Bethel. ⁵ He deposed the idolatrous priests whom the kings of Judah had ordained to make offerings in the high places at the cities of Judah and around Jerusalem; those also who made offerings to Baal, to the sun, the moon, the constellations, and all the host of the heavens. ⁶ He brought out the image of Asherah from the house of the LORD, outside Jerusalem, to the Wadi Kidron, burned it at the Wadi Kidron, beat it to dust and threw the dust of it upon the graves of the common people. ⁷ He broke down the houses of the male temple prostitutes that were in the house of the LORD, where the women did weaving for Asherah. ⁸ He brought all the priests out of the towns of Judah, and defiled the high places where the priests had made offerings, from Geba to Beer-sheba; he broke down the high places of the gates that were at the entrance of the gate of Joshua the governor of the city, which were on the left at the gate of the city. ⁹ The priests of the high places, however, did not come up to the altar of the LORD in Jerusalem, but ate unleavened bread among their kindred. ¹⁰ He defiled Topheth, which is in the valley of Ben-hinnom, so that no one would make a son or a daughter pass through fire as an offering to Molech. ¹¹ He removed the horses that the kings of Judah had dedicated to the sun, at the entrance to the house of the LORD, by the chamber of the eunuch Nathan-melech, which was in the precincts; then he burned the chariots of the sun with fire. ¹² The altars on the roof of the upper chamber of Ahaz, which the kings of Judah had made, and the altars that Manasseh had made in the two courts of the house of the LORD, he pulled down from there and broke in pieces, and threw the rubble into the Wadi Kidron. ¹³ The king defiled the high places that were east of Jerusalem, to the south of the Mount of Destruction, which King Solomon of Israel had built for Astarte the abomination of the Sidonians, for Chemosh the abomination of Moab, and for Milcom the abomination of the Ammonites. ¹⁴ He broke the pillars in pieces, cut down the sacred poles, and covered the sites with human bones. ¹⁵ Moreover, the altar at Bethel, the high place erected by Jeroboam son of Nebat, who caused Israel to sin—he pulled down that altar along with the high place. He burned the high place, crushing it to dust; he also burned the sacred pole. ¹⁶ As Josiah turned, he saw the tombs there on the mount; and he sent and took the bones out of the tombs, and burned them on the altar, and defiled it, according to the word of the LORD that the man of God proclaimed, when Jeroboam stood by the altar at the festival; he turned and looked up at the tomb of the man of God who had predicted these things. ¹⁷ Then he said, "What is that monument that I see?" The people of the city told him, "It is the tomb of the man of God who came from Judah and predicted these things that you have done against the altar at Bethel." ¹⁸ He said, "Let him rest; let no one move his bones." So they let his bones alone, with the bones of the prophet who came out of Samaria. [19] Moreover, Josiah removed all the shrines of the high places that were in the towns of Samaria, which kings of Israel had made, provoking the LORD to anger; he did to them just as he had done at Bethel. [20] He slaughtered on the altars all the priests of the high places who were there, and burned human bones on them. Then he returned to Jerusalem. [21] The king commanded all the people, "Keep the passover to the LORD your God as prescribed in this book of the covenant." [22] No such passover had been kept since the days of the judges who judged Israel, or during all the days of the kings of Israel or of the kings of Judah; [23] but in the eighteenth year of King Josiah this passover was kept to the LORD in Jerusalem. [24] Moreover Josiah put away the mediums, wizards, teraphim, idols, and all the abominations that were seen in the land of Judah and in Jerusalem, so that he established the words of the law that were written in the book that the priest Hilkiah had found in the house of the LORD. [25] Before him there was no king like him, who turned to the LORD with all his heart, with all his soul, and with all his might, according to all the law of Moses; nor did any like him arise after him. [26] Still the LORD did not turn from the fierceness of his great wrath, by which his anger was kindled against Judah, because of all the provocations with which Manasseh had provoked him. [27] The LORD said, "I will remove Judah also out of my sight, as I have removed Israel; and I will reject this city that I have chosen, Jerusalem, and the house of which I said, My name shall be there." [28] Now the rest of the acts of Josiah, and all that he did, are they not written in the Book of the Annals of the Kings of Judah? [29] In his days Pharaoh Neco king of Egypt went up to the king of Assyria to the river Euphrates. King Josiah went to meet him; but when Pharaoh Neco met him at Megiddo, he killed him. [30] His servants carried him dead in a chariot from Megiddo, brought him to Jerusalem, and buried him in his own tomb. The people of the land took Jehoahaz son of Josiah, anointed him, and made him king in place of his father.

Upon hearing Huldah's report, Josiah had the people gathered together. Standing next to the pillar at the entrance of the temple (as Joash did in 2 Kings 11:14), he reads the book—here called the book of the covenant— to the community and makes a covenant, a declaration of loyalty to God and intention to follow the precepts of the book in ordering the community (see Exod. 24:3–8; Deut. 31:9–13). Then the people join him in this covenant renewal rite (see the separable aspects in 2 Kings 11:12–18). The language used here is strongly reminiscent of Deuteronomy (see 5:1–5; 6:4–7; 29:2–28).

Upon completion of the covenant ritual, Josiah commands that reforms of Israel's worship be carried out (vv. 4–25). Note that Josiah personally is made the subject of many of these actions; that is, they are carried out exactly according to this command. These reforms are shaped most fundamentally by the principles and precepts of the book of Deuteronomy. The bulk of the reforms are focused on issues relating to the First Commandment, especially syncretistic practices associated with Canaanite worship of Baal. That Josiah extended the reform to the Northern Kingdom (see Bethel in vv. 4, 15, 19) indicates that his reform had political implications regarding the entire kingdom of David. In its detailed description the reform comprehensively links up with every idolatrous innovation by prior kings and names the key culprits (Solomon; Jeroboam I (especially); Ahaz; Manasseh). Note also that Josiah defiles or desecrates these objects (vv. 6, 8, 10, 13–14, 20) by linking them to death (graves, bones). Josiah's thirteen separable reform actions can be ordered as follows:

1. He removes from the temple and its immediate area all foreign elements and destroys them (v. 4, with further detail given in vv. 6–7, 11–12). Note the references to astral deities (vv. 5, 11).

2. He deposes all the idolatrous priests both in Jerusalem and at the various local sanctuaries (v. 5, with further detail in vv. 7–9), and does not allow them to sacrifice in Jerusalem (as permitted in Deut. 18:6–8).

3. He destroys the local sanctuaries and associated objects across the country (v. 8; the gate of Joshua is otherwise unknown; further detail in vv. 13–15). This includes high places and shrines in the immediate environs of Jerusalem (see 1 Kings 11:5–7; the Mount of Destruction is a word play on the Mount of Olives).

4. He extends the reform to the North, specifically undoing the religious innovations of Jeroboam (see 1 Kings 12:25–33) and slaughtering the priests of Samaria (vv. 4, 15–20). These practices had continued in the repopulated areas of the North (17:24–34). This action fulfills the word of the prophet (see 1 Kings 13:2–3, 32), whose tomb Josiah honors because of these links (vv. 16–18).

5. He destroys the installations associated with child sacrifice (=Topheth, a play on the word for shame, v. 10; cf. 16:3–4; 21:6);

6. He commands that Passover, that foundational ritual of Israel's deliverance, be reinstituted (vv. 21–23; see Deut. 16:5–6). The law in Deuteronomy ("the book of the covenant") specified that Passover be celebrated only at the central sanctuary; Josiah thus renews the practice from an early time (see Josh. 5:10–12; cf. 2 Chronicles 30 for a celebration under Hezekiah).

7. He puts away all the diviners and, in summary fashion, various associated idolatrous objects (v. 24; see 21:6, 11, 21). The reference to the

"book" in this last cleansing action returns to the law that prompted the reform in the first place.

All this reform activity does not turn God's wrath away (see below), built up especially in view of the abominations of Manasseh (vv. 26–27). The oracle in verse 27 recalls 21:10–15; the specific rejection of Jerusalem and the temple creates tension with the "forever" of 21:7, suggesting that this rejection is only temporary. Remarkably, nothing is said about the end of the Davidic dynasty.

Josiah is killed (609 B.C.) in an encounter with the Egyptians over relationships with Assyria (see the expanded account in 2 Chron. 35:20–25, including Jeremiah's lament for him). This death stands over against the word of Huldah in 22:20 (a not uncommon lack of specific fulfillment of prophecy). The "people of the land" (compare 11:14) see to his son's succession. But Josiah's death seems to portend the death of the community.

Covenant, Reform, and Prophecies of Judgment

Some interpreters suggest that Josiah's reform was an exercise of futility in view of the prior prophetic word that disaster will come. Or, less negatively, his reform is a sign of faithfulness, even though it would not redound to Israel's benefit (except by extending Josiah's life). But these interpretations are tied to a mechanistic view of prophecy, that the word would inevitably be (fully and precisely) fulfilled. It is clear from various texts (most closely, 20:1–7; cf. 1 Kings 19:14–19) that the response of people can deflect the trajectory of a prophetic word (see also Jer. 26:2–3, 18–19; 36:3; and the theme of divine repentance). The covenant ritual and the reforms that follow are undertaken in the assumption that divine judgment might be turned aside, that Huldah's prophetic word does not necessarily set the future in concrete. That verses 26–27 expressly report that God's anger was not turned aside assumes that (Josiah thought) it might have been otherwise. Moreover, Josiah's extension of the reform to the North suggests a more long-range interest in the restoration of the kingdom to its Davidic and Solomonic extent. It might also be noted that no rigid doctrine of retribution is assumed in these texts (nor in most Old Testament texts), as if, say, repentance and reform necessarily (!) lead to blessing or the amelioration of judgment. Remarkably, given some caricatures of Deuteronomistic theology, the narrator never wonders about this matter at this key juncture in the narrative, which is to his theological credit. Readers should not find any theological tension at this particular point either. That is not the issue to ponder (on judgment, see at 17:7–20).

The narrator does not clarify why Josiah's reforms were insufficient to turn aside the divine anger or whether Judah's sufferings were less severe or less final because of him. It may be surmised that the buildup of the forces of destruction were too great to be turned aside, but this could not be determined with certainty at the time of the reform. The threat was real and prophecies were known to be deflected in view of human response; these motivations were sufficient for Josiah and the nation to make every effort to counteract the threat and seek to shape a different future. To do so would be to stand in the Davidic tradition. When David was faced with a prophetic word about the death of his child (2 Sam. 12:14), he engaged in fervent prayer and fasting because "Who knows? The LORD may be gracious to me, and the child may live" (12:22; see Joel 2:14; Jonah 3:9). Josiah may well function with a comparable "Who knows?"

A point of contrast in these stories comes to the fore when David is forgiven, but the child still dies. A clear distinction is made between forgiveness and deliverance; for the latter to occur (in any situation), further divine (and often human) work is needed. In Kings, however, not only is no deliverance forthcoming, but, except for Josiah (22:19), forgiveness is withheld as well (24:4; for a time, see Isa. 43:25; but God's work through Cyrus is still needed for deliverance). In other words, no divine action that might effect a reversal of the slide to judgment is forthcoming. The divine decision not to forgive adds to the weight of already existing forces that make for destruction and exile. This does not mean, finally, that God's promises no longer stand (see below at 23:31–25:30). Again and again, God's judgment has been in the service of God's ultimate salvific will, though (as here) that may be hidden deeply within the impenetrable folds of disastrous events. Any future the people may have must come from God, who at such moments has given people only a few slim words to hang on to; and it is not always easy to live on words alone.

When the human community is faced with a threat in any time or place, it is both natural and appropriate that it make every effort to turn things around, rather than be passive. Claims for a word from God interpreting such moments will need to be assessed with discernment; for example, is God behind the threat or not? Whether the answer is positive or negative, human response may well be the same. At the same time, such communities should learn to live with a "Who knows?" regarding future divine action. Even to be assured of divine forgiveness will not necessarily lead to deliverance from the threat to the community. But the very nature of the divine-human relationship calls for active engagement, for God has determined that human will, insight, and energy truly count in the shaping of the future. In some cases, finally, as here, death and destruction are experienced, human will and power and institutions are gone, and new life can only come from God (see Deut. 32:36). But even then, human agency remains important, as when a Persian named Cyrus appears on the scene.

From another perspective, this text (if not Josiah's actions) may look more to a future beyond the destruction of Jerusalem than to correcting the past (and hence, finally, Josiah has an impact different from that of Manasseh). Even though the situation is too far gone to pull the community back from the brink, human activity of a reforming sort may provide both impetus and a kind of road map for a restored community, generating energies and guidelines for tending to the law and the reestablishment of Israel's life of worship, with a special eye to preventing a recurrence of idolatrous practices. From such a perspective, this activity would constitute an implicit hope for life for the community beyond destruction and exile.

THE END OF JUDAH
(2 Kings 23:31–25:30)

24:1 **In his days King Nebuchadnezzar of Babylon came up; Jehoiakim became his servant for three years; then he turned and rebelled against him.** [2] **The LORD sent against him bands of the Chaldeans, bands of the Arameans, bands of the Moabites, and bands of the Ammonites; he sent them against Judah to destroy it, according to the word of the LORD that he spoke by his servants the prophets.** [3] **Surely this came upon Judah at the command of the LORD, to remove them out of his sight, for the sins of Manasseh, for all that he had committed,** [4] **and also for the innocent blood that he had shed; for he filled Jerusalem with innocent blood, and the LORD was not willing to pardon.** [5] **Now the rest of the deeds of Jehoiakim, and all that he did, are they not written in the Book of the Annals of the Kings of Judah?** [6] **So Jehoiakim slept with his ancestors; then his son Jehoiachin succeeded him.** [7] **The king of Egypt did not come again out of his land, for the king of Babylon had taken over all that belonged to the king of Egypt from the Wadi of Egypt to the River Euphrates.** [8] **Jehoiachin was eighteen years old when he began to reign; he reigned three months in Jerusalem. His mother's name was Nehushta daughter of Elnathan of Jerusalem.** [9] **He did what was evil in the sight of the LORD, just as his father had done.** [10] **At that time the servants of King Nebuchadnezzar of Babylon came up to Jerusalem, and the city was besieged.** [11] **King Nebuchadnezzar of Babylon came to the city, while his servants were** besieging it; [12] King Jehoiachin of Judah gave himself up to the king of Babylon, himself, his mother, his servants, his officers, and his palace officials. The king of Babylon took him prisoner in the eighth year of his reign. [13] He carried off all the treasures of the house of the LORD, and the treasures of the king's house; he cut in pieces all the vessels of gold in the temple of the LORD, which King Solomon of Israel had made, all this as the LORD had foretold. [14] He carried away all Jerusalem, all the officials, all the warriors, ten thousand captives, all the artisans and the smiths; no one remained, except the poorest people of the land. [15] He carried away Jehoiachin to Babylon; the king's mother, the king's wives, his officials, and the elite of the land, he took into captivity from Jerusalem to Babylon. [16] The king of Babylon brought captive to Babylon all the men of valor, seven thousand, the artisans and the smiths, one thousand, all of them strong and fit for war. [17] The king of Babylon made Mattaniah, Jehoiachin's uncle, king in his place, and changed his name to Zedekiah. [18] Zedekiah was twenty-one years old when he began to reign; he reigned eleven years in Jerusalem. His mother's name was Hamutal daughter of Jeremiah of Libnah. [19] He did what was evil in the sight of the LORD, just as Jehoiakim had done. [20] Indeed, Jerusalem and Judah so angered the LORD that he expelled them from his presence. Zedekiah rebelled against the king of Babylon.

25:1 And in the ninth year of his reign, in the tenth month, on the tenth day of the month, King Nebuchadnezzar of Babylon came with all his army against Jerusalem, and laid siege to it; they built siegeworks against it all around. [2] So the city was besieged until the eleventh year of King Zedekiah. [3] On the ninth day of the fourth month the famine became so severe in the city that there was no food for the people of the land. [4] Then a breach was made in the city wall; the king with all the soldiers fled by night by the way of the gate between the two walls, by the king's garden, though the Chaldeans were all around the city. They went in the direction of the Arabah. [5] But the army of the Chaldeans pursued the king, and overtook him in the plains of Jericho; all his army was scattered, deserting him. [6] Then they captured the king and brought him up to the king of Babylon at Riblah, who passed sentence on him. [7] They slaughtered the sons of Zedekiah before his eyes, then put out the eyes of Zedekiah; they bound him in fetters and took him to Babylon. [8] In the fifth month, on the seventh day of the month—which was the nineteenth year of King Nebuchadnezzar, king of Babylon—Nebuzaradan, the captain of the bodyguard, a servant of the king of Babylon, came to Jerusalem. [9] He burned the house of the LORD, the king's house, and all the houses of Jerusalem; every great house he burned down. [10] All the army of the Chaldeans who were with the captain of the guard broke down the walls around Jerusalem. [11] Nebuzaradan the captain of the guard carried into exile the rest of the people who were left in the city and the deserters who had defected to the king of Babylon—all the rest of the population. [12] But the captain of the guard left some of the poorest people of the land to be vine-dressers and tillers of the soil. [13] The bronze pillars that were in the house of the LORD, as well as the stands and the bronze sea that were in the house of the LORD, the Chaldeans broke in pieces, and carried the bronze to Babylon. [14] They took away the pots, the shovels, the snuffers, the dishes for incense, and all the bronze vessels used in the temple service, [15] as well as the firepans and the basins. What was made of gold the captain of the guard took away for the gold, and what was made of silver, for the silver. [16] As for the two pillars, the one sea, and the stands, which Solomon had made for the house of the LORD, the bronze of all these vessels was beyond weighing. [17] The height of the one pillar was eighteen cubits, and on it was a bronze capital; the height of the capital was three cubits; latticework and pomegranates, all of bronze, were on the capital all around. The second pillar had the same, with the latticework. [18] The captain of the guard took the chief priest Seraiah, the second priest Zephaniah, and the three guardians of the threshold; [19] from the city he took an officer who had been in command of the soldiers, and five men of the king's council who were found in the city; the secretary who was the commander of the army who mustered the people of the land; and sixty men of the people of the land who were found in the city. [20] Nebuzaradan the captain of the guard took them, and brought them to the king of Babylon at Riblah. [21] The king of Babylon struck them down and put them to death at Riblah in the land of Hamath. So Judah went into exile out of its land. [22] He appointed Gedaliah son of Ahikam son of Shaphan as governor over the people who remained in the land of Judah, whom King Nebuchadnezzar of Babylon had left. [23] Now when all the captains of the forces and their men heard that the king of Babylon had appointed Gedaliah as governor, they came with their men to Gedaliah at Mizpah, namely, Ishmael son of Nethaniah, Johanan son of Kareah, Seraiah son of Tanhumeth the Netophathite, and Jaazaniah son of the Maacathite. [24] Gedaliah swore to them and their men, saying, "Do not be afraid because of the Chaldean officials; live in the land, serve the king of Babylon, and it shall be well with you." [25] But in the seventh month, Ishmael son of Nethaniah son of Elishama, of the royal family, came with ten men; they struck down Gedaliah so that he died, along with the Judeans and Chaldeans who were with him at Mizpah. [26] Then all the people, high and low and the captains of the forces set out and went to Egypt; for they were afraid of the Chaldeans. [27] In the thirty-seventh year of the exile of King Jehoiachin of Judah, in the twelfth month, on the twenty-seventh day of the month, King Evil-merodach of Babylon, in the year that he began to reign, released King Jehoiachin of Judah from prison; [28] he spoke kindly to him, and gave him a seat above the other seats of the kings who were with him in Babylon. [29] So Jehoiachin put aside his prison clothes. Every day of his life he dined regularly in the king's presence. [30] For his allowance, a regular allowance was given him by the king, a portion every day, as long as he lived.

This final section of Kings is obviously written from the perspective of exile. The mirroring periods of rule of the last four kings (three months—Jehoahaz, Jehoiachin; eleven years—Jehoiakim, Zedekiah) signals a certain spiraling rhythm to events; they finally make little difference in the scheme of things and have no known theological sensitivities. No sign of Josiah's reform is in evidence. The material is straightforward reporting with little emotional energy, considering the topic (contrast the book of Lamentations). Yet the relentless litany of one thing after another being destroyed and removed carries its own impact. There are few explicitly theological references (24:2–4, 20), especially when one compares the text with 17:7–23, but enough to solidify a point already made.

23:31–37. After the death of Josiah, Judah's situation rapidly deteriorates. His son Jehoahaz (whose "evil" is unspecified) rules for only three months in 609 B.C. before he is deposed by the Egyptians. Under Pharaoh Neco the Egyptians take control of Judah and place another son of Josiah (Eliakim/Jehoiakim) as a puppet on the throne. Jehoiakim (609–598 B.C.) in turn supports Egypt from existing treasuries and an imposed land tax, levied on the "people of the land."

24:1–17. During the reign of Jehoiakim, Judah comes under the control of Babylon and its king Nebuchadnezzar. Nebuchadnezzar is explicitly identified as one whom Yahweh "sent against" Judah to destroy it (24:2; cf. 17:20). Babylon had conquered Assyria in 612 B.C. (at Nineveh) and defeated Egypt in 605 B.C. (at Carchemish in Syria). In 604 B.C., Jehoiakim concludes a treaty with the Babylonians (=Chaldeans) but then rebels in 602 B.C. when the Egyptians regain power for a brief period. But Babylon comes back in force shortly thereafter and uses the armies of neighboring Aram, Ammon, and Moab (former vassals of Israel) to overrun Judah. This turn of events is understood as the fulfillment of the prophetic word against Judah (vv. 2–4, see 20:17; 21:10–16; 23:26–27). This judgment is from God, but not in isolation from what the people have done. The basis for God's noncapricious action—focused in the sins of Manasseh—is once again made crystal clear. God even determines not to forgive (v. 4; see above at 22:1–23:30).

During the Babylonian siege Jehoiakim dies and is succeeded by his son Jehoiachin, who rules for just a few months before he surrenders to Nebuchadnezzar and is deported with his family to Babylon (March of 597 B.C.; see 25:27–30). Nebuchadnezzar takes all the treasuries of the temple as Isaiah had prophesied (20:17), deports the cream of Judah's society to Babylon (either eight or ten thousand, vv. 14, 16), and puts Jehoiachin's uncle (another son of Josiah), Mattaniah/Zedekiah, on the throne as a puppet king.

24:18–25:21. This account of the destruction of Jerusalem is repeated in condensed form in 2 Chronicles 36:11–21 and with variations in Jeremiah 52 (which adds an account of deportees, 52:28–30); a shortened form of 25:1–11 is also found in Jeremiah 39:1–14. More information about Gedaliah is found in Jeremiah 40–44. These repetitions indicate the importance of this event for Israel.

The reign of Zedekiah (597–586 B.C.) is evaluated as "evil" and further prompted the divine anger (24:20). Zedekiah finds himself caught between Babylon and a resurgent Egypt; he opts to side with the latter in rebellion against Babylon and suffers the disastrous consequences. In response, Babylon lays siege to Jerusalem; the siege, with accompanying famine, lasts for eighteen months. When the end becomes obvious, Zedekiah and his guards flee the city. The king is captured near Jericho (the place where Israel entered the land 600 years or so before), his guard scatters, his sons are killed in his presence, and he is blinded and imprisoned in Babylon. The temple, palace, and all the houses are destroyed (August, 586 B.C.), the city walls are broken down, and a second group of Israelites and also the temple treasures are carried away to Babylon (vv. 13–17; departed is Solomon's glory!), leaving only poor farmers behind (again; cf. 24:14). Several court officials and other leaders are put to death (25:18–21). Thus Judah goes "into exile out of its land" (v. 21; cf. 17:23).

25:22–30. This appendix briefly describes ensuing events. For purposes of continuity and stability, an important Israelite leader, Gedaliah, a grandson of Shaphan (22:3), is appointed governor of Judah. His "capital" was Mizpah, about eight miles north of Jerusalem. In an attempt to establish some order in the land, Gedaliah encourages some remaining Judahite leaders to be tolerant of Babylonian rule and live as best they can (25:24; similarly Jeremiah, see 27:12–22; 40:1–6). But some Judahites under Ishmael (a member of the royal family) raid Mizpah and put Gedaliah and other officials to death, and then flee to Egypt with others sympathetic to their efforts; the final exile finds them back in a "pre-exodus" place (see Deut. 28:68). Yet Jehoiachin lives on in Babylon, from which the next exodus will take place.

Do God's Promises
to David Still Hold?

The final verses of Kings (25:27–30; see Jer. 52:31–34) contain a hopeful note (though not everyone agrees; see also above at 22:1–23:30). A special interest accrues to the Davidic king Jehoiachin (unlike Zedekiah), whose family had also gone into exile (24:15). No connection is made with the word of Isaiah about Hezekiah's sons becoming "eunuchs" in Babylon (20:15; contrast Zedekiah in 25:7). Jehoiachin is released from prison by King Evil-merodach (562–560 B.C.). He is treated in a kindly manner and given new robes and special provision at the king's table, symbols of honor and power (see 1 Kings 4:27). At the least, the text claims that the people of God can survive under Babylonian rule (25:24; see Jer. 27:12–22; 29:1–9; see 1 Kings 8:46–50). Finally, Babylon has not put an end to these people, however precarious their future seems.

While this text is reticent about a restoration (for political reasons?), there may be more here than at first appears. Initially important is the narrative recognition that history has not somehow gotten beyond God; God is caught up in the disaster itself and is involved in what happens. God remains the subject of verbs, and hence who this God is believed to be becomes important for thinking about the future. For one thing, the divine wrath is "provoked" (22:13, 17; 23:26; 24:20; see at 1 Kings 14:21–16:34); that is, it is a contingent response to human sin and not an eternal attribute. If there were no sin, there would be no wrath. This means that God cannot be defined fundamentally in terms of wrath and its effects; this God is believed to be essentially something more. And Israel, in continuing to speak of "Yahweh" until the end (e.g., 24:20), hangs on to that something more in the midst of wrath (see Lam. 3:22–33), while not knowing for sure where God might turn next.

It should also be remembered that the final chapters of Kings nowhere claim that the Davidic dynasty has come to an end (see 21:10–15; 23:26–27). Conditional statements about the dynasty could have been called upon to support such a claim if it were true (for example, 1 Kings 9:3–9), but no such assertion is made. Given the propensity of Kings to link up with previous prophetic words, that absence is important, and signals a hopeful future. Hence, the unconditional statements ("forever") about the Davidic dynasty in the prior narrative come to the fore (2 Sam. 7:14–16; 1 Kings 11:36, 39; 15:4; 2 Kings 8:19), as do the citation of the ancestral promises undergirding those of David (2 Kings 13:23; 14:26–27). These are only words, not much comfort perhaps in the middle of a Babylonian siege or exile to a foreign land. But at the end of Kings these words of promise are never retracted. With only words to hang on to, the future remains in the hands of the one who spoke them. We know from the larger canonical picture that these promises still hold for Israel and those who have been grafted into that tree (see Jer. 23:1–8; 30:1–11; Ezek. 37:1–14; Haggai 2:20–23; Matt 1:10–11).

Works Cited and Select Bibliography

Balentine, Samuel E. *Prayer in the Hebrew Bible: The Drama of Divine-Human Dialogue*. Minneapolis: Fortress Press, 1993.

Brenner, Athalya. *A Feminist Companion to Samuel and Kings*. Sheffield: Sheffield Academic Press, 1994.

Brueggemann, Walter. *1 Kings*. Atlanta: John Knox Press, 1982.

———. *2 Kings*. Atlanta: John Knox Press, 1982.

Brueggemann, Walter, and Hans Walter Wolff. *The Vitality of Old Testament Traditions*. Atlanta: John Knox Press, 1975.

Cohn, R. L. "Form and Perspective in 2 Kings 5." *Vetus Testamentum* 33 (1983): 171–84.

———. "The Literary Logic of 1 Kings 17–19." *Journal of Biblical Literature* 101 (1982): 333–50.

Dutcher-Walls, P. *Narrative Art, Political Rhetoric: The Case of Athaliah and Joash*. Journal for the Study of the Old Testament Supplement, 209. Sheffield: Sheffield Academic Press, 1996.

Fewell, Danna Nolan. "Sennacherib's Defeat: Words at War in 2 Kings 18:13–19:37." *Journal for the Study of the Old Testament* 34 (1986): 79–90.

Fretheim, Terence E. *Deuteronomic History*. Nashville: Abingdon Press, 1993.

———. *Exodus*. Louisville, Ky.: John Knox Press, 1991.

———. *The Suffering of God: An Old Testament Perspective*. Philadelphia: Fortress Press, 1984.

Hamilton, J. M. "Caught in the Nets of Prophecy? The Death of King Ahab and the Character of God." *Catholic Biblical Quarterly* 56 (1994) 649–63.

Hauser, Alan J., and Russell Gregory. *From Carmel to Horeb: Elijah in Crisis*.

Journal for the Study of the Old Testament Supplement. Sheffield: Sheffield Academic Press, 1990.

Hobbs, T. R. *2 Kings.* Dallas, Tex.: Word, 1985.

Knoppers, Gary N. *Two Nations under God: The Deuteronomistic History of Solomon and the Dual Monarchies.* Vol. I, *The Reign of Solomon and the Rise of Jeroboam.* Vol. II, *The Reign of Jeroboam, the Fall of Israel, and the Reign of Josiah.* Harvard Semitic Monographs, 52 and 53. Atlanta: Scholars Press, 1993, 1994.

Lasine, S. "Jehoram and the Cannibal Mothers (2 Kings 6:24–33): Solomon's Judgment in an Inverted Word." *Journal for the Study of the Old Testament* 50 (1991): 27–53.

Lindström, Fredrik. *God and the Origin of Evil: A Contextual Analysis of Alleged Monistic Evidence in the Old Testament.* Lund: Gleerup, 1983.

Long, Burke O. *1 Kings, with an Introduction to Historical Literature.* Forms of the Old Testament Literature 9. Grand Rapids: Wm. B. Eerdmans Publishing Co., 1984

————. *2 Kings.* Forms of the Old Testament Literature 10. Grand Rapids: Wm. B. Eerdmans Publishing Co., 1984.

McKenzie, Steven L. *The Trouble with Kings: The Composition of the Book of Kings in the Deuteronomistic History* (Leiden: E. J. Brill, 1991).

Moore, R. D. *God Saves: Lessons from the Elisha Stories.* Journal for the Study of the Old Testament Supplement 95. Sheffield: Sheffield Academic Press, 1990.

Nelson, Richard D. *First and Second Kings.* Louisville, Ky.: John Knox Press, 1987.

Olyan, S. "*Hăšālôm:* Some Literary Considerations of 2 Kings 9," *Catholic Biblical Quarterly* 46 (1984): 652–68.

Provan, I. W. *1 & 2 Kings.* Sheffield: Sheffield Academic Press, 1997.

Provan, I. W. *1 and 2 Kings.* Peabody, Mass.: Hendrickson, 1995.

Rad, Gerhard von. *Studies in Deuteronomy.* Studies in Biblical Theology 9. London: SCM Press, 1953.

Rice, Gene. *1 Kings: Nations under God.* Grand Rapids: Wm. B. Eerdmans Publishing Co., 1990.

Trible, Phyllis. "Exegesis for Storytellers and Other Strangers." *Journal of Biblical Literature* 114 (1995): 3–19.

Viviano, P. A. "2 Kings 17: A Rhetorical and Form-Critical Analysis." *Catholic Biblical Quarterly* 49 (1987) 548–59.

Walsh, J. T. *1 Kings.* Collegeville, Minn.: Michael Glazier Books, 1996.